# COMBINATIONS

## BEGINNING STRATEGIES IN THINKING AND WRITING

# COMBINATIONS ▬▬

## BEGINNING STRATEGIES IN THINKING AND WRITING

**Dorothy M. Berger**
**San Diego Mesa College**

Scott, Foresman and Company
Glenview, Illinois
Boston
London

**Cover:** *Painter's Progress*, 1981 by Elizabeth Murray. Oil on canvas in 19 parts, 9'8" × 7'10". Collection, The Museum of Modern Art, New York. Acquired through the Bernhill and Agnes Gund Funds. Photograph © 1987 The Museum of Modern Art, New York.

**Photo Credits: 2** Harry Redl/Black Star; **41** Dennis Brack/Black Star; **77** Co Rentmeester; **113** Courtesy of the National Broadcasting Company, Inc.; **148** Focus On Sports; **180** Scott Foresman; **194** John Whitman/*People Weekly.* © *1986 Time, Inc. All rights reserved;* **233** Bill Eppridge/*Sports Illustrated.* Time, Inc.

**Library of Congress Cataloging-in-Publication Data**

Berger, Dorothy M.
  Combinations : beginning strategies in thinking
and writing.

  Includes index.
  1. English language—Sentences. 2. English
language—Text-books for foreign speakers. I. Title.
PE1441.B47 1988    808'.042    87-16653
ISBN 0-673-18294-0

23456—EBI—92 91 90 89 88

# PREFACE

## Audience and Scope

The materials in *Combinations* have been used successfully with two groups of college students: those in the course just before standard freshman composition and ESL students at the advanced or advanced-intermediate level. In either case, the book contains material for a one-semester course concentrating on syntactic and stylistic flexibility, grammatical correctness, and the elements of paragraph development and essay structure.

The text is designed for classes in which students write more than they study theory or listen to lectures.

## How the Text Is Organized

The text is divided into two parts: the *Writing Practice* and the *Writing Guide*. *Writing Practice*, the heart of the text, contains six working chapters that lead a student—via a series of paired sentence combining and independent writing exercises—from considerations of the well-mannered sentence through essay assignments that approximate those in standard freshman composition courses. Unlike more usual sentence-combining exercises that deal with grammatical concepts in isolation (*e.g.,* Combine the following two sentences so that the second becomes an adverb clause.), the exercises here are sustained passages ranging over the spectrum of rhetorical types. A student is thus always confronted with issues of writing in a particular context and cannot separate issues of meaning and style from strict grammatical correctness.

The *Writing Guide* is divided into two sections: *Composition Notes* and *Grammar Notes.* That this part of the text is composed of "notes" rather than exhaustive discussions, and that the notes follow—rather than precede—the exercises is a key to the central concept of the text. Traditionally, exercises are appended to detailed discussions. Here, the exercises take precedence and the explanations, analyses, and prescriptions follow, to be used as need arises. Since this arrangement is somewhat unusual, it needs a word or two of explanation.

One of the basic assumptions underlying *Combinations* is that the more students work with language—via exercises or their own writing—the better they learn about language. Learning grammar all too often has no relationship to learning to write. Many students who write poorly do quite well on grammar quizzes, but there is little transfer of what they are learning to how they write. So *Combinations* deliberately deemphasizes the study of formal grammar and emphasizes using language. The standard principles of grammar and composition are discussed in some detail in the Notes in Part II, but the discussions are not the primary focus. In addition, at appropriate points in the early chapters are Mini-Notes—minimal discussions of points of grammar relevant to a particular exercise. These are brief summaries of the longer Notes that can get students started on an exercise and often see them through it without overwhelming them with grammar and without deflecting them from the main purpose: using language well.

Another reason for giving the exercises major prominence is that in most cases the students likely to use *Combinations* do not yet have the habit of digesting abstract principles of grammar and composition and then applying those principles to their own writing. The exercises tap the student's existing language sense, intuition, and independent ability to discover principles of language and composition primarily by working with language and composition rather than by reading about them.

## The Arrangement of Sentence-Combining Exercises

The material in the chapters progresses from simple to complex in terms of a changing focus on individual parts of a sentence, sentence structure, paragraph structure, and essay structure. Each of the first five chapters requires students not only to work sentence-combining exercises but to write independently. The writing assignments also follow a progression from more simple to more complex.

Chapter 1 requires students to use a wide variety of grammatical structures, but each exercise singles out only one such structure for particular emphasis. The degree to which formal grammar is stressed, however, may be adjusted according to the needs of the students or the preference of the instructor. For example, an early exercise focuses on the placement of adverbs. Students may work that exercise without any discussion of what an adverb is or where adverbs may be placed in a sentence. Or students may be required to read and discuss the fairly detailed grammar note on adverbs (in Part II) before they begin the exercise. Another possibility is that the decision may be left to the students: they can begin an exercise and refer to the grammar note only if they run into trouble. In any event, there is more emphasis on *using* than on *studying about*.

In this chapter, the independent writing assignments require students to write sentences according to directions, for example, sentences with noun clauses in a variety of positions. Each assignment focuses on only one aspect of structure, the same one emphasized in the combining exercise.

Chapter 2 is an extension of the first chapter with the prime difference being more complexity in structure and content. Transitions between sentences are stressed. The independent writing assignments in this chapter require students to write paragraphs according to directions. That is, a topic and a structure are both suggested. The subject of each writing assignment is related to the subject of the combining exercise it follows.

Chapter 3 emphasizes variety. Students are required to produce at least two versions of each sentence in the exercises. Then the sentences are written in paragraph form, with students asked to choose which of their versions for each sentence works best in the flow of the paragraph. Students see that sentences do not exist in isolation but depend on what comes before and after. The writing assignments in chapter 3 are also paragraphs, but there is much less direction about how to structure them than there was in chapter 2. The chapter begins with several paragraphs for analysis. Students thus become more independent in planning and organizing.

In chapter 4, the sentences in the exercises are not grouped. Students must decide how much information a sentence can reasonably contain. Here opportunity is provided for students to write sentences that are either too short or too long and to see the consequences of either decision. This chapter requires students to do several new things. Most of the combining exercises are in the form of essays, but paragraph divisions are not indicated. As they do the exercises, students must identify where one paragraph ends and a new one begins. Students are also directed to examine, discuss, and evaluate the structure of the completed combining exercises. Then they are required to write short essays of their own. As in the second chapter, specific instructions are provided for structuring the essays. And again, the subjects are related to the content or rhetorical form of the preceding combining exercise. This chapter begins with several full essays to analyze as an introduction to the examination of structure that is one of the main focuses of the rest of the chapter.

Chapter 5 is the most complex in terms of structure and subject matter and requires the most complex original writing. Various rhetorical types—argumentation, comparison and contrast, classification—are demonstrated in the combining exercises. The completed forms of these exercises approximate the kinds of writing students will have to do in freshman composition courses. Chapter 5 requires the most complex independent writing. The first combining exercises are in the form of paragraphs, essays, or letters from which something essential has been omitted—a topic sentence or a concluding paragraph, for example. As they do the combining exercises, students must also comprehend the material and its structure well enough to write the missing portions. Throughout the chapter there are assignments for writing complete essays, but no suggestions for structure are provided.

The sixth chapter is a complete break from the others. Editing and proofreading are the subjects of the exercises. The focus is on grammatical correctness, syntactic sophistication, and essay structure.

The writing assignments throughout the text call for a balanced mix of personal and objective writing of increasing complexity. In each case, the accompanying combining exercise serves as either a rhetorical example or a prompt for independent thinking and writing.

# Acknowledgments

I am grateful to a number of people for their support and clear thinking during the writing of *Combinations*. William Covino (San Diego State University), Muriel Davis (San Diego Mesa College), Philip Eggers (Borough of Manhattan Community College), Sandra Flake (University of Minnesota), Carolyn Madden (University of Michigan), Fritz Pasierbsky (Universitat Paderborn, West Germany), and Frank Pialorsi (University of Arizona) read the manuscript in various stages and gave both encouragement and sensible suggestions. Anne Smith, Patricia Rossi, and Elizabeth Fresen provided intelligent and hassle-free editorial support. My colleagues Myra Harada and Sally Wyte used an early draft of *Combinations* in their classes—a real act of faith as well as a source of practical revisions. My own students, too, helped with their questions, comments, and interest. Warmest thanks to all.

Dorothy M. Berger

# OVERVIEW

# CONTENTS

# COMBINATIONS

BEGINNING STRATEGIES IN THINKING AND WRITING

# WRITING PRACTICE

I

# 1 REVIEWING THE BASICS

Now to work. This first chapter is designed to accomplish two things: to let you become accustomed to sentence combining and to review the basic elements of sentence structure.

The exercises are relatively uncomplicated so that you can concentrate on becoming familiar with the process of sentence combining. If you are using this book in class, you will also have an opportunity to see how others do sentence combining, for what seems obvious to one person isn't always so obvious to another. This is true both for the sentences you write and for the method you use to combine. For example, some people just look at the sentences and ''see'' right away how they want to combine them. Other people cross out words that appear in more than one sentence before they decide how to combine the remaining words. It's useful to work with several people and to ask them about how they ended up where they did. In any case, try to become aware of what method works best for you. In addition, pay attention to the sentences that other people write if they are different from yours. You will quickly learn that the first way of writing a sentence isn't always the one that you will use in your final version.

In addition to familiarizing you with the process of sentence combining, this chapter provides a review of the basic elements of the sentence—things such as adverbs and clauses and, indirectly, punctuation. In reviewing, you have some choices, depending on what you need to accomplish or on what your instructor assigns you to do. For each element of the sentence that is covered in this chapter, there is a Mini-Note on the page where the sentence element is first introduced and a Grammar Note at the end of the book in chapter 8. Each note explains that particular element of the sentence and shows you examples of using it in your writing. The Mini-Notes in the chapters are brief summaries of the Grammar Notes in chapter 8. This book includes Composition Notes as well, and it would be a good idea for you to look at their titles in the tables of contents now. The titles will give you an idea of what is discussed and may help you to determine what you want to concentrate on now and what can be saved for later.

You can use the notes in several ways. First, suppose you are going to work on an exercise about adverb clauses. You could read the Mini-Note and begin working on the exercise. If you find that you need a more detailed explanation, you could turn to the full Grammar Note in chapter 8 and find the information you want. Or you could turn to the full Grammar Note first, read and study it carefully, and then do the exercise. The purpose of the Grammar Notes is to help you become more aware of what you do when you write sentences and to help you write better ones. They aren't designed to make you an expert in grammar.

In working the exercises, a useful procedure is to combine all the sentences in one group into one sentence, to write it down, and to follow it with the other newly written sentences, writing them in list form down the page. Check things such as spelling and punctuation, and read the new sentences carefully to be certain you did not accidentally leave out an idea. Then rewrite the sentences into paragraph form, read the paragraph aloud to yourself, and change anything that doesn't sound good to your ear. Then you are done.

## SUNDAY MORNING

As you do this exercise, think carefully about commas. You won't use many. In fact, you may not need any commas at all.

## MINI-NOTE ON COMPOUND PARTS OF SENTENCES

### Definition:

Compound means two or more parts.

### Examples:

1.  Tea and coffee contain caffeine.
2.  I read and summarized the chemistry assignment.
3.  Her smile was cheerful, sincere, and spontaneous.

### Punctuation:

1.  He combed and trimmed his beard. (two parts, no comma)
2.  They tried to eat, drink, and be merry. (use a comma before the final ''and'')

**See Grammar Note 8 for more details.**

1.  Sunday morning is quiet.
    It is leisurely.*
    Sunday morning is in the Davidson's house.

*slow and relaxed

2.  George has a tradition.
    Sylvia has a tradition.
    The tradition is long-standing.*

*done for a long time

    (Use ''they'' only once in combining the following sentences.)

3.  They sit together.
    [Their sitting] is in the living room.
    [Their sitting] is peaceful.
    They read the newspaper.

4. They drink coffee.
   They drink juice.
   The coffee is strong.
   The coffee is in cups.

*very old and
sometimes expensive*

   The cups are antique.*
   The juice is orange.
   The juice is cold.
   The juice is in glasses.

*high-quality glass*

   The glasses are crystal.*

5. George doesn't talk much.
   Sylvia doesn't talk much.

   (Use ''they'' only once in combining the following sentences.)

6. They read the paper.
   They think about the news.
   The news is of the world.
   They enjoy their time.
   Their time is with each other.

*parts*

7. They pick up all the sections.*
   The sections are of the paper.
   [Their picking up] is later.
   They put them away.
   [Their putting] is neat.

8. They are cheerful.

*satisfied*

   They are content.*
   They begin the day.
   (Try putting ''cheerful'' and ''content'' in front of ''they.'')

## On Your Own

Write 10 sentences about what you do on Saturday evening (or Monday morning or Friday afternoon). Include in those sentences a variety of different compound parts. For example, read the following:

> On Monday morning, <u>my roommate and I</u> <u>scramble</u> to finish our <u>algebra and French homework</u> and then <u>race</u> off to class by <u>bus or car</u>.

Underline each compound part in your sentences.

## GETTING OLD _____

When you combine the sentences on page 7, write all of them as compound sentences, even though you will probably see other ways to combine. Think carefully about commas.

# MINI-NOTE ON COMPOUND SENTENCES————

## Definition:

A compound sentence is made up of two or more sentences (independent clauses) correctly joined into one longer sentence.

## Examples:

1. Harriet loves Paris, but her husband refuses to go there.
2. Abner couldn't find his wallet, so he telephoned his wife.
3. Salads are healthy; nevertheless many people don't eat them often enough.
4. Jack kissed his neighbor; she stared at him in surprise.

## Punctuation:

Any of these methods for combining may be used:

1. a comma and a coordinating conjunction
2. a semicolon
3. a semicolon followed by a conjunctive adverb

(See examples above.)

## Common Problems:

1. Don't confuse a sentence containing a compound verb with a compound sentence and therefore use an unnecessary comma:

**Incorrect:** George sailed all the way around the lake, but still couldn't find his friends.

**Correct:** George sailed all the way around the lake but still couldn't find his friends.

2. The comma splice—using only a comma between the parts of a compound sentence—is a common error:

**Incorrect:** George sailed all the way around the lake, he still couldn't find his friends.

**Correct:** George sailed all the way around the lake, but he still couldn't find his friends.

**See Grammar Note 8 for more details.**

1. Mr. Jenkins is quite old.
   He still drives his car.
   [His driving] is frequent.

2. He drives very carefully.
   His children don't worry about him.

3. It is difficult for him to see well at night.
   He tries to drive in daylight.
   [His trying] is usual.

4. Today he is going to a party.
   It is at 6:00 in the evening.
   He is not sure how to go.

   (Use two different conjunctions in combining the following sentences.)

5. It is at the Welden's house.
   He has been there many times.
   Someone else has always driven him.

6. Should he drive his car?
   Should he ask a younger friend to pick him up?

7. He decides to drive.
   He feels nervous.
   [His nervousness] is slight.
   He studies the map.
   [His study] is careful.

   (In combining the following sentences, if you use ''then,'' think about punctuation. If you use ''he'' more than twice, think again. The sentence may be too choppy.)

8. He drives on the freeway.
   [His driving] is for 10 miles.
   He takes the exit to Greenville.
   He drives north.

9. He makes a wrong turn.
   The turn is at an intersection.
   The intersection is confusing.
   He corrects his mistake.
   [The correction] is easy.

10. Mr. Jenkins is old.
    He is independent.

## On Your Own

Write one compound sentence for each of the coordinating conjunctions (and, but, or, nor, for, so, yet). Check your use of commas.

Now write *one* long sentence that uses each of those conjunctions. Read that sentence aloud. It probably sounds pretty bad. Remember how bad it sounds if you find yourself tempted to write long sentences with many clauses joined with conjunctions.

## A SPECIAL DESSERT

Since many adverbs can be correctly placed at several different points in a sentence, you may want to write two or more versions of some sentences in this exercise.

## MINI-NOTE ON ADVERBS

### Definition:

An adverb describes a verb by telling how, why, when, or where the action occurred. It can also intensify an adjective or another adverb.

### Examples:

1. They jogged yesterday. (when?)
2. He shouted angrily. (how?)
3. The sky turned very dark. (how dark?)
4. Diane took the book upstairs. (where?)

### A Common Problem:

Don't forget the "ly" at the end of an adverb that needs it:

**Incorrect:** They held hands and walked slow.

**Correct:** They held hands and walked slowly.

**Incorrect:** When he's angry, his face gets real red.

**Correct:** When he's angry, his face gets really red.

**See Grammar Note 4 for more details, especially about where adverbs may be placed in a sentence.**

1.  Fred likes to bake a cake.
    He likes it once a year.
    He likes it for Mother's Day.

2.  He looks through the cookbook.
    [His looking] is slow.
    The cookbook is thick.

3.  He takes out the ingredients.
    The ingredients are correct.
    He measures them.
    [His measuring] is careful.

4.  He mixes butter and sugar.
    [His mixing] is thorough.
    He mixes for four minutes.
    The four minutes is exact.

5.  He beats the egg whites.
    [His beating] is slow.
    Then he increases the speed.
    *little by little*    [The increase] is gradual.*

6.  He stirs everything together.
    [His stirring] is delicate.
    [His stirring] is with concentration.
    The concentration is great.
    *a mixture of unbaked ingredients*    He pours the batter* into the cake pan.

    (In combining the following sentences, think carefully about where the adverb goes.)

7.  He waits for the cake to bake.
    [His waiting] is anxious.

8.  He takes the cake out of the oven.
    *crooked; uneven*    The cake is lopsided.*
    He smiles.
    [His smiling] is regretful.

## On Your Own

Write one sentence for each of these adverbs: bashfully, competently, annoyingly, secretly, haughtily, intuitively. Make the sentences longer and more interesting than, "He smiled bashfully."

# WALKING TO WORK_____

## MINI-NOTE ON ADVERB PHRASES_____

### Definition:

A phrase is a group of words without a subject and verb. Phrases sometimes act as adverbs.

### Examples:

1.    Some people are grouchy <u>in the morning.</u> (when?)
2.    <u>Under the table</u>, the dog silently begged for food. (where?)
3.    Jason walked home <u>to save money</u>. (why?)

**Grammar Note 4 discusses the position of adverbs in sentences.**

1.    Professor Robinson lives.
      [His living] is near the university.

2.    He walks.
      [His walking] is usual.
      [His walking] is to his office.
      [His walking] is in fine weather.

3.    However, he takes the bus.
      [His taking] is when it rains.
      [His taking] is general.

4.    He goes.
      [His going] is early in the morning.
      [His going] is down.
      [His going] is to the lobby.*
      The lobby is of his apartment building.

*an area just inside the door of a building

5.    Then he looks.
      [His looking] is in his mailbox.
      [His looking] is for the letters.

6.    He leaves his building.
      He strolls.*
      [His strolling] is under a row of walnut trees.
      The trees are at the edge of a field.
      [His strolling] is on the way to the university.

*to walk in a slow, relaxed manner

7. As he walks, he thinks.
   [His thinking] is a little.
   [His thinking] is about his lecture.
   His lecture is next.

   (In the preceding sentence, is "next" an adverb or an adjective?)

8. But he also listens to the wind.
   The wind is blowing.
   [The blowing] is quiet.
   [The blowing] is through the trees.
   He feels the morning sun.
   The sun is on his face.

9. He turns.
   [His turning] is after crossing the main street.
   *to the north*
   [His turning] is northward.*
   He walks.
   [His walking] is along the path.
   The path is to his office building.

10. His walk has given him a clear mind.
    His walk has given him energy.
    The energy is to face the day.
    [His facing] is with calmness.

## On Your Own

Make a list of 20 adverbs and adverb phrases. Include adverbs of manner, of time, of place, and so on. Now use all those adverbs in five or six sentences—that is, about four of the adverbs in each sentence. Vary their position in the sentences. Here is an example:

> On payday, the family anxiously gathers in the dining room, and Dad calculates with care how much can be added to the vacation fund.

# THE OLD MAN

## MINI-NOTE ON PREPOSITIONAL PHRASES

### Definition:

Prepositions (words such as to, at, by, near, of, between, and under) show relationships between parts of sentences.

The noun or pronoun following a preposition is called the object of the preposition.

A prepositional phrase is made up of a preposition, its object, and any adjectives modifying the object.

A prepositional phrase can act as an adverb or an adjective.

## Examples:

1. She bought a bouquet of tulips. (an adjective phrase telling what kind of bouquet)

2. Evelyn drinks coffee in the morning. (an adverb phrase telling when she drinks)

3. All around the mulberry bush, the monkey chased the weasel. (an adverb phrase explaining where the chasing took place)

1. The man sits.
   [His sitting] is on the ground.
   [His sitting] is quiet.

2. Eyebrows cover his eyes.
   [The covering] is partial.*
   The eyebrows are thick.
   The eyebrows are white.

*not complete*

3. A few hairs grow.
   [The growing] is from his ears.
   The hairs are white.

4. He wears a robe.
   The robe is blue.
   [The wearing] is over his shoulders.
   His shoulders are thin.

5. One leg is bent.
   [The bending] is up to his chest.

6. His hands are folded.
   [The folding] is across his shin.*

*the part of the leg between the knee and the ankle*

7. He has a look.
   The look is of peace.
   The look is of humor.
   The look is on his face.

8. His struggles are finished.
   His struggles are with life.

9. He looks at the world.
[His looking] is with interest.
The interest is quiet.

10. He is made.
[The making] is of clay.
The clay is brown.

11. He is a statue.
The statue is Chinese.
The statue is small.
The statue is on my table.

## Suggestion:

Do your sentences for numbers 6 through 11 all begin with ''he'' or ''his''?
Try to move some words or phrases so the sentences don't all begin in the
same way.

# A JOGGING STORY _____

In this exercise, concentrate on adverbs and adverb phrases. Remember that
many adverbs end in ''ly.''

1. Jack Higgins jogs.
[The jogging] is usual.
[The jogging] is brisk.*
[The jogging] is around the reservoir.*
[The jogging] is in the morning.

*rather fast
*a man-made lake for
storing water

2. He saw a woman.
[The seeing] was last week.
[The seeing] was on the trail.
The trail was jogging.*
The woman was attractive.

*an adjective, not a
verb!

3. She was jogging.
The jogging was rather slow.
The jogging was in the direction.
The direction was opposite.

4. Women jog.
[The jogging] is hardly ever.
[The jogging] is at the reservoir.
Jack was surprised.

## MINI-NOTE ON COMMA SPLICES AND RUN-ON SENTENCES

Two common errors—the comma splice and the run-on sentence—result from uncertainty about where one sentence ends and another begins.

A comma splice is the joining of two sentences with only a comma:

**Incorrect:** Jack was tired, he walked to his car.

A run-on sentence is the joining of two sentences without any punctuation at all:

**Incorrect:** Jack was tired he walked to his car.

These errors can be corrected as follows:

Jack was tired, so he walked to his car.
Because Jack was tired, he walked to his car.
Jack was tired; he walked to his car.
Jack was tired; therefore he walked to his car.
Jack was tired. He walked to his car.

**See Grammar Note 14 for more details.**

5. He passed her.
    [The passing] was three or four times.
    She smiled.
    [The smiling] was distant.*
    [The smiling] was at him.

*not too friendly*

6. Jack walked.
    [The walking] was slow.
    [The walking] was after 45 minutes.
    [The walking] was to his car.

7. One car was there.
    The car was other.
    Jack thought [something].
    It must be the car.
    The car is the woman's.

8. A dog sat.
    The dog was huge.
    [The sitting] was in the back seat.
    [The sitting] was protective.
    The seat was of the convertible.*
    The convertible was open.

*car with a folding roof*

9.  Jack walked.
    [The walking] was near.
    The dog growled.
    [The growling] was low.
*threatening*　　　[The growling] was menacing.*

10. Jack decided [something].
    It was not to wait.
    [The waiting] was for the woman.
*not gladly*　　　[The deciding] was reluctant.*

# ANOTHER JOGGING STORY _____

1.  Beth Graves hasn't jogged.
    [The jogging] was for weeks.
    The weeks were a few.

2.  She had been jogging.
    [The jogging] was regular.
    [The jogging] was in the park.
    [The jogging] was with enjoyment.
    The enjoyment was great.

3.  Something happened.
    The something was frightening.
    [The happening] was then.
    [The happening] was one morning.
*storage building*　　　[The happening] was behind a tool shed.*

4.  A group attacked some runners.
    The group was of boys.
    [The attack] was for no reason.
*with violence*　　　[The attack] was vicious.*

5.  Beth decided not to jog.
    [The deciding] was immediate.
    [The jogging] was in the park.
    [The jogging] was any longer.

6.  She is running.
    The running is at the reservoir.
    The running is today.
    The running is for the first time.

    (Sentence 7 on the following page should be a compound sentence.
    See Grammar Note 8.)

7.  However, people are there.
    The people are hardly any.
    Beth feels nervous.
    [The nervousness] is slight.

8.  One man passes her.
    The man is tall.
    [The passing] is repeated.
    He smiles.
    [The smiling] is each time.

    (The following should be a compound sentence. You will probably find that ''and'' doesn't sound right.)

9.  Beth jogs.
    [The jogging] is in a different direction.
    [The jogging] is to avoid the man.
    She feels silly.
    [The silliness] is a little.
    She feels overly* cautious.

*too much

10. She also feels silly.
    [The silliness] is about having left the dog.
    The dog is large.
    The dog is her neighbor's.
    [The leaving] was in her car.

11. Everyone told her [something].
    It was to be careful.
    Perhaps she has taken their advice.
    [The taking] is too serious.
    (This sentence will also be compound.)

## On Your Own

Each of the following sentences contains a commonly used adverb or adverb phrase—in fact, the adverbs are so common that they are almost boring. Substitute a less commonly used adverb or adverb phrase to give the sentences some life. If you wish, you can add details to the sentences to make the new adverbs ''fit'' better. For example,

**Ordinary:** The coach blew his whistle loudly.

**More Lively:** The coach blew his whistle fiercely in a futile attempt to end the fight.

1.  Sylvia studied <u>hard</u> all weekend.
2.  The skaters moved <u>gracefully</u> across the ice.
3.  George ate <u>quickly</u>.

4. Henry slept <u>soundly</u>.
5. Alice smiled <u>sweetly</u> at the old man in the trench coat.
6. Bill gathered his books <u>in a hurry</u> and ran <u>quickly</u> to class.
7. Grandpa snored <u>loudly</u> all night.
8. The children argued <u>all the time</u>.
9. We looked <u>high and low</u> for the missing keys.
10. The sun shone <u>brightly</u>.

## THE END OF THE JOGGING STORY

Include an adverb clause in each sentence. Think carefully about the use of commas.

## MINI-NOTE ON ADVERB CLAUSES

### Definition:

A clause is a group of words with a subject and a verb. Some clauses modify verbs, so they are called adverb clauses. An adverb clause must be part of the sentence that contains the verb it modifies. It cannot be punctuated as a separate sentence.

### Examples:

1. I felt much better <u>when I had eaten</u>. (tells when I felt better)
2. <u>Because it was raining,</u> Tracy stayed home. (tells why Tracy stayed home)
3. Aunt Gladys found her false teeth <u>where she had left them</u>. (tells where she found her teeth)

### Punctuation:

A comma is used after an adverb clause but not before. See the examples above.

### A Common Problem:

Punctuating an adverb clause as if it were a complete sentence results in the error known as a fragment.

> **Incorrect:** I ate four bananas. Because I was hungry.
>
> **Correct:** I ate four bananas because I was hungry.
>
> **See Grammar Note 5 for full details.**

1.  Beth Graves is tired.
    She had a day.
    The day was busy.
    The day was at work.
    She has to go out.
    [The going] is this evening.

    (This first sentence may need two adverb clauses.)

2.  She is going to a meeting.
    The meeting is political.
    She wants to work.
    [The working] is for the election.
    The election is of a new mayor.

3.  She arrives.
    [The arrival] is at the meeting.
    She looks around.
    She doesn't know anyone.

*begins
4.  The meeting is called to order.*
    She thinks she recognizes the chairman.

*remember where she
saw before
5.  She isn't able to place* him.
    The meeting ends.
    [The ending] is at 10:30.

    (Consider ''until'' in combining the preceding sentences.)

6.  He walks.
    [The walking] is toward her.
    He smiles.
    He knows her.

    (You will probably need ''as if'' to combine the previous sentences. An ambitious thing to do would be to combine sentences 5 and 6—perhaps using the word ''when.'' An even more ambitious thing would be to combine sentences 4, 5, and 6.)

7.  He introduces himself.
    [The introduction] is as Jack Higgins.
    He asks about her jogging.

8. She tells him about the park.
   She tells him about the dog.
   He understands her behavior.
   Her behavior was at the reservoir.
   Her behavior was last week.

9. They leave the meeting.
   They have a plan.
   The plan is to meet.
   [The meeting] is again.
   [The meeting] is in the morning.
   [The meeting] is to jog.
   [The meeting] is together.

### On Your Own

Write ten sentences with adverb clauses. Place some of them at the beginning of the sentence, some of them in the middle, and some at the end. Check your punctuation carefully.

## GETTING OLD AGAIN _____

Yes, you have seen this exercise before, for practice in writing compound sentences. This time, combine them using as many adverb clauses as you can. Not every sentence will have an adverb clause, but most of them will. See Grammar Note 5 if necessary.

1. Mr. Jenkins is quite old.
   He still drives his car.
   [His driving] is frequent.

2. He drives very carefully.
   His children don't worry about him.

3. It is difficult for him to see well at night.
   He tries to drive in daylight.
   [His trying] is usual.

4. Today he is going to a party.
   It is at 6:00 in the evening.
   He is not sure how to go.

5. It is at the Welden's house.
   He has been there many times.
   Someone else has always driven him.

6. Should he drive his car?
   Should he ask a younger friend to pick him up?

7. He decides to drive.
   He feels nervous.
   [His nervousness] is slight.
   He studies the map.
   [His study] is careful.

8. He drives on the freeway.
   [His driving] is for 10 miles.
   He takes the exit to Greenville.
   He drives north.

9. He makes a wrong turn.
   The turn is at an intersection.
   The intersection is confusing.
   He corrects his mistake.
   [The correction] is easy.

10. Mr. Jenkins is old.
    He is independent.

## On Your Own

Sometimes students rely too much on a few sentence structures that they have mastered and feel confident of. The result can be a monotonous style that sounds somewhat immature. Overreliance on compound sentences, for example, is a relatively common problem. Read the following passage—preferably aloud—to get the feel of its unsatisfactory style. Then revise the passage so that the sentence structure is more varied. Look especially for opportunities to use adverb clauses (but too many of them could also sound awkward).

### About Mr. Jenkins

Mr. Jenkins had a very interesting career, and he didn't want to retire, but company policy prohibited elderly employees, so he was forced into retirement five years ago. He was a diamond merchant, and his work took him all over the world, so he saw many interesting places, and he met many interesting people. Once a year he went to Africa, and three times a year he went to Europe, and once in a while he was sent to South America. He felt uneasy after he retired, and for a few months he didn't know what to do with his time, but then he learned to play bridge, and he also developed an interest in oil painting, and those things began to occupy more and more of his time. He also met a retired woman, and she enjoys bridge, too, and they care very much for each other, but they think they are too old to consider marriage, so they spend a lot of time together, but their children keep suggesting that they marry, so they are thinking of changing their minds.

# WORK TABLE

---

**MINI-NOTE ON ADJECTIVES**

**Definition:**

An adjective describes a noun. It can tell which noun, or what kind of noun, or how many.

**Examples:**

1. The silver necklace was expensive.
2. The poem was long and boring.
3. Sleek and glossy, the cat purred in contentment.
4. A small, hungry kitten cried on the porch.
5. Two dry old sandwiches had been left in the sink.

**See Grammar Note 2 for more details, especially about the order of adjectives and whether to use a comma between two of them.**

---

1. The table is in the middle of the room.
   The table is messy.

2. Six books lie on the left.
   The books are open.
   The books are in a pile.
   The pile is disorganized.

3. A cup is near the notebook.
   The notebook is yellow.
   The cup is white.
   The cup is empty.

4. A bowl is at the edge of the table.
   The bowl is plastic.
   The bowl is blue.
   The blue is bright.

5. The bowl holds popcorn.
   The popcorn is stale.*
   The popcorn is old.

   *not fresh*

6. Scattered* everywhere are notecards.
   The cards are white.

   *spread out*

The cards are yellow.
The cards are green.

7. On the right is a composition.
   It is neatly typed.
   It is long.

8. A student has been at work.
   The student is serious.

## On Your Own

Write five sentences crowded with adjectives. Put adjectives in front of the nouns they modify and after. Put them after the verb. Put them in strings of three or four and practice with the punctuation. The sentences will probably sound rather strange, but they are just for practice. So when you write paragraphs or compositions, don't use this many adjectives—except, perhaps, once in a while for a special effect.

# THE BLACK CUP

1. Coffee cups are unusual.
   *fine china for dishes*    The cups are porcelain.*
   The cups are black.

2. This cup was made in Japan.
   *delicate; easily broken*    The cup is fragile.*
   The cup is handsome.

3. The surfaces are black.
   The surfaces are inner.
   The surfaces are outer.
   The black is deep.
   *shiny*    The black is glossy.*

4. One side is decorated.
   The side is of the cup.
   *a kind of flower*    [The decoration] is with a peony.*
   The peony is red.
   The red is brilliant.
   The peony is on a branch.
   *twisted*    The branch is gnarled.*

5. Leaves surround the flower.
   The leaves are green.
   The green is pale.
   The leaves are heart-shaped.

*unopened flowers*

6. Two buds* are on branches.
    The buds are round.
    The buds are small.
    The branches are off to one side.

*flies in one place*

7. A butterfly hovers.*
    [The hovering] is on the right.
    The butterfly is brown.
    The brown is light.
    The butterfly is with spots.
    The spots are red.
    The spots are blue.

8. The cup seems too beautiful.
    [The beauty] is for use.
    The use is daily.

## On Your Own

The adjectives in the following passage are not very effective because they are quite general and are the ones that usually come to mind first. Revise the passage so that the adjectives are more precise and interesting:

> Sheila McNair is the prettiest girl in her first grade class. She has shiny black hair and blue eyes that are bright and intelligent. Her pink cheeks are round and chubby. Her sweet smile frames straight, pearly teeth. Her behavior is as nice as her looks. Her voice is soft, and her manners are polite. Mr. Phillips, her teacher, worries about her, however, because she seems too good to be true.

When you finish revising that passage, write seven or eight interesting sentences using these adjectives—or other adjectives that you like but don't use too often:

| | | |
|---|---|---|
| gaseous | mottled | unbecoming |
| waxy | pungent | elliptical |
| rotund | bulging | matted |
| ingenuous | disoriented | inky |

# IN THE BOOKSTORE

Include one adjective clause in each sentence in the exercise beginning on page 24. You may need such expressions as ''in which'' and ''of whom'' as well as the more common relative pronouns.

## MINI-NOTE ON ADJECTIVE CLAUSES_____

### Definition:

A clause is a group of words with a subject and a verb. If a clause describes a noun, it is called an adjective clause.

### Examples:

1.   She wore a pair of shoes <u>that pinched her toes.</u> (tells which shoes)

2.   I want a teacher <u>who can control children without being unkind.</u> (tells what kind of teacher)

3.   They found the drawer <u>in which Grandpa had hidden his diary.</u> (which drawer)

4.   St. Louis, <u>where they first met,</u> remained their favorite city. (describes St. Louis)

5.   Mr. Jones, <u>who drinks too much beer,</u> is quite stout. (describes Mr. Jones)

Words that introduce adjective clauses (<u>that, which, who,</u> for example) are called relative pronouns.

**See Grammar Note 3 for more details, especially about the adjective clauses that must be separated from the rest of the sentence by commas.**

1.   John Robinson goes to bookstores.
     John Robinson is a professor of English.
     [His going] is often.

2.   He likes bookstores.
     He can also drink coffee [there].
     He can sit in a comfortable chair [there].

3.   ''The Bookshelf'' is the name of his favorite bookstore.
     He goes [there] on Sunday afternoons.
     The afternoons are rainy.

4.   His second favorite bookstore is downtown.
     He goes [there] after busy days on campus.
     It is called ''The Book Inn.''

5.   Coffee is served at ''The Book Inn.''
     The coffee is stale.
     The coffee is bitter.
     The coffee is lukewarm.*

*not very warm

6. Nevertheless, Professor Robinson likes that shop.
   There are good chairs [there].
   *partly hidden;* There are secluded* corners.
   *private* There are low prices.

7. The coffee is much better.
   The coffee is at "The Bookshelf."
   And there are poets [there].
   The poets sit quietly.
   [Their sitting] is all day.
   They write.

8. The shop owner is a shy woman.
   She is a pleasant woman.
   She is a well-informed woman.
   Her father and grandfather were also bookdealers.

9. Professor Robinson had a talk with her.
   The talk was last Sunday.
   The talk disturbed him.
   *a lot* [The disturbance] was considerable.*

10. The owner is planning to retire.
    Professor Robinson has grown fond of the owner.
    She is planning to close the shop.

11. Professor Robinson will have to find another bookstore.
    He can be comfortable [there].
    He can be relaxed [there].

## On Your Own

Write six sentences with adjective clauses. Use "that" in only one of them.

# DISCOUNT STORES

Not every sentence in this exercise will have an adjective clause. Some sentences can be written with or without. It is usually better to use a single-word adjective than to express the same idea in a clause.

1. People like to shop in stores.
   *prices are lower than* The stores are discount.*
   *in other stores* The people are many.
   The people are careful about money.

2. These stores do business in a way.
   The way permits them to offer prices.
   The prices are low.

*not downtown*

**3.** Discount stores are often in areas.
The areas are suburban.*
The rents are not too high [there].

**4.** The stores have interiors.
The stores have exteriors.

*last for a long time; strong*

The interiors and exteriors are simple.
They are durable.*

*business methods*

**5.** These practices* keep the cost down.
The cost is of running the business.
The prices can be low.
The customers pay the prices.

**6.** Buying also keeps costs down.

*buying a lot*

The buying is in quantity.*

**7.** This is true.
It is true for the stores.
It is true for the customers.

**8.** A store can buy cheaply.
The store buys in quantities.
The quantities are large.
It can sell cheaply.

**9.** A customer can save money.
The customer can buy 30 pounds of potatoes.
The customer can buy 100 plates.
The plates are paper.

**10.** This can be a disadvantage for people.
The people are single.
The people don't usually need so much.

**11.** Discount stores can help families.
The families are young.

*don't have extra money*

The families are on tight budgets.*
The stores have existed for only about 25 years.

**12.** They also attract people.
The people don't like to pay prices.
The prices are unnecessarily high.

## On Your Own

The following passage contains some unsatisfactory adjective clauses. As you revise it, think of punctuation and relative pronouns. In some cases, you may want to eliminate the clause and use a single-word adjective instead.

Herb Johnson is a man that doesn't like to waste money. His family does most of its shopping at Thrifty City which is a large discount store on the far north side of Westborough. The Johnsons live on the south side, and the long drive, that goes through the crowded downtown district, annoys Herb's wife who has a busy schedule. Sandra has always argued that they spend on gas what they save on groceries at Thrifty City, and Herb has always disagreed. This minor argument that has lasted for ten years would probably have continued forever except that Sandra recently got a new job, that requires significant changes in the way the family operates. Sandra can't work, take the children to their piano lessons and ball games, and shop for groceries. Herb's schedule that is rather flexible can be changed to include grocery shopping. Sandra who has a good sense of humor, is amused that Herb now calls the drive to Thrifty City unhealthy. The explanation, that he presented in detail last night, is that the heavy traffic that is downtown raises his blood pressure and makes him irritable. He added that spending a little extra money at the neighborhood supermarket is worth the benefit to his health and their marriage which has always been harmonious.

# MINI-NOTE ON COMMAS WITH ADJECTIVE CLAUSES

Some adjective clauses must be separated from the rest of the sentence with commas; others should not be separated. Here is an easy and almost foolproof method for determining which is which:

Look at the noun being modified by the clause and ask yourself if it is already identified without the information in the clause. If the answer is Yes, then Yes you need a comma. If the answer is No, then No you don't need a comma.

## Examples:

1.  The man <u>who lives upstairs</u> snores every night. Is the man identified without the information in the clause? No, it could be any man. No commas.

2.  Mr. Appleby, <u>who lives upstairs,</u> snores every night. Is Mr. Appleby identified without the information in the clause? Yes, we know his name. Yes, commas are used.

## A WEDDING PRESENT_____

Every sentence in this exercise will contain a noun clause.

---

### MINI-NOTE ON NOUN CLAUSES_____

#### Definition:

A clause is a group of words with a subject and a verb. A clause that functions the way a noun does (for example, as a subject or direct object) is called a noun clause.

#### Examples:

1.   I forgot <u>what I wanted to say.</u> (direct object—what did I forget?)
2.   <u>Whoever stole my car</u> will be sorry. (subject—who will be sorry?)
3.   The fact <u>that she was 20 minutes late</u> didn't seem to bother her. (appositive—renames "fact")

**Grammar Note 11 discusses noun clauses in more detail.**

---

1.   Cathy Benson just remembered [something].
     She must buy a wedding present.
     The present is for her aunt.

*\*unusual; strange*
     The aunt is eccentric.*

     (If you are tempted to end the following with a question mark, don't do it. Can you see why it would be incorrect?

2.   She wonders [something].
     It is what you buy.
     [The buying] is for a woman.
     The woman is getting married.
     The getting married is for the fourth time.

*\*choice of style*
3.   The fact worries her.
     The fact is that her aunt has taste.*
     The taste is unpredictable.

4.   Perhaps [someone] can advise her.

*\*what a salesperson
does to help customers*
     It is whoever waits on* her.
     [The waiting on] is in the gift section.
     The section is of Mallon's Department Store.

*looks here and there*    **5.**  Cathy browses* around.
        She examines [something].
        It is whatever seems unusual.

    **6.**  She asks the saleswoman [something].
        It is what those plates are.
        The plates are metal.
        The plates are small.

    **7.**  [Something] interests her.
        It is what she hears.

    **8.**  They are plates.
*snails*         The plates are for baking escargots.*
        Cathy decides [something].
*be acceptable*    It is that they will do.*

    **9.**  [Something] will probably be wrong.
        It is whatever she chooses.

  **10.**  Her aunt can exchange the plates for [something].
        It is whatever she likes.
        [The liking] is real.

        (Try combining sentences 9 and 10.)

  **11.**  Cathy feels relieved.
        She has done [something].
        It is what she can.

### On Your Own

Write five sentences of your own with noun clauses in them. Vary the position of the clauses—some subjects, some direct objects, etc.

## AT THE COMPUTER_____

In the exercise beginning on page 30, use a participial phrase in every sentence but the third. Some sentences will also contain single-word participles.

## MINI-NOTE ON PARTICIPIAL PHRASES_____

### Definition:

A participle is a verb used as an adjective. A present participle ends with "ing" (running shoes). A past participle ends with "ed" or "en" or "t" (a baked potato, a broken arm).

A participial phrase is made up of a participle, its object, and any modifiers (eating a scrambled egg).

### Examples:

1. Shouting into the microphone, the announcer informed his listeners that there was a winner at last.

2. The shelf, bent from the weight of too many books, finally cracked.

3. The dog crept under the bed, terrified by the thunder.

**See Grammar Note 12, especially for the difference between a past and a present participle.**

1. Ben Fox stretched.
   [The stretching] was tired.
   He sat.
   [The sitting] was at his desk.

*felt dull pain*
*tense; stiff*

2. His neck ached.*
   His neck was cramped.*
   [The cramping] was from hours.
   The hours were long.
   The hours were of work.

   (Use an appositive in combining the following sentences. See Grammar Note 6 for an explanation.)

3. Nevertheless, his computer had been a help.
   The computer was a gift.
   The gift was unexpected.
   The gift was from his grandparents.
   The help was big.
   The help was in writing his term paper.

4. He took one look.
   The look was last.
   The look was at the pages.
   The pages were finished.

He felt satisfied.
[The satisfaction] was with himself.

*looked quickly*

5. He glanced* at the fifth page.
[The glancing] was casual.
He saw something.
The something was annoying.

(In combining the following sentences, change "showed" to a participle.)

*form of a language spoken in a particular region*
*English spoken before 1500 A.D.*

6. The chart was not centered.
The chart showed the dialects.*
The dialects were of Middle English.*
[The centering] was proper.
[The centering] was on the page.

7. Ben reached.
[The reaching] was for the manual.*
*book of instructions*
The manual was thick.
He sighed.
[The sighing] was in frustration.
The frustration was mild.

8. He was confused.
[The confusion] was by the instructions.
The instructions were complicated.
He decided to wait.
[The waiting] was until evening.

9. Besides, the sunshine was calling him.
*mirrored*
The sunshine was reflected.*
[The reflection] was on the screen.
The screen was of the computer.
The calling was to come out.

10. He walked out.
[The walking] was to the volleyball court.
*an old saying: All work and no play makes Jack a dull boy.*
He told himself.
[The telling] was about all work and no play.*

## On Your Own

Revise the passage on page 32 to eliminate all dangling modifiers. Some sentences may require considerable rewriting in order to eliminate the error.

# MINI-NOTE ON DANGLING MODIFIERS————

## Definition:

A participial phrase that modifies the wrong word or no word at all is called a dangling modifier.

## Examples:

**Incorrect:** Frightened by his anger, large tears streamed down her face. (This says that her tears were frightened.)

**Incorrect:** Studying all night, the test was still too hard. (This says that the test was studying.)

To correct the error, you must place the participial phrase close to the word it actually modifies. Sometimes the sentence is better written in a completely different way.

**Correct:** Frightened by his anger, she wept, and large tears streamed down her face.

**Correct:** Henry studied all night, but the test was still too hard.

**See Grammar Note 15 for a more detailed discussion.**

Stretching for the spinning ball hurtling over the net, a terrible thought came into Ben's head. The letter he had written to his grandparents to thank them for the computer was still in the backpack he had accidentally left hanging in his gym locker. He abruptly left the game and his friends annoyed by his thoughtlessness.

Racing across campus, his parents' voices echoed in his ears: ''To be an adult, responsibilities must be taken seriously. Going off to college, your family shouldn't be neglected. Your grandparents are proud of you, so don't let them sit at home waiting to hear from you.'' Embarrassed by his negligence, Ben's feet ran even faster, as if to get away from the voices. Reaching the gym red-faced and out of breath, Ben could hardly explain to the locker room attendant why he was there after hours, but he retrieved his backpack, raced to the mailbox, and, exhausted by the long run, the letter was finally mailed.

Now write five sentences of your own that contain participial phrases. Use present and past participles, and don't put them all at the beginning of the sentences.

# WINTER CACTUS_____

Use a gerund in numbers 1, 3, 4, 5, 6, 8, 9, and 10.

---

## MINI-NOTE ON GERUNDS_____

### Definition:

A gerund is a verb with an "ing" ending used as a noun, that is, as the subject, direct object, or object of a preposition.

### Examples:

1.  Jogging is quite popular. (subject) (But in the following sentence, jogging is used as a present participle: Jogging shoes can be expensive.)
2.  Helga enjoys walking in the rain. (direct object)
3.  Mother ignored Bobby's whining. (direct object)
4.  By insisting on perfection, Mr. Grimes made himself very unpopular. (object of a preposition)

**See Grammar Note 9 for a more detailed discussion.**

---

1.  [Something] sounds impossible.
    It is to grow cactus.
    [The growth] is in a cold climate.

2.  Most people believe [something].
    It is that cactus can survive.
    [The survival] is only in the heat.
    [The survival] is only in the dryness.
    The heat and dryness are of the desert.

    (Now try combining the first and second sentences you have written.)

3.  [Something] is the secret.
    It is to keep the plant indoors.
    It is to keep the plant at a window.
    The secret is to success in cold weather.

4.  [Something] is a surprise.
    It is to see cactus.
    The cactus are large.
    The cactus are in bloom.*
    The surprise is in the north of Germany.

*producing flowers

5.  There people appreciate [something].
    It is to have green plants.
    The plants are in their homes.
    [The appreciation] is because of the winter.
    The winter is long.
    The winter is hard.

6.  People have difficulty in [something].
    The people are from climates.
    The climates are warm.
    The difficulty is to imagine the effect.
    The effect is of so many winter months.
    The months are without color.

7.  The sky presses down.
    The sky is gray.
    The trees are brown.
    The brown is pale.
    Even the houses have lost their color.
    The houses are brick.
    The brick is red.

8.  [Something] is a reminder.
    It is to be able to see green plants.
    The plants are at the window.
    The reminder is important.
    The reminder is that nature is not dead.

    (The following one isn't easy. You might want to look at Grammar
    Note 9 again to review the use of a gerund after a preposition and the
    use of the possessive in front of the gerund.)

*grow in a healthy way*

9.  The cactus plants thrive.*
    [The thriving] is in spite of [something].
    It is that the winter is so dark.

10. It is difficult.
    [The difficulty] is to imagine.
    But it proves the truth.

*a saying*

    The truth is of the adage.*
    The adage is old.
    The adage is ''To see is to believe.''
    (In combining the sentences above, change ''to see'' and ''to believe''
    into gerunds.)

# WALKING HOME

Each sentence in this exercise should have a gerund phrase.

1. [Something] was a pleasure.
   It was to walk home.
   [The walk] was after school.
   The pleasure was great.
   [The walk] was when we were children.

2. The pleasure was [something].
   It was to feel free of rules.
   The rules were strict.
   It was to feel free of discipline.
   *related to studies*      The discipline was academic.*
   The pleasure was of the first few minutes.

3. [Something] was allowed.
   It was to run.
   It was to shout.
   [The allowance] was just beyond the playground.

   (Since dry leaves and snowballs occur in different seasons, you may not want to use ''and'' in the next sentence.)

4. Then came the pleasure of [something].
   It was to kick leaves.
   The leaves were dry.
   It was to make snowballs.
   The snowballs were giant.
   The snowballs were of snow.
   The snow was soft.
   The snow was damp.

5. There was the pleasure of [something].
   It was to walk home.
   [The walk] was with a group of girlfriends.
   [This was] a few years later.

6. [Something] filled our time.
   *laugh in a silly way*      It was to giggle* about boys.
   The boys were silly.
   It was to gossip about teachers.
   The teachers were our favorite.

7. In high school came the pleasure of [something].
   It was to walk home.
   [The walk] was with a boy.

*damp (from
nervousness)*

It was to hold hands.
The hands were clammy.*

(In combining the following sentences, use two adverb clauses as well
as a gerund.)

8.  We got close to home.
    We let go.
    We were afraid of [something].
    It was to be seen by our mothers.

(In combining the following sentences, begin with "now that.")

9.  We are adults.
    Most of us drive home.
    We have lost the habit of [something].
    It is to take time out.
    [This is] between work and family.

### On Your Own

Write a fairly long gerund phrase that has something to do with your childhood. Now use that same phrase in as many sentences as you can. For example: Hanging around the pool parlor was strictly forbidden when I was a
child. My father forbade hanging around the pool parlor when I was a child.
You might also try using the same phrase as a present participle: Hanging
around the pool parlor, Hank learned about the ways of the world.

## A BORING LECTURER

1.  Professor Bateson knows history.
    The history is American.
    [The knowing] is in detail.
    The detail is great.
    He delivers lectures.
    The lectures are boring.

(If you make this first sentence compound, think carefully about what
conjunction to use. The sentence can also be complex.)

2.  The problem is [something].
    It is that he is shy.
    [The shyness] is extreme.
    The problem is major.

3.  His voice is low.
    His voice is monotonous.*
    He looks.

*doesn't change*

[The looking] is rare.
[The looking] is at the class.

*stopped

4. He forgets [something].
   It is where he left off.*
   [The leaving off] was at the last lecture.
   [The forgetting] is often.
   He repeats himself.
   [The repeating] is frequent.

5. He loses his place.
   The place is in his notes.
   His face turns red.
   He says, "Uh, let's see here."

6. Students like him.
   [The liking] is nevertheless.
   He is kind.
   He is fair.
   He cares about them.

   (In combining the following sentences, try "although" or "even if.")

7. And the subject is interesting.
   The subject is of his lectures.
   The style is awful.

   (Use an adverb clause in combining the following sentences.)

8. He is a man.
   The man is different.
   [The difference] is complete.
   He is in his office.

9. There he is relaxed.
   He is confident.
   He looks at the people.
   The people come to talk.

10. The enrollment is huge.
    The enrollment is in his classes.
    He was voted [something].
    It was the teacher.
    The teacher was the most popular.
    The teacher was of the year.
    [The voting] was recent.

11. His students forgive [something].
    It is the way he lectures.
    They wish [something].
    It is that he would improve his style.

**On Your Own**

Write between six and ten sentences about a teacher you once had. Include in those sentences a variety of structures that you have recently practiced with, things such as participial phrases and noun clauses.

# THE HORSE THAT RAN AWAY
# (A CHINESE FABLE)

1. Once there was a man.
   The man was old.
   The man raised horses.
   The horses were fine.*

*beautiful and expensive*

2. The horse ran.
   The horse was his best.
   [The running] was away.
   [The running] was into the woods.
   [The running] was one day.

3. The friends came.
   The friends were the old man's.
   [The coming] was to sympathize.*

*to say they felt sorry for him*

4. They said [something].
   "Your horse is lost."
   "The horse is the best."
   "What bad luck!"

5. The man looked.
   The man was old.
   [The looking] was down.
   He said [something].
   "Perhaps."

6. The horse came back.
   [The coming] was three weeks later.
   [The coming] was with horses.
   The horses were five.
   The horses were wild.
   The horses were magnificent.*

*very handsome*

7. The neighbors came.
   [The coming] was to congratulate the man.
   The man was old.
   [The congratulation] was on his luck.
   His luck was good.

8. They said [something].
   ''You have five horses.''
   ''The horses are new.''
   ''You didn't have to pay.''
   ''[The paying] was one penny.''
   ''How fortunate you are!''

9. The old man looked.
   [The looking] was up at the sky.
   He said [something].
   ''We'll see.''

   (Use an adverb clause in combining the following sentences.)

10. The son was riding.
    The son was the old man's.
    [The riding] was on the back.
    The back was of one of the horses.
    The horses were new.
    He fell off.
    He broke his leg.

11. All the neighbors came.
    [The coming] was once again.
    [The coming] was to sympathize.

12. They said [something].
    ''What bad luck!''

13. The old man looked.
    [The looking] was down.
    He said [something].
    ''Perhaps.''

    (The sentence you write to combine the following will probably have to be compound and complex.)

14. The soldiers came.
    The soldiers were the emperor's.
    [The coming] was soon.
    [The coming] was to take all the men.
    The men were young.
    [The taking] was to fight in a war.
    They couldn't take the son.
    The son was the old man's.
    He had a leg.
    The leg was broken.

15. The neighbors came.
    [The coming] was again.

[The coming] was to congratulate the man.
The man was old.

16.  They said [something].
"Your son doesn't have to go."
"[The going] is to war."
"What good luck!"

(Try combining sentences 15 and 16 by changing "said" to a participle. See Grammar Note 12.)

17.  The old man looked.
[The looking] was up at the sky.
All he said was [something].
"We'll see."

## On Your Own

Write a few sentences explaining the old man's attitude toward life.

# EXPANDING THE BASICS AND DESIGNING PARAGRAPHS

# 2

This chapter is quite similar to the first, but the sentences you will be writing are longer and more complex. As part of the process of learning to write in a more varied and flexible way, you will also be asked to use some words (such as "consequently") and structures (such as restrictive clauses) that you may not have used too frequently before. You will also be asked to write some paragraphs of your own. To assist you, each paragraph assignment includes a general outline for you to follow. Reading Composition Note 3 on paragraphs will be helpful.

If punctuation has been a problem for you—especially using commas— it would be useful to concentrate on punctuating the sentences in these exercises. There are two ways you can improve your punctuation skills. One way is to read Grammar Note 13 on punctuation. Skim through it rather rapidly, noting the parts you will need to refer to in more detail. That note, however, makes reference to various types of sentences and various elements of the sentence, so you might prefer to begin your work on punctuation in another way. That way is to begin by studying Grammar Note 8, if you haven't done so already, on compound sentences and compound parts of sentences. Once you understand how compounds work, you will find using commas less of a problem. Then study the grammar notes on adverb clauses, adjective clauses, and noun clauses. When you have done that, you should feel confident that you can avoid making the common errors in punctuation. You can refer quickly to the note on punctuation whenever you have a question, perhaps going directly to an example that you remember rather than reading through the entire explanation. If you occasionally spend five minutes browsing through the rest of that note, looking over the discussions of other punctuation marks, you will probably find that you remember more than if you spend one long session trying to memorize all the rules.

## WAITING TOO LONG

In this exercise, write as many adverb clauses as you can. Concentrate particularly on using these words as you combine: because, as, since, so . . . that, such . . . that. Some sentences, however, will require other words.

1.   It is late in May.
   The end is coming.
   The end is of the semester.
   [The coming] is soon.

   (In combining the following sentences, use "so . . . that.")

2.   Hubert Nelson has much work to do.
   He feels anxious.
   [His anxiety] is extreme.

## MINI-NOTE ON TROUBLE SPOTS WITH ADVERB CLAUSES_____

1.  The structures "so . . . that" and "such . . . that" may be unfamiliar. Here are some examples of how to use them:

    The meal was so large <u>that no one could finish it.</u> (the clause modifies "large")
    He built up such anger <u>that he couldn't control himself.</u> (the clause modifies "such")

2.  The word that introduces an adverb clause is called a subordinating conjunction. In sentence combining and in your own writing, be sure to attach the subordinating conjunction to the right idea. If it gets in the wrong place, the result will be illogical.

**Illogical:** Although he didn't eat breakfast, he was hungry.

**Logical:** Although he was hungry, he didn't eat breakfast.

Also, be sure to use the subordinating conjunction that expresses the exact relationship between the ideas in the sentence.

**Illogical:** Even though George forgot to water the plant, it dried up and died.

**Logical:** Because George forgot to water the plant, it dried up and died.

**See Grammar Note 5 for other subordinating conjunctions.**

3.  He doesn't like science.
    [His liking] is very much.
    He has neglected his chemistry class.
    [His neglect] was for several months.

4.  Now he has so many experiments.
    He must do the experiments.
    He is afraid he won't finish.
    [His finishing] is on time.

5.  The lab assistant likes Hubert.
    She is giving him a chance.
    The chance is to spend time.
    The time is extra.
    [The spending] is in the lab.

(In combining the following sentences, use ''such . . . that.'')

**6.** But he has dislike.
The dislike is of working.
[The work] is there.
He cannot force himself.
[The forcing] is to go.

*to delay or postpone
an unpleasant task

**7.** He procrastinated.*
[His procrastination] was this morning.
[His procrastination] was so long.
It is too late to do anything.
[The doing] is today.

**8.** He told himself [something].
It was that he had to do his laundry.
He realizes [something].
It was only an excuse.
[His realization] is now.

**9.** He feels guilty.
He feels quite ashamed.
The lab assistant has been so kind.

**10.** He cannot work on chemistry.
[His working] is today.
He decides to write the paper.
The paper is for his history class.
He does not feel happy.
[His happiness] is with himself.

## On Your Own

Write six sentences containing adverb clauses. Do not use ''because'' or ''although.'' Vary the positions of the adverb clauses.

Next, write a paragraph by completing the following outline. For each blank, write at least three sentences.

> Topic sentence: Guilt can sometimes cause people to improve their behavior. Hubert Nelson feels guilty because _____. He could avoid a repetition of this situation if he _____. But if he continues to procrastinate, his guilt will _____.

# HOMEMADE NOODLES

Use an infinitive in numbers 1, 2, 4, 5, 7, 11, 13, and 15 of the exercise beginning on page 45.

## MINI-NOTE ON INFINITIVES

### Definition:

An infinitive is the "to" form of a verb: to swallow, to hop, to listen.

    An infinitive (and the infinitive phrase) can be used as a noun (subject, direct object), an adjective, or an adverb. Sometimes only part of the infinitive is needed.

### Examples:

1. Beulah likes to sleep in the afternoon. (direct object)
2. It is difficult to ride a bicycle in the woods. (delayed subject)
3. Ben should have cleaned the garage, but he didn't want to. (incomplete infinitive)
4. A small box to put the kitten in was what they needed. (adjective)
5. To keep the children quiet, Mrs. Jasper promised them a special dessert. (adverb)

**Grammar Note 10 contains a more detailed discussion of infinitives.**

1. [Something] is not difficult.
   It is to make noodles.
   The noodles are your own.
   [The making] is at home.

2. Most of the steps are simple.
   One of them takes practice.
   The practice is to master* [it].

   *do it perfectly

3. Add three cups.
   The three is approximate.
   The cups are of flour.
   [The adding] is to three eggs.
   The eggs are beaten.

4. Use your fingers.
   [The using] is to mix the dough.
   [The mixing] is thorough.

5. Then knead* the dough.
   Look in a cookbook.
   [The looking] is first.
   [The looking] is if you have forgotten how to do [something].

   *mix with the heel of the hand

It is to knead.
[The kneading] is correct.

6.  Form the dough into a ball.
    The ball is smooth.
    The ball is round.

*make flat*

7.  Use a rolling pin.
    [The use] is to flatten.*
    [The flattening] is of the ball.
    [The flattening] is slight.

8.  Now roll it out.
    [The rolling] is into a sheet.
    The sheet is paper-thin.

    (In combining the following sentences, use the participial form of ''begins.'')

9.  Curl the sheet.
    [The curling] is careful.
    [The curling] begins at one edge.
    [The curling] is into a jelly roll shape.

10. The step comes next.
    The step is difficult.

11. Use a knife.
    The knife is very sharp.
    [The use] is to make slices.
    The slices are fine.
    [The fineness] is extreme.
    The slices are in the dough.
    The dough is rolled up.

*rolled up*

12. Loosen the coiled* slices.
    [The loosening] is with your fingers.
    [The loosening] is with two forks.
    [The loosening] is a little.

13. You can dry the noodles.
    The drying is for a while.
    The drying is in the air.
    You don't have to [do something].
    It is to dry them.

14. Boil the noodles.
    [The boiling] is in a pot.
    The pot is large.
    The pot is filled with water.
    The water is salted.

(In combining the following sentences, remember that ''let'' is followed by the incomplete infinitive. See Grammar Note 10.)

15. You can let a friend [do something].
    It is to taste the noodles first.
    [The tasting] is if you feel unsure.
    [The unsureness] is of your work.

## On Your Own

Write eight sentences, each with an infinitive or infinitive phrase. Use the infinitives as subjects, direct objects, adverbs, and adjectives. Write one sentence with an incomplete infinitive.

Next, write a paragraph according to the following outline. Write several sentences for each blank except in the last sentence where a phrase and a clause will be sufficient.

Topic sentence: There are several common ways to eat spaghetti. One way is to use a fork and a large spoon. The spoon is used to _____. Another way is to use only a fork. In this method, _____. The last way is to use a knife and fork. The diner first _____. The ''best'' method is _____ because _____.

# ONE THING LEADS TO ANOTHER (I)_____

This exercise focuses on transitional words and phrases. You might want to look at Composition Note 2 before you begin. Remember that it is possible to use too many transitions as well as too few. Reading your work aloud as you go can help in deciding where transitions are needed.

1. Mary Calvin should have spent the afternoon [doing something].
   It was studying for an exam.
   The exam is in biochemistry.
   Biochemistry is the last course.
   She needs the course in order to graduate.

   (Use an appositive in combining the previous sentences.)

## MINI-NOTE ON APPOSITIVES_____

### Definition:

An appositive is a noun, a noun phrase, or a noun clause that follows another noun and renames it.

### Examples:

1.    Abner's gift, a large box of coconuts, surprised Mrs. Abernathy.
2.    The class was shocked by the news that Henry was dropping out of
      school.

**Grammar Note 6 discusses appositives in greater detail.**

(In combining the following sentences, you should probably begin
with a transitional word or phrase. Also, try changing "photographed" to a present participle.)

2.    She spent the afternoon at the window.
      The window is of her dining room.
      She photographed birds.
      The birds were in the tree.
      The tree is just outside.

(In combining the following sentences, try using "despite the fact
that.")

3.    She did this.
      The exam is less than two weeks away.
      She must do well on the exam.
      [The doing] is to assure her admission.
      The admission is to medical school.

(The following sentence needs a transitional word or phrase at the beginning. Also, try a very long dependent clause after "camera.")

*so interesting that it*
*cannot be resisted*

4.    Her camera is irresistible.*
      She bought the camera.
      [The buying] was recent.
      [The buying] was because a friend kept saying [something].
      It was that she would be a photographer.
      The photographer is excellent.

(Begin the following sentence with another transitional device.)

5.    Something was going on.
      She had never seen [it] before.

*a kind of bird; also a symbol of peace*

[The going on] was in the tree.
Some doves* were emerging from their eggs.
The doves were tiny.

6. Mary had been watching the nest.
The watching was all week.
The watching was with interest.

*not strong*

The interest was mild.*
She had taken photographs.
The photographs were a few.

7. She had seen the dove.
[The seeing] was first.
[The seeing] was last Monday.
The dove was sitting.
[The sitting] was on its nest.

(In the following sentence, be careful not to write a run-on sentence or a comma splice. Check Grammar Note 14 if necessary.)

8. The dove never left the nest.
Sometimes it faced north.
Sometimes it faced south.

(In combining the following sentences, use ''if'' and omit the question mark.)

9. Sometimes the dove looked large.
Sometimes the dove looked small.
Mary began to wonder [something].
Were the male and female taking turns?
The turns were on the nest.

10. She didn't know.
She didn't have enough curiosity to find out.
She didn't have enough time to find out.

11. There was no bird on the nest.
[It] was when she looked out.
[The looking] was this morning.

12. The nest appeared to be filled.
[The filling] was with feathers.
The feathers were gray.

(Try combining sentences 11 and 12.)

13. The bird was sitting.
The sitting was on the nest.
The sitting was at mid-morning.
The sitting was again.

14. The bird was gone again.
[It] was at noon.

The gray feathers were moving.
The feathers were in the nest.
Mary saw a tiny head.
Mary saw a tiny wing.
[The seeing] was sudden.

(In combining the following sentences, add at least one transitional word or phrase.)

15. Mary realized [something].
    It was that the nest wasn't empty.
    The nest was filled.

*baby birds    [The filling] was with chicks.*
    The chicks were small.

16. That was the end of studying.
    She could not stay away.
    [The staying] was from the window.

# ONE THING LEADS TO ANOTHER (II) _____

*went on        1. The afternoon progressed.*
    The birds became more active.
    The birds were small.

    (In combining the first group of sentences, begin with an adverb clause.)

2. Mary used a roll.
   The roll was of film.
   The roll was entire.
   [This] was to capture the hours.
   The hours were the birds'.
   The hours were the first.

3. The small doves were resting.
   Mary watched other birds.
   They were robins.
   They were jays.
   They were hummingbirds.

4. She had never paid attention.
   [The paying] was to them.
   [The paying] was before.
   She photographed them all.
   [The photographing] was today.
   [The photographing] was because they were so interesting.

5. She put a lens.
   The lens was more powerful.

[The putting] was in the middle of the afternoon.
[The putting] was on her camera.

6. She began to notice bees.
   The bees were flying.
   The flying was from flower to flower.

   (Try combining sentences 5 and 6.)

7. She photographed them.
   [The photographing] was extensive.*
   She wondered [something].
   It was if bees ever stop to rest.

   *a lot*

   (Begin the following sentence with a transition word.)

8. She had no more film.
   She had to go back to studying.

   (Make the following sentence compound. If you use ''photographs''
   twice, think again.)

9. She got the photographs back.
   [The getting] was a few days later.
   The photographs were wonderful.

10. She was still studying.
    The studying was for the exam.
    The studying was feverish.*
    The exam was crucial.*

    *very busy; with anxiety*
    *most important*

11. She began to wonder [something].
    It was if she wanted to be a doctor.
    [The wanting] was real.

    (Begin the preceding sentence with a transitional word or phrase. Or
    combine sentences 10 and 11.)

12. Perhaps she should be a photographer.
    Perhaps she should be an ornithologist.*
    Perhaps she should be an entomologist.*

    *one who studies birds*
    *one who studies insects*

    (Begin the following sentence with a transitional word or phrase.)

13. Life seemed to offer choices.
    The choices were too many.

    (In combining the following sentences, should you use ''because of''
    or ''because''?)

14. Perhaps these ideas came.
    The ideas are new.
    [The coming] was because of [something].
    It was that she was afraid of failing the exam.
    The exam is in biochemistry.

15. Mary will decide.
[The deciding] will be when she sees her grade.
The grade is final.
[The deciding] will be what to do.

### On Your Own

Write a paragraph following this outline:

Topic sentence: Accidental discoveries can be very interesting. Once, when I was (*something you were doing or were supposed to be doing*), I saw (*several sentences explaining what you saw and what was interesting about it*).

End with one sentence that refers back to what you were originally doing.

## THE TOW-TRUCK DRIVER

Combine each of the following so that you have a compound sentence. In all but number 8, use a conjunctive adverb. Choose from this list: however, nevertheless, then, otherwise, furthermore, consequently.

## MINI-NOTE ON COMPOUND SENTENCES WITH SEMICOLONS

Remember that either a semicolon or a comma followed by a coordinating conjunction is needed to join the parts of a compound sentence. When conjunctive adverbs (for example, *therefore, however, nevertheless*) are used, a semicolon is required.

1. His glasses slid down his nose, and he slept peacefully.
2. His glasses slid down his nose; however he didn't notice.
3. His glasses were always sliding down his nose; his wife, therefore, urged him to get contact lenses.

**Grammar Note 8 has more details.**

1. Sandy's car was repaired.
[The repair] was last week.
It would not start.
[The starting] was this morning.

2. She tried to start it.
   [Her trying] was three or four times.
   She went back.
   [Her going] was into the house.

*slightly angry; annoyed*

3. She was irritated.*
   [Her irritation] was because the car had just been fixed.
   She had promised [something].
   It was to be at work early.

4. She called her neighbor.
   He knows a lot about cars.
   He had already left his house.

5. She knew she had to [do something].
   It was to call her office.
   Her staff* would be worried.

*the people who work for her*

6. She made that call.
   She called the garage.
   The garage had repaired her car.

7. A man arrived.
   He was very young.
   [His arrival] was two hours later.
   [His arrival] was in a tow truck.
   He did not apologize.
   [His apology] was for being so late.

8. He turned the key.
   [His turning] was confident.
   The key was in her car.
   The car started.
   [The starting] was immediate.

*suggesting superiority*

9. He smiled.
   [His smiling] was supercilious.*
   [His smiling] was at Sandy.
   He jumped in his truck.
   He roared away.

10. Sandy was angry.
    She was puzzled.
    She decided [something].
    It was to take the day off.

## On Your Own

Write five compound sentences, each with a semicolon and a conjunctive adverb. Make the sentences fairly long.

Write a paragraph according to the following outline. Your paragraph should be more than five sentences long.

Topic sentence: People react to frustration in a variety of ways. Sandy reacted to the frustration of her stalled car by _____. Someone else might have _____. If I had been in Sandy's situation, I would have _____.

End with a general statement about the three different responses.

## MAKING THE BEST COFFEE

In this exercise, concentrate on adding transitional words, phrases, and clauses, but don't add too many. See Composition Note 2 for some suggestions.

1. Making coffee is not difficult.
   The coffee is good.
   There are a few things to remember.
   The things are simple.

2. The best coffee needs some equipment.
   The equipment is special.
   You will need a pan or kettle.
   The pan or kettle is to boil water.
   You will need a coffee grinder.
   You will need a drip coffeepot.
   You will need a paper filter.

3. The secret is to start with coffee beans.
   The beans are fresh.
   Coffee loses its flavor.
   [The losing] is quick.
   Coffee has been ground.

4. Put four cups of water.
   The water is cold.
   [The putting] is into a pan.
   Pour out half a cup.
   Keep it nearby.

5. The water is heating.
   Put four tablespoons of coffee beans.
   [The putting] is into the grinder.
   Grind the coffee until you have a powder.
   The powder is fine.
   Pour the coffee into the filter.

6. The water is boiling.
   Remove it from the heat.
   Pour in the half cup of water.
   The water is cold.
   [The pouring] is to lower the temperature.
   [The lowering] is slight.

7. Boiling water releases acid.
   The acid is bitter.
   The acid is in the coffee.
   The water should be below the boiling point.
   You use the water to make coffee.

8. Pour a little of the water.
   The water is hot.
   [The pouring] is over the coffee.
   The coffee is in the filter.
   Wait until it drips down.
   [The dripping] is into the coffeepot.

9. Pour a little more in.
   It is gone.
   Pour in the rest of the water.

*chopped up into a powder*

10. The water is dripping through the coffee.
    The coffee is ground.*
    You may want to heat the pot.
    [The heating] is a little.
    Don't let the coffee boil.
    [Boiling] will make it bitter.

11. You can drink the coffee.
    The coffee is the best.
    You have ever tasted [the coffee].

## On Your Own

Think of something that can be done in three steps. Write a paragraph following this outline:

Topic sentence: _____ is easier to do if you think of it as involving three separate steps.

Explain each step. Provide transitions between them. End with a general comment.

# THINGS GO WRONG (I) _____

On the following page, all sentences but the second should include an adverb clause.

1. Dale Parnot is taking his children.
   [The taking] is to Maine.
   [The taking] is for the month of August.
   He can finish writing his book.
   His children can avoid the summer heat.
   The heat is of New York City.

   (Use "so that" in the preceding sentence.)

2. Evelyn is remaining at home in the city.
   Evelyn is Dale's wife.
   [The remaining] is to supervise the workers.
   *water pipes*            The workers will be replacing the plumbing.*
   *sinks, bathtubs, etc.*  The workers will be replacing the fixtures.*

3. She wants the family to fly.
   Their car is unreliable.
   [The unreliability] is somewhat.
   Dale wants to drive.
   He can have the car.
   [The having] is in Maine.

   *worried*
4. She is apprehensive.*
   [The apprehension] is about the drive.
   The drive is long.
   She agrees.
   [The agreement] is reluctant.

   (Use "as soon as" in the following sentence.)

5. The space is filled.
   The space is the last available.
   The space is in the car.
   [The filling] is with all the things.
   The children cannot live without the things.
   Dale and the children begin their trip.

   (Use "no sooner . . . than" in the following sentence. The Mini-Note on the following page gives examples.)

6. They have gone the first mile.
   The child announces [something].
   The child is the youngest.
   The child is Anne.
   It is that she feels carsick.

> ## MINI-NOTE ON "NO SOONER . . . THAN"
>
> The construction "no sooner . . . than" can cause some difficulties. Study the word order in the following examples:
>
> 1.  No sooner <u>had</u> the bell <u>rung than</u> the children raced into the hallways.
> 2.  The bell <u>had</u> no sooner <u>rung than</u> the children raced into the hallways.

(Think carefully about what subordinating conjunction to use in the following sentence.)

7.  The older children don't believe her.
    They feed her candy.
    The candy is hard.
    *make her think of something else* They distract* her.
    [The distraction] is with songs.
    The songs are silly.

(In the following sentence, there should not be a word between the two parts of the infinitive.)

8.  They leave the area.
    *of a large city* The area is metropolitan.*
    The car begins to overheat.
    [The overheating] is bad.

9.  Dale had insisted on [something].
    It was to drive to Maine.
    He wishes they had listened to Evelyn.
    [The wishing] is at that moment.

(In combining the following sentences, change "include" to a present participle.)

10. Several other things go wrong.
    [The going] is before they reach the house.
    The house is in Maine.
    The other things include getting lost.
    The other things include almost running out of gas.

(Begin the following sentence with some sort of transition.)

11. Evelyn calls.
    Evelyn asks about their trip.
    They all smile.
    They all say [something].
    *nothing unusual or unpleasant happened* It is that it was uneventful.*

## THINGS GO WRONG (II)

Each sentence in this exercise should include an adjective clause. You may need expressions such as "some of whom," "whose," "to whom," and "when." Remember that some adjective clauses require commas.

---

# MINI-NOTE ON UNFAMILIAR ADJECTIVE CLAUSES

Certain adjective clauses are not used very frequently in informal speech or writing; therefore they may be unfamiliar. They contribute, however, to a more formal, polished style and are worth practicing.

1. All men whose hair is getting thin will be interested in this product.
2. Henry Clayton, whose office is upstairs, reported a burglary.
3. I bought sixteen eggs, some of which were quite rotten.
4. He studied chemistry with Dr. Henrikson, about whom very little is known.

## A Reminder About Commas:

Is the noun described by the adjective clause already identified? If yes, then yes, a comma should be used. If no, then no comma should be used. See the examples above.

---

1. Evelyn Parnot is alone in her apartment.
   Her family has gone to Maine.
   [The going] is for a month.

2. Today is the day.
   The workers come today.
   [The coming] is to replace all the pipes.
   [The coming] is to replace all the fixtures.
   The fixtures are in her kitchen.
   The fixtures are in her bathrooms.

3. Evelyn is not looking forward to the confusion.
   Peace and order are very important to Evelyn.

4. She answers the doorbell.
   [The answering] is at 10 o'clock.
   She lets the workers into the apartment.

Some of the workers look young.
Some of the workers look inexperienced.

5. The house is filled with the confusion.
[The filling] is within half an hour.
*fearing*   She has been dreading* the confusion.

6. A worker drops Evelyn's guitar.
[The dropping] is in the middle of the afternoon.
The worker is young.
The guitar is handmade.
Evelyn's grandfather had brought the guitar.
[The bringing] was from France.
[The bringing] was 60 years ago.

7. Evelyn calls Dale.
Evelyn doesn't know [something].
It is how she will survive the next month.

8. He doesn't answer the phone.
He is at the beach.
[There] the children are forgetting the drive.
The drive was terrible.

(Try combining sentences 7 and 8.)

9. Dale telephones Evelyn.
[The telephoning] is that night.
Evelyn has recovered.
Evelyn says everything is fine.

10. Have Dale and Evelyn lied?
They are honest people.
[The lying] is to each other.

## On Your Own

Write five sentences with adjective clauses. Use these words to begin the clauses: whose, of whom, for whom, which, when.

Now write a few sentences answering the question at the end of this exercise. Can you identify any adverb or adjective clauses in what you have written? If there aren't any, it's possible that your response is written in too simple a style. Try combining some of your sentences.

# LEARNING TO DRIVE

Each sentence in the exercise beginning on page 60 should include an infinitive.

# MINI-NOTE ON INFINITIVES _____

### Definition:

An infinitive is the "to" form of a verb: to swim, to think, to grasp.

### Examples:

1. It is easy <u>to learn</u> the Greek alphabet. (It would be correct to write "To learn the Greek alphabet is easy," but that form is quite formal and infrequently encountered.)

2. His parents made him <u>do</u> his homework. (After some verbs—such as "made"—only part of the infinitive is used; the "to" is left out.)

3. Ben Fox cleaned up his desk because he had <u>to.</u> (Here is another partial infinitive. Writing "because he had <u>to clean up</u> his desk" would be repetitious.

---

1. [Something] is possible.
   It is getting a driver's license.
   The getting is at the age of 16.
   The getting is in many states.

   (Use a delayed subject in the preceding sentence.)

2. This fact causes [something].
   It is that many arguments occur.
   The arguments are between parents and teenagers.

   (In combining the following sentences, use "teenager" and "to drive" only once.)

3. Some parents argue [something].
   The teenager is old enough to drive.
   The teenager is not responsible enough to drive.

   (In the following sentence, use the infinitive form of "done" and omit the other parts of the verb.)

4. They say [something].
   It is that the teenager has chores.*
   The chores must be done.
   But he or she forgets.
   [The forgetting] is often.

*small jobs that are done regularly

5. This proves that the teenager is not ready [for something].
   It is taking on the responsibility.
   The responsibility is of a driver's license.

6. Teenagers want their licenses.
[The wanting] is in order to feel independent.
[The wanting] is to feel mature.

7. They give many arguments.
The arguments are to make their parents [do something].
It is to change their minds.

*finally agree, but not gladly*

8. Many parents give in.*
They feel they have to give in.
They are not happy.

*numbers*

9. The statistics* make some parents [do something].
It is to refuse.

*deaths*

The statistics are about fatalities.*
The fatalities are among teenage drivers.

10. The cost makes other parents [do something].
It is to refuse.
The cost is of insurance.
The insurance is for teenage drivers.

11. Some parents agree, only to [do something].
It is to change their minds.
[The changing] is after an accident.
The accident is careless.

12. There are many issues.
The issues are about teenage drivers.
The issues are too serious to ignore.

## On Your Own

Choose an infinitive and use it in five different sentences. Use these expressions: learn to X, too frightened to X, him to X, careless of her to X, only to X. If you can't think of an infinitive that will make sense in all these situations, use different infinitives.

Write a paragraph following this outline:

Topic sentence: Teenagers should/should not be allowed to drive at 16.

Give three specific reasons, using several sentences to explain each one.

## COMMUTER COLLEGES: DISADVANTAGES_____

1. Going to college used to mean [something].
It was leaving home.

It was living on campus.
[The living] was in a dormitory.

2. Going to college means [something].
It is driving to class.
It is then driving home.
[The meaning] is now.
[The meaning] is more often.

3. Colleges are economical.
The colleges are commuter.*
They have some disadvantages.

*one travels there but doesn't live there

4. Part is getting to know one's classmates.
[The part] is of college life.
[The knowing] is intimate.*

*in great detail

5. Many friendships have been made.
The friendships lasted a lifetime.
[The making] was in college dormitories.

6. Students complain.
[The complaining] is often.
The students commute.
[The complaint] is that the campus is unfriendly.
Students go to class.
Students leave.
[The leaving] is without talking.
[The talking] is to one another.

(Use ''by the time'' or ''before'' in the following sentence.)

7. [Something] is difficult at commuter campuses.
It is to organize social events.
It is to organize cultural events.
Most students have left.
These events can begin.

8. Students find [something] difficult.
It is to see their professors.
[The seeing] is outside of class.
Many professors have office hours.
The hours are inconvenient.
[The inconvenience] is to commuters.

9. These colleges are located downtown.
[The locating] is frequent.
The colleges are often housed* in buildings.
The buildings are concrete.
The buildings are brick.
The buildings are uninteresting.
Nothing beautiful can be found in the buildings.

*located

10. [Something] is missing.
    It is the "old college spirit."
    [The missing] is at commuter colleges.

## On Your Own

Write a paragraph following this plan:

> Topic sentence: Going to college right after graduating from high school is quite common, but there are some disadvantages.

Explain two or three disadvantages. End with a sentence that begins with "nevertheless."

# RESIDENTIAL COLLEGES: DISADVANTAGES_____

Insert transitions in this exercise wherever they are needed.

1. Tradition says [something].
   Students should go away.
   [The going] is to college.
   There are some disadvantages.
   The disadvantages are to doing that.

*students live there

2. Residential* colleges are expensive.
   Some cost more than $12,000.
   The cost is per year.

3. This cost limits attendance.
   [The limiting] is primarily to the children.
   The children are of wealthy families.
   Some scholarships are available.
   [The availability] is to those in need.

   (Try "although" or "but" in the following sentence.)

*the group of all the students
**made up; contain
*unusual

4. Some residential colleges are not so expensive.
   The student bodies* are composed.**
   [The composition] is of similar people.
   [The similarity] is remarkable.*

*what someone wishes to accomplish

5. Almost all are between 18 and 24 years of age.
   Almost all have the same values.
   Almost all have the same aspirations*
   Almost all have the same lack of experience.

6.  This means [something].
    The students do not learn to mix.

*varied; different*

    [The mixing] is with diverse* people.
    [The mixing] is as they will have to do.
    [The doing] is after graduation.

*separated*

7.  Students can be isolated.*
    [The isolation] is in another way.
    [The isolation] is from the world.
    The world is real.

8.  They concentrate only on [something].
    It is their studies.
    It is their lives.
    Their lives are social.
    They do not see [something].
    It is how protected they are.

9.  They are not prepared for lives.
    The lives can be filled with disappointment.
    The lives can be filled with struggle.
    The lives can be filled with failure.

*to face successfully*

10. [Something] comes after graduation.
    It is learning to cope.*
    [The coping] is with those realities.

## On Your Own

Write a paragraph following this outline:

> Topic sentence: Going back to college at an "older" age is becoming quite common, but there are some disadvantages.

Explain several disadvantages. End with a sentence beginning with "however."

# WHICH COLLEGE?

Some sentences in this exercise need transitions.

1.  The decision to go to college is made.
    The question needs to be answered.
    The question is what kind of campus to choose.

    (Try "once" as the first word in the preceding sentence. In sentence 2 on the following page, "each" is considered to be singular.)

2. The choices include colleges.
   The colleges are residential.
   The colleges are commuter.
   Each has advantages.
   The advantages are its own.

3. The residential campus provides an opportunity.
   The opportunity is to gain some independence.
   The opportunity is for a young person.
   The independence is from his or her parents.
   There are some restrictions.
   The restrictions are on behavior.

   (In combining the following sentences you have several decisions to make: infinitives or gerunds? singular or plural?)

4. [Some things] are the steps.
   It is to choose one's own friends.
   It is to meet deadlines.
   [The meeting] is without a parent's reminder.
   It is to set one's own hours.
   The steps are the first.
   The steps are important.
   The steps are to independence.

5. [Something] is important.
   *surroundings; place*     It is to be in an environment.*
   The environment is studious.
   The environment is intellectual.

6. The fact can encourage behavior.
   The fact is that others are studying.
   The fact is that others are discussing.
   [The discussion] is of ideas.
   The ideas are serious.
   The behavior is similar.

7. Write a transitional sentence that prepares for a change to a discussion of the advantages of commuter colleges.

8. *varied; different*     The students are diverse.*
   The students are at commuter colleges.
   [The diversity] is usually more than those at residential colleges.

9. Young and old exchange ideas.
   Married and single exchange ideas.
   Experienced and inexperienced exchange ideas.
   All exchange ideas.

10. People can be students.
    The people have families.

The people have jobs.
The jobs are full-time.
The students are part-time.

11. [Something] is comforting.
It is to know that everyone else is busy.
It is to know that everyone else is pressed for time.*

*doesn't have enough time

12. Write a sentence to end the paragraph.

# NEIGHBORHOOD DISAGREEMENT

1. Dave is giving a party.
The party is this evening.
The party is for Chris.
Chris has just graduated.
[Her graduation] was from nursing school.

(The preceding will probably have an adjective clause in it. If necessary, check Grammar Note 3 to see if the clause needs commas.)

2. He wants it to be a party.
The party is very special.
He has hired a band.

*made louder by electronic equipment

3. It will play in the backyard.
The music will be amplified.*

(In combining the following, consider changing ''lives'' to a present participle.)

4. Dave is the only person.
The person is young.
The person lives on the block.

*calm; no excitement

5. The neighborhood is quiet.
The neighborhood is sedate.*
[The quietness and sedateness] are usual.

*a little

6. He is worried about noise.
[His worry] is slight.*
The noise is loud.

(Try combining sentences 4, 5, and 6.)

7. He visited his neighbors.
[His visit] was this morning.
[His visit] was to tell them.
[His telling] was about the band.

8. He said [something].
The music might be loud.

It would end.
[The ending] would be by 10 o'clock.

(In combining the following, write your sentence as a compound sentence. Try using a transitional phrase in the middle.)

*disapprove; think it shouldn't happen*

9. The neighbors didn't object.*
They thought he was being thoughtful.
[His thoughtfulness] was extreme.
[His thoughtfulness] was to tell them about the band.
[His telling] was in advance.

10. The band members came.
[The coming] was in the afternoon.
[The coming] was to hook up their equipment.
[The coming] was to test their equipment

(Use "so . . . that" in the following sentence.)

11. The music was loud.
One neighbor changed his mind.
He objected to the party.

*complete*

[His objection] was altogether.*

12. He even called the police.
He asked them [something].
It was to order Dave to call off the party.

13. The police said [something].
They couldn't prevent the party.
They could stop it.
It became too loud.

(Consider adding "also" or "either" in combining the following sentences.)

14. Dave can't move the party.
[The moving] is at the last minute.
He doesn't want to be a bad neighbor.

15. He has asked the band to play softer.

*satisfy; reduce anger*

He hopes that will mollify* the neighbor.
The neighbor is angry.

*lowered*

16. Dave's spirits are dampened.*
[The dampening] is considerable.
[The dampening] is right now.

(Try combining sentences 15 and 16. Or, if you don't want to do that, begin sentence 16 with a transition word.)

### On Your Own

Do you think Dave's neighbor was reasonable or unreasonable when he called the police? Explain in a paragraph. Be sure to begin with a clear statement of your opinion.

## THE NEIGHBOR APOLOGIZES _____

See the preceding exercise for the first part of this story.

1. The guests are beginning to arrive.
   *nervous*
   Dave feels apprehensive.*
   [His apprehension] is about his neighbor.
   The neighbor is angry.

2. He hopes the party will be a success.
   He hopes [this] for Chris's sake.
   He is afraid that his neighbor will call the police.

3. He takes a breath.
   The breath is deep.
   The breath is to calm himself.
   He begins to greet his friends.
   He begins to serve drinks.

4. The band is playing.
   The playing is soft.
   The playing is at the end.
   The end is far.
   The end is of the yard.

5. Dave knows [something].
   The music will get louder.
   *gets more lively*
   [The loudness] will be when the party warms up.*
   He wants to relax.
   [The relaxation] is until then.

6. A problem appears.
   The problem is new.
   [The appearance] is sudden.

7. Several guests have just arrived.
   The guests are uninvited.
   *ready to argue*
   They look argumentative.*
   *very strange*
   They look bizarre.*

8. One fellow is wearing clothes.
   The clothes are leather.
   The leather is black.

The clothes are with designs.
The designs are satin.
The satin is red.
The red is shiny.
The designs are sewn everywhere.

9. A woman is talking.
   The talking is loud.
   The talking is to herself.
   The talking is in front of the band.
   The woman has a head.
   The head is clean-shaven.*

*all the hair has been cut off

10. The noise gets louder.
    Dave can't do anything about it.
    He stops worrying.
    He enjoys himself.

11. The police never come.
    The party ends.
    [The ending] is on a happy note.*

*everyone is cheerful

12. Something surprising happens.
    [The happening] is the next morning.
    [The happening] is just after Dave wakes up.

13. The neighbor comes to the door.
    The neighbor had been so angry.
    [His coming] is to apologize.

14. He says he remembered [something].
    It is what it is to be young.
    [His saying] is with a grin.
    The grin is embarrassed.

15. Dave shakes his hand.
    Dave invites him in.
    [The invitation] is for coffee.
    [The invitation] is for cake.
    The cake is leftover.

## On Your Own

Write a paragraph according to the following plan:

Topic sentence: Apologies are sometimes very difficult to make.
Once I *(explain something you did that made you feel sorry)*. Apologizing for my behavior was difficult because _____.

End with a short discussion of what happened and how you felt about it.

# EMBARRASSMENT _____

1. Bob Johnson is a teacher.
   Beth Elliot is a teacher.
   The teachers are young.
   The teachers are at Morgan High School.
   They have a meeting.
   The meeting is tomorrow morning.

   (Use an appositive in combining the previous sentences. See Grammar Note 6 if necessary. Use ''even though'' in combining the following.)

2. They are excited.
   [The excitement] is about this meeting.
   It is summer vacation.
   They will not be paid.
   [The payment] is for their time.

3. Six teachers have been chosen [to do something].
   It is to participate in a program.
   The program is experimental.
   The program is college-preparatory.

   (In combining the following, make the sentence both compound and complex.)

4. The other teachers are experienced.
   The other teachers are well known.
   Bob and Beth were surprised.
   [The surprise] was to be included.
   They are quite pleased.

5. Beth has offered [something].
   It is to pick Bob up.
   It is to drive him to the meeting.

   (Use ''so that'' and ''even if'' in the following.)

6. They plan to leave early.
   They will be on time.
   There is traffic.
   The traffic is heavy.

7. It is now 8 P.M.
   Beth is reading [something].
   It is the agenda.*
   The agenda is long.
   The agenda is for tomorrow's meeting.
   [The reading] is careful.

*list of subjects to be discussed at a meeting

8.  A telephone call interrupts her work.
    The call gives her some news.
    The news is shocking.

9.  The meeting was this morning.
    The meeting is not tomorrow morning.
    Bob and Beth missed the meeting!

    (In combining the following, begin with the word "embarrassed.")

10. Beth is embarrassed.
    Beth is upset.
    She asks herself [something].
    It is how she could have made such a mistake.
    The mistake is awful.

    (Begin with a present participial phrase when you combine the following.)

11. She looks at her calendar.
    She discovers [something].
    The meeting is marked.
    [The marking] is clear.
    [The marking] is for the day.
    The day is correct.

## MINI-NOTE ON PRESENT PARTICIPIAL PHRASES

When two events occur at the same time, one of them can be expressed in a present participial phrase.

> <u>Looking into her coffee cup,</u> Alicia saw the contact lens she had lost.

Without a participial phrase, the sentence might look like this:

> Alicia looked into her coffee cup and saw the contact lens she had lost.

The second sentence is correct, but the version with the participial phrase emphasizes more strongly that the two events occurred at the same time. Careful use of participial phrases can contribute to the development of a polished and flexible writing style.

Be careful, however, with where you place participial phrases.

**Confusing:** Alicia saw the contact lens she had lost looking into her coffee cup.

Written this way, the sentence suggests that the lens was looking into the cup—an impossibility, of course—or that Alicia lost the lens while she was looking into her cup. In any case, the sentence is confusing.

**Grammar Note 15 discusses the dangling modifier error.**

12. She telephones Bob.
    She tells him [something].
    *foolish mistake*   It is about their blunder.*

13. They each apologize.
    [The apology] is the next day.
    [The apology] is to the other committee members.
    *full; complete*   [The apology] is profuse.*

    (Use ''even though'' in combining the following sentences.)

14. No one is angry.
    Bob and Beth still feel embarrassed.

## On Your Own

Write a paragraph according to this plan:

> Topic sentence: Helping someone else to recover from an embarrassing situation isn't easy.

Describe a situation you were involved in when someone else was embarrassed. Explain what you did or wish you had done. End with a sentence explaining whether or not what you did made the other person feel better.

# THE CAFÉ HABIT

1. There is a custom.
   The custom is in some parts.
   The parts are of the world.
   The custom is to go.
   The going is to cafés.
   The going is frequent.

   (In combining the preceding sentences, you will need to use the expression ''custom of,'' so think about what form of ''to go'' is needed. In combining the next group of sentences, experiment with where you can place ''without'' and the words that follow it.)

2. One can sit.
   [The sitting] is there.
   [The sitting] is for a long time.

[The sitting] is without [something].
It is to be rushed to leave.
*required It is to feel obligated* to order some thing else.

3. Friends meet in cafés.
The friends are old.
[The meeting] is to talk.
The talk is about their lives.
Lovers meet to look.
[The looking] is at one another.
[The looking] is shy.
Students write their papers.
Shoppers rest.
[The resting] is from their search.
The search is for bargains.

4. Certain people have tables.
[The having] is in some cafés.
The tables are their own.
This means [something].
It is that no one else may sit there.
[The sitting] is at a specific hour of the day.

5. A language teacher has been giving lessons.
[The giving] is in one café.
The café is in Budapest.
[The giving] has been for twenty years.
[The giving] is at the same table.
The table is marble-topped.

(In combining the following, try using "some . . . others . . . still others.")

6. Each café has its own spirit and style.
The spirit and style are special.
Some are old-fashioned.
Some are modern.
Some attract university students.
Some attract poets.
Some attract actors and actresses.

(Try using a colon in the following.)

7. But one thing is true.
[The truth] is of all cafés.
*customers Patrons* may do as they like.
[The doing] is for as long as they like.

(In combining the following, see Grammar Note 11 for use of the noun clause as a delayed subject.)

8.  [Something] is unfortunate.
    It is that the United States does not have the "café habit."

    (Think carefully about where to put "here" in combining the following.)

9.  The waiter brings the bill.
    [The bringing] is here.
    [The bringing] is with the food.
    [The bringing] is often.

10. [Something] is impossible.
    It is not to feel pressured.*
    The pressure is to leave.
    [The leaving] is as soon as the meal is over.

*pushed; forced*

11. Customers want to stay.
    [The staying] is for a long time.
    [The staying] is to read.
    [The staying] is to talk.
    They must ask for permission.
    They must leave a large tip.

*fit; match*

12. The café habit just does not suit.*
    The habit is leisurely.
    [The suiting] is of the hustle and bustle.*
    The hustle and bustle is of American life.

*constant activity*

13. [Something] would be good.
    [The goodness] is for this country.
    It is to adopt the café habit.

## On Your Own

Write a paragraph giving three reasons the United States should or should not adopt the café habit. Be sure to begin with a clear statement of your opinion.

# THE BOW ON THE WALL _____

*person of lower rank*

1.  Once an official invited his subordinate.*
    [The invitation] was to drink wine.
    [The drinking] was with him.
    [The drinking] was during a festival.

*used to shoot an arrow*

2.  A bow* was hanging on the wall.
    The bow was red.

*threw

The bow cast* its reflection.
[The casting] was into the wine cup.
The cup was the subordinate's.

3.  The reflection looked just like a snake.
    The subordinate was terrified.
    He did not dare to refuse.
    [The refusal] was of the drink.

4.  He drank the wine.
    He developed a pain.
    The pain was severe.
    The pain was in his stomach.
    No medicine could cure the pain.

5.  He could not eat.
    He became very thin.
    He drew close to death.

6.  The official heard about the problem.
    He visited his subordinate.
    [The visiting] was to ask [something].
    It was how he had gotten so sick.

7.  The man explained [something].
    It was that his pain was caused by the snake.
    He had swallowed the snake.
    [The swallowing] was at the official's house.

8.  The official was puzzled.
    He returned home.
    He saw the bow on the wall.
    He understood.
    [The understanding] was sudden.

9.  He sent for his subordinate.
    He placed a cup of wine.
    [The placing] was in the same way as before.
    The "snake" appeared.
    [The appearance] was once again.

10. The official showed the man [something].
    The snake was only the reflection.
    The reflection was of the bow.
    The bow was hanging on the wall.

11. The man felt better.
    [The feeling] was immediate.
    He made a full recovery.
    [The making] was in a time.
    The time was short.

## On Your Own

Write one very long (and very correct) sentence explaining this fable. If you can, make the sentence compound and complex, and include as many different kinds of phrases and clauses as you can. Of course such exaggerated sentences shouldn't be used in ''normal'' writing assignments, but this will be a good test of your command of sentence structure.

# VARYING SENTENCE STRUCTURE AND PRACTICING PARAGRAPHS

**3**

77

The exercises in chapter 3 look quite similar to those you have done so far. There are some important differences, however. First, square brackets ([]) are no longer used to tell you what to leave out of your finished sentence. So you will have to decide, for example, whether to use ''walked'' or ''walking.'' By now, that shouldn't be a problem.

A more important difference is that, for each group of sentences, instead of writing just one combined version you will have to write at least two versions. Each exercise has been designed so that the sentences can be written in at least two different ways—even if the second way is not too obvious at first. For some sentences, there are more than two different possibilities. Write as many as you can think of, but write at least two. The purposes of this chapter are first to give you practice in the many ways there are to say the same thing and second to give you practice in choosing which version expresses more precisely what you mean to say. A change in meaning or emphasis always occurs when you change the wording. The change may be slight, but it exists. As part of the process of refining writing skills, this chapter asks you to pay attention to those slight differences.

A short example might help you understand. Read through these two groups of sentences:

*an African language*   **1.**   George Lawson is studying Swahili.*
He is going to spend a year.
The spending is in Tanzania.
He will work on a research farm.

**2.**   He is having trouble.
The trouble is with Lesson 16.
He doesn't understand direct objects.
The direct objects are in English.
Learning about direct objects is difficult.
The direct objects are in Swahili.

Write two different versions for the first group. You might write it this way:

George Lawson is studying Swahili because he is going to spend a year in Tanzania working on a research farm.

Or, you might write it another way:

George Lawson is going to spend a year in Tanzania, where he will work on a research farm, so he is studying Swahili.

There are other possibilities, too: Because he is going to spend a year in Tanzania working on a research farm, George Lawson is studying Swahili. George Lawson is going to spend a year in Tanzania, where he will work on a research farm; therefore, he is studying Swahili. Perhaps you thought of other versions, but for the moment, we have enough.

Now combine the second group. Some possibilities: He is having trouble with Lesson 16 because he doesn't understand direct objects in English, so learning about Swahili direct objects is difficult. Learning about Swahili direct objects is difficult because he doesn't understand them in English, so George is having trouble with Lesson 16. Now take a moment to study these versions and others that you have written. Try to see the differences in meaning and emphasis that occur when the word order is changed.

Next, choose one version of each sentence and write them one after another as you would do in a paragraph:

> Because George Lawson is going to spend a year in Tanzania working on a research farm, he is studying Swahili. Because he doesn't understand direct objects in English, learning Swahili direct objects is difficult, so he is having trouble with Lesson 16.

Most people would object to two sentences in a row that begin with long clauses introduced by the word "because." Try another way:

> George Lawson is going to spend a year in Tanzania working on a research farm, so he is studying Swahili. He is having trouble with Lesson 16 because he doesn't understand direct objects in English; learning Swahili direct objects, therefore, is difficult.

This version avoids the awkward repetition of "because." It also puts the idea "learning Swahili direct objects" close to "Lesson 16"—two related ideas. In this way, we also avoid the long, awkward jump from "Swahili" to "direct objects" in the first version. Try some other possibilities until you find a combination that satisfies you.

Another difference in chapter 3 is that you will be asked to write your own paragraphs, usually with only suggestions about how to structure them—not the outlines that were provided in the last chapter. To help you plan your own paragraphs, this chapter opens with several relatively well structured examples for you to examine and analyze. The purpose of these exercises is to make you more aware of paragraph structure so you can better plan and evaluate your own paragraphs.

The following paragraph classifies; that is, it takes a relatively large topic—ways of using credit cards—and shows the different categories into which specific examples may be organized. Classification is a common pattern in paragraph structure because it can be used to bring order to a large or diverse subject.

## USING CREDIT CARDS

Since credit cards became a major characteristic of the American economy, they have been used in a variety of ways. One method of classifying the use of credit cards is to say that their use can be either conservative, modest, or extravagant. People who use credit cards conservatively pay their bills in full each month. They think of the credit card not as a way to buy more than they can afford but as a way to avoid carrying large sums of cash. Modest use of the credit card is similar to conservative use except that on occasion the card is used to buy a large item such as a refrigerator or an airline ticket, which is paid for over a few months. People who use credit cards extravagantly often get into trouble. Each month, they buy the most they can and pay the least they can. In this way, everything costs more, for there is a 1.8 percent charge each month on the unpaid balance. Recently, companies have been formed to teach people how to get out—and stay out—of credit card trouble. These companies would be wise to require that their fees be paid in cash!

### Thinking About Structure

1.  Does the first or the second sentence contain the topic of this paragraph? Could (or should) the first sentence be eliminated?

2.  What is the order in which the three types of credit card use are described? Is this a logical order? Could they be described in reverse order?

3.  How many sentences are devoted to each category? Is each category described in enough detail?

4.  Explain the slight humor in the final sentence. Do you think the ending is appropriate?

## On Your Own

Pick a group of people (students in your class, lifeguards, or relatives, for example) and write a paragraph in which you classify them into two or three categories. Include in your topic sentence what the categories are. A topic sentence like this one:

> Although lifeguards look pretty much the same—tall, tan, and muscular—they are either conceited, flirtatious, or boring.

is more interesting than one like this:

> There are three kinds of lifeguards.

The paragraph below is a description. Like all descriptions, it attempts to translate what the eye can see into words written on a page. One of the important principles of writing description is order. Unless individual details are presented in some clear and logical order, the reader will have a hard time seeing the whole picture.

# TREES IN SNOW

Simply framed in dark wood edged in gold, the rectangular painting is 24 inches wide and 18 inches high. The subject is three fully grown trees that cast their shadows on the snow-covered ground. The trees form a rough triangle surrounding a white sapling that leans sharply to the right. The reddish-brown trees, whose tops cannot be seen, occupy the top one third of the canvas. Yellow-tinted snow, covered with the turquoise shadows of the trees, occupies the remainder of the canvas. The paint has been heavily applied, and brush strokes can be seen from a distance of several feet. This is a landscape painted in a rather traditional style.

## Thinking About Structure

1. Does this paragraph have a topic sentence?

2. The details are presented in the order of most general (size and shape) to most specific (the way the paint was applied to the canvas). Look at each sentence and explain how it fits in this general pattern. That is, what follows size and shape? State what comes next, and so on. Is there any place where the general-to-specific pattern is broken? Does beginning with size and shape seem appropriate?

3. Underline all the adjectives in this paragraph. Do any of them indicate the attitude of the writer? If you wanted to show that you didn't care much for the painting, how would you change the adjectives? What would you change if you wanted to show admiration?

4. This is a rather objective description. (An exercise later in this chapter presents a warmer view of the same painting.) Can you think of situations in which objective description would be appropriate?

## On Your Own

Write a paragraph describing a painting or a picture. A trip to the library's collection of art books might make this assignment more interesting. Try a collection of reproductions of Picasso or Breughel, for instance. When you have chosen the painting to describe, decide whether the general-to-specific pattern used in this exercise is appropriate or whether some other pattern would be more effective.

Next is a paragraph that defines or explains what a ghost town is.

## GHOST TOWNS

Scattered here and there in the western United States are ghost towns, abandoned communities that were once populated and thriving. Various situations—flood, drought, or sickness—caused the inhabitants to abandon their homes, but the most common cause was the closure of a gold mine. In the middle of the 19th century, thousands of people moved west, believing that they would make their fortunes in gold. Towns grew up near the mines, but when the gold ran out, the people left. Now, crumbling churches, homes, and shops serve only as reminders that entire families participated in the search for wealth and adventure. Some ghost towns have been restored for tourists, but no restoration can capture the excitement or harshness of daily life in those earlier years.

### Thinking About Structure

1. What is the topic sentence of this paragraph?

2. The second sentence explains why people abandoned their homes, but the third sentence explains why they built their homes there in the first place. Should these two sentences be reversed?

3. Comment on the final sentence. Does it seem appropriate, or does it go off in a new direction?

4. Does the paragraph contain sufficient detail to make clear what the term ''ghost town'' means? Do you think the paragraph would be more effective if at least one particular ghost town were mentioned?

### On Your Own

Think of another general location of human activity (a shopping center, an amusement park, a beauty parlor) and explain or define what it is. As you write, assume that your audience has never heard of your subject before. Remember that you are not describing the place; you are explaining what it is.

The following paragraph uses examples to support a general observation, a conclusion that the writer wishes to convince the audience to share.

# HAVE A NICE DAY

Most people would agree that words are supposed to have meaning, but very often the words people use are empty. People sometimes speak only to make a noise that acknowledges the presence of another person, and some sentences do not reflect what is in the mind or heart of the speaker. A common interchange between two people who pass each other in a hallway or on a sidewalk is "Hi! How are you?" "Fine, thanks. How are you?" Often the questioner has no real interest in how the other person is, and frequently the person who answers "Fine, thank you" is not fine. "Good to see you again" is often only a polite way of saying that the conversation must end, and foreigners are quick to learn that Americans don't necessarily mean it when they say "We should get together soon." In many restaurants, the waiter doesn't expect or wait for an answer to his question "How is your dinner?" and would be shocked to hear a negative response. The sentence "Have a nice day" is the most recent to become empty. When it follows an angry discussion between a policeman and a driver about a speeding ticket, what does that sentence mean? None of this is to suggest that people should give up good manners; it does, however, suggest that human relationships might profit from more sincerity in speech.

## Thinking About Structure

1. What is the main idea of this paragraph, and where is it stated?
2. According to this paragraph, what are empty words? Where did you find the answer to that question?
3. The second sentence names two situations in speaking. Do the examples that follow illustrate both situations?
4. Are there too many examples? Too few? Is the purpose of each example clear?
5. Comment on the final sentence.

## On Your Own

Think of a commonly used expression such as "You know what I mean?" or "Excuse me." Write a paragraph in which you explain whether the expression helps communication or has become an empty phrase. Or, if you disagree with the above paragraph, show how those or similar expressions are helpful in human relationships.

The paragraph below explains how to do something. Giving directions requires some care because the audience may know little or nothing about the process and can be easily confused. Equipment and supplies need to be discussed together, and the various steps need to be handled in order. For example, when a cake is ready for the oven, it is too late to inform the reader then that it requires a special, hard-to-locate baking pan.

## DRYING FLOWERS

A pressed flower used to be a fine, sentimental reminder of a holiday or a first love, but in the last 80 years drying flowers has become a lost art. It is an art, however, that is worth reviving. Hardly any equipment is needed—only a thick book and some paper of good quality. Almost any flower can be dried, but it is better not to choose one that is too thick in the middle; it may rot before it dries. The first step is to fold the paper in half or in thirds so that it fits completely in the book. Then open the paper, lay the flower in the middle, away from the fold, and, pressing it very gently with your fingers, make sure the flower is lying perfectly flat. Now refold the paper, but take care that the flower isn't disturbed in the process. Put the paper in the middle of the book, and after you have left it undisturbed for several days, you will have an attractive dried flower that will last almost forever.

### Thinking About Structure

1. Does the opening of the paragraph clearly indicate that an explanation of how to dry flowers is going to follow? If not, how would you revise the opening?

2. What is the first thing that is discussed?

3. How many steps are there?

4. What signals that one step is finished and another about to begin?

5. Are there any steps that are not clear enough?

### On Your Own

Pick a simple procedure (such as making tea or watering houseplants) and write a paragraph explaining how to do it.

# FLOWERING CACTUS _____

Write two versions of each sentence.

*a desert plant*

1.  The cactus* orchid bloomed.
    The blooming was last night.
    The orchid is outside my window.

2.  It is the only spot.
    The spot is of color.
    I can see the spot.
    My seeing is this morning.
    The morning is foggy.

*deep purple-red*

3.  The petals are crimson.*
    The petals are of the flower.
    The petals are five inches long.
    The crimson is brilliant.

4.  The blossom is the size.
    The size is of a dinner plate.
    The blossom is odorless.

5.  It is heavy.

*hangs down*

    It droops.*
    The drooping is graceful.
    The drooping is to the left.

    (In combining the following, try using ''loveliness'' in one version.)

6.  It is lovely.

*takes your breath away; used to describe beautiful things*

    The loveliness is breathtaking.*
    It will be gone.
    Its going is by this evening.

## On Your Own

Look out a window, choose one object (such as the flowering cactus), and describe it in a paragraph. Take some time to plan before you begin to write. You might want to make a list of details first, or see Composition Note 1 for other ways of getting started.

Take some time, also, to plan your topic sentence. What is the main idea that your description is going to convey? A topic sentence such as ''The tree outside my window is interesting'' is probably too general to help you organize the details. And it's not a very interesting beginning. ''The tree outside my window looks ready to survive another brutal Chicago winter'' can lead you into concrete details about the tree's strength, loss of leaves, and stillness.

# HOUSE-SITTING _____

Remember to write at least two versions of each sentence.

1.  Sarah Miller has been baby-sitting.
    The baby-sitting has been since she was twelve.
    The baby-sitting was for the Harrisons.
    Now she is house-sitting.
    The house-sitting is for the first time.
    The house-sitting is for them.

    (In combining the previous sentences, try an adjective clause in one version.)

2.  The Harrisons are visiting their relatives.
    The relatives are in England.
    They will be gone for six weeks.

3.  Several burglaries have occurred.
    The occurrence was in the neighborhood.
    The occurrence was recent.
    The Harrisons asked Sarah to do something.
    It is to live in their house.
    The living is during their absence.

4.  Sarah agreed.
    She won't have to pay rent.
    She will have more money.
    The money is for tuition.
    The tuition is next semester's.

5.  Now she is not sure of something.
    It is that her decision was wise.
    She feels a little uncomfortable.
    She feels a little unsure.
    The unsureness is about being alone.
    The being alone is in their house.

6.  The house is large.
    The house is empty.
    The house seems unfriendly.
    The seeming is sudden.
    She has known the house for years.

    (For the following, try a past participial phrase in one version.)

    *moved away

7.  The two dogs have withdrawn.*
    The withdrawal is to the garage.
    The dogs are displeased.
    The displeasure is at being left behind.
    One of them even gave a growl.

The growl was half-hearted.
The giving was when Sarah scratched its head.

8. Sarah walks.
*without a clear purpose*  The walking is aimless.*
The walking is through the house.
She wonders something.
It is what she would do if the washing machine were to spring a leak.
It is what she would do if someone were to ring the doorbell.
The ringing is after dark.

9. The knowledge permits her to relax.
The relaxation is a little.
The knowledge is comforting.
The comforting is slight.
The knowledge is that the neighbors are home.

10. She turns on the TV.
The turning on is for company.
She opens a book.
She has wanted to read the book.
The wanting has been for weeks.

11. A noise disturbs her peace of mind.
*low; not clear*  The noise is faint.*
The peace of mind is fragile.
She looks around.
The looking is apprehensive.

*walk quietly*  12. The two dogs pad.*
The padding is into the room.
They wag their tails.
The wagging is slight.
The wagging is as if to apologize.
The apology is for their coolness.
The coolness was earlier.

13. Sarah settles down.
The dogs settle down.
The settling is comfortable.
They spend an evening.
The evening is uneventful.
The spending is together.

## On Your Own

Write a paragraph about a time when you felt nervous or uneasy while you were alone. The topic sentence should contain a general comment about the experience; for example, ''I thought I had outgrown my childhood fear of the dark, but reading Robin Blake's *Ghostly Times* proved me wrong.'' Include more than the details of what happened. You might end by commenting on how you felt about your fear. Embarrassed? Surprised?

## A QUIET PAINTING

*painting of a nature scene*

1. The landscape* is rectangular.
   The landscape is powerful but serene.
   The landscape is framed.
   The framing is in wood.
   The framing is in gold.
   The wood and gold are delicate.

*controlled; major part is taken up by*

2. The scene is simple.
   The scene is dominated.*
   The domination is by a field.
   The field is of snow.
   The snow is covered.
   The covering is with the shadows.
   The shadows are of three trees.

3. The trees are seen.
   The seeing is only partial.
   The trees occupy the upper third.
   The upper third is of the canvas.

*outer layer of a tree trunk*

4. Their bark* contrasts with the snow.
   The bark is reddish brown.
   The reddish brown is warm.
   The contrast is sharp.
   The snow is yellowing.

5. There is another contrast.

*a very young tree*

   Standing in the triangle is a sapling.*
   The triangle is formed by the trees.

*strong*

   The trees are sturdy.*
   The trees are well grown.
   The sapling is white.
   The sapling is delicate.

*leans as if it will fall*

   The sapling lists.*
   The listing is to the right.

6. The shadows provide the contrast.
   The contrast is the most startling.
   They are turquoise.

*very intense*

   The turquoise is vibrant.*

*marks left by the paintbrush*

*showing much energy*

7. The strength and depth are captured.
   The strength is of the trees.
   The depth is of the snow.
   The capturing is by the paint.
   The paint is heavily applied.
   The capturing is by the brush strokes.*
   The brush strokes are vigorous.*

8. The quietness makes this a painting.
   The painting is powerful.
   The quietness is of the scene.
   The scene is snow-covered.
   The quietness is in contrast to something.
   It is the vividness.*
   The vividness is of the colors.

*brightness*

### On Your Own

Without worrying about your artistic ability, draw a picture of a landscape. Now write a paragraph describing it—either as it really looks or as it would look if it had been painted by a great artist.

## FRIENDSHIP AND CULTURE

1. Many problems exist.
   The existence is for people.
   The people come from cultures.
   The cultures are different.
   The people come in contact.
   The contact is with one another.

   (In combining the preceding sentences, try using "when" as the first word in one of your versions.)

2. Making friends can be a problem.
   Cultures have ideas.
   The ideas are different.
   The ideas are about friendship.

3. Misunderstandings can occur.
   The occurrence is easy.
   The occurrence is when people are unaware of something.
   It is their beliefs.
   The beliefs are their own.
   The beliefs are about friendship.

   (Add a phrase to the following sentence to show how it is related to sentence 3.)

4. Americans confuse foreigners.
   The confusing is frequent.
   The confusing is with their behavior.
   The behavior is friendly.
   The behavior is warm.
   The behavior doesn't lead.
   *closeness*       The leading is to intimacy.*

5. Friends expect to tell everything.
   The telling is to each other.
   The expectation is in some cultures.
   Many things may be held back.
   The holding back is in other cultures.
   The holding back is without damaging the friendship.

6. Friends see each other.
   The seeing is very frequent.
   This is in some cultures.
   Friends may not see each other.
   The seeing is for months at a time.
   This is in other cultures.

7. Something is required.
   It is self-awareness.
   It is tolerance.
   People make friends.
   The people are from different cultures.

## On Your Own

Write an account of some other cultural difference that you know of. Consider things such as differences in behavior toward parents or differences in the distance between two people who are talking with one another. Do something more than simply explain what the cultural difference is. For example, a topic sentence such as "The Japanese and Chinese have different sitting habits" tells what you are going to discuss but doesn't indicate why the reader should care about the difference. "My Americanized nephews cause problems in the family because they forget to greet my grandparents in the traditional way" shows the result of the cultural difference and so promises a more interesting paragraph.

## WELFARE OR NOT?

1. Welfare is a subject.
   People have feelings about the subject.
   The feelings are strong.

2. Something can be difficult.
   Something can be painful.
   It is to decide to apply.
   The application is for welfare.

3. Kathy Thomas has worked.
   The working was as a lab assistant.
   The working was at Midtown Hospital.
   The working was for eight years.

4. Kathy has always been self-supporting.
   She doesn't know what she is going to do.
   The knowing is now.
   She had a baby.
   The having was two weeks ago.
   Her husband left her.
   The leaving was at the same time.

5. Her salary is too small to cover something.
   It is her expenses.
   The expenses are usual.
   It is the new expenses.
   The expenses are of the baby.
   The expenses include child care.

6. She has learned something.
   She can receive welfare.
   She can go back to school.
   The going is at the same time.
   The going is to learn new skills.

   *upset    Her mind has been in turmoil.*

7. She would like a degree.
   The degree is in radiation therapy.
   She is embarrassed.
   The embarrassment is at the idea.
   The idea is of welfare.

8. Her relatives say something.
   It is that she should avoid welfare.

   *takes away dignity    Welfare is demeaning.*

9. Her friends tell her something.
   It is that welfare was designed.
   The designing was for people.
   The people are in her situation.
   It is that she should apply for welfare.

10. She will decide.
    The deciding is tomorrow.
    She will spend a night.

The spending is first.
The night is sleepless.

### On Your Own

Write a paragraph explaining what you think Kathy should do and why.
Consider a topic sentence that includes a clause beginning with "although"
or "because."

## DOWN WITH FAIRY TALES? _____

In this exercise, you may want to add some transitions, and you may feel
that some of the sentences can be combined. Don't forget to write at least
two versions of each sentence.

1. People have begun to worry.
   The beginning is in recent years.
   The worry is about the messages.
   Children get the messages.
   The messages are from fairy tales.
   The tales are traditional.

2. These stories present pictures.
   The pictures are incorrect.
   The pictures are of how men and women act.
   The pictures are of how men and women should act.

   (The following sentence will probably need "either . . . or." And try
   an adjective clause after "men" in one version.)

3. The women are passive and beautiful.
   The women are evil and ugly.
   The men are heroic.
   The heroism is unbelievable.
   The men marry only women.
   The women are beautiful.

4. Cinderella never defends herself.
   The defense is against her stepmother.
   The stepmother is wicked.
   The stepmother is selfish.

5. She does nothing.
   Her fairy godmother comes.
   The fairy godmother gives her clothes.
   The fairy godmother gives her transportation.
   The fairy godmother gives her a chance.
   The chance is to meet the prince.

6.  The prince has a requirement.
    The requirement is odd.
    The requirement is for a wife.
    The wife must have feet.
    The feet are tiny.
    Most people agree.
    The agreement is that feet don't influence the success.
    The success is of a marriage.

    (In combining the following, try a present participial phrase in one version.)

7.  Sleeping Beauty is another woman.
    The woman is passive.
    She lies in sleep.
    She looks lovely.
    The lying is until the prince kisses her.

8.  The prince can find her.
    He must kill dragons.
    He must fight giants.
    He must perform other acts.
    The acts are impossible.

9.  Fairy tales are part.
    The part is of our culture.
    Many parents don't want something.
    It is these ideas.
    The ideas are old.
    The ideas are for their children.

## On Your Own

Write a paragraph that summarizes a fairy tale and explains what message the story gives to children who read it.

# PATIENCE: ANOTHER FABLE

1.  A man was preparing.
    The preparation was to leave.
    The leaving was of his hometown.
    He had been promoted.
    The promotion was to an office.
    The office was high.
    The office was in another city.

    (Consider an adjective clause for one version of the previous sentence.)

2.  A friend came.
    The coming was to see him off.
    The friend was close.
    The friend gave him some advice.

3.  "You must remember something."
    "It is to be patient."
    "The remembering is always."
    "The remembering is when you are an official."
    "The official is high."

    (Try a participial phrase in combining the following sentences.)

4.  The man agreed.
    The man nodded his head.

5.  The friend repeated his advice.
    The repetition was three times.
    The man nodded his head.
    The nodding was in agreement.
    The nodding was each time.

    (In combining the following, don't try to put all the words in quotes in one sentence.)

6.  The friend repeated his advice.
    The repetition was for the fourth time.
    *got very angry*      The man exploded.*
    He shouted.
    "Do you think something?"
    "It is that I am a fool."
    "Why do you repeat?"
    "The repetition is of this idea."
    "The repetition is so many times."

    (In one version of the following, try a gerund as the subject.)

7.  His friend sighed.
    His friend replied.
    "Something is not easy."
    "It is to be patient."
    "I have said that."
    "The saying was only four times."
    "You are already impatient."

## On Your Own

Write a paragraph explaining what is funny or ironic about this story. Or write a paragraph about a time when you should have been patient but weren't.

# HALLOWEEN

**1.** Halloween is one of the celebrations.

*\*not too important*

The celebrations are minor.\*
The celebrations are in the United States.
It is colorful.
It is lighthearted.
It has a history.
The history is long.
The history is interesting.

**2.** Children go.
The children are in strange costumes.
The going is from house to house.
The going is to demand candy.
The going is to demand other things.
The things are good.
The things are to eat.

(In combining the following, think carefully about what conjunction to use.)

**3.** The children disguise themselves.
The disguising is frequent.
The disguising is as witches.
The disguising is as ghosts.
The disguising is as skeletons.
Any kind is acceptable.
The kind is of costume.

**4.** They ring doorbells.
They say, ''Trick or treat.''
This means something.
It is that they will play a trick.
The trick is on you.
You do not give them a treat.

**5.** The decoration is a jack-o'-lantern.
The decoration is most common.
It is a pumpkin.

*\*the insides have been removed*

The pumpkin is hollowed out.\*
The pumpkin is with a face.
The face is carved on it.
The face is frightening.
A candle is inside.
The candle is burning.

*\*origins*

**6.** The roots\* of Halloween go back.
The going is about 2000 years.
The going is to the Celts.

The Celts were a group of people.
They lived in England.
They lived in Ireland.
They lived in Scotland.

7. The Celts celebrated a festival.
The celebration was once a year.
The festival was of the dead.
The festival was called Samhain.

8. They believed something.
It was that the dead walked on earth.
The walking was on that day.
Large fires would keep people safe.
The people were living.
Gifts would keep people safe.
The gifts were of fruit.
The gifts were of vegetables.

9. That explains something.
It is why death is a theme.
The theme is common.
The theme is during this celebration.
The celebration is happy.

## On Your Own

Write a paragraph that explains the purpose of another holiday. You might want to go to the library to look up some details.

# HOT FUDGE SUNDAE

*having to do with good food*

1. The hot fudge sundae is a pleasure.
The pleasure is gastronomical.*
The pleasure is for people.
The people have digestions.
The digestions are strong.

(Keep going. This long sentence isn't finished yet.)

2. The sundae is made with ice cream.
The ice cream is vanilla.

*thickly covered*

The ice cream is smothered.*
The smothering is in a sauce.
The sauce is hot.
The sauce is chocolate.
The chocolate is dark.

It is covered with cream.
The cream is whipped.
It is sprinkled.
The sprinkling is with nuts.
It is served.
The serving is usual.
The serving is in a glass.
The glass is tall.

*\*the edge is waved or grooved*

The glass is fluted.*

(In one version of the following, try beginning the sentence with ''The contrast.'')

3.     One of the things is the contrast.
The things are best.
The things are about eating a hot fudge sundae.
The contrast is between the ice cream and the sauce.
The ice cream is cold.
The sauce is hot.
The contrast is between the sauce and the whipped cream.
The sauce is heavy.
The whipped cream is airy.

4.     The sauce hardens.
The sauce is next to the ice cream.
The sauce sticks to your teeth.
That is the sign.
The sign is perfect.
The sign is of a sundae.

*\*the most excellent*

The sundae is supreme.*

5.     Teeth can be cleaned.
The teeth are chocolaty.
The cleaning is without much trouble.
Something is not easy.
It is to recover.
The recovery is from the guilt.
The guilt is of consuming.
The consumption is of so many calories.

## On Your Own

Think of some food that you like or dislike very much. Write a description that includes details about its appearance and taste. You may want to include details about texture and smell, too. The more specific you can be, the better the paragraph will be. Your first draft may include adjectives such as ''delicious'' or ''disgusting,'' but revise to include more vivid details such as ''tangy'' or ''crunchy'' or ''overpowering.''

# TALKING _____

|  |  |  |
|---|---|---|
| *medical treatment of children | **1.** | Le Phong is a doctor.<br>He practiced pediatrics*<br>The practicing was in his country.<br>The practicing was for six years.<br>He came to the United States. |

**2.** Now there are many requirements.
He must meet the requirements.
The requirements are to get a medical license.
The license is American.
One requirement troubles him.
The troubling is the most.

*great ability The requirement is proficiency* in English.

**3.** He is enrolled in three classes.
The classes are English.
The enrollment is this semester.
He has taken two others.
The taking is already.
He is not satisfied.
The satisfaction is with his progress.

**4.** He studies.
*constant; careful His study is diligent.*
Someone speaks to him.
He gets nervous.
He doesn't understand.
His understanding is frequent.

**5.** He goes to an office.
He goes to a bank.
He practices sentences.
The practicing is in his head.
The practicing is before he enters.

**6.** He is always tense.
The tension is slight.
This makes speaking more difficult.
It makes listening more difficult.
It makes him tired.

**7.** He reads English well.
He writes English well.
He knows something.
He must use spoken English.
The using is more frequent.
*force himself He cannot bring himself* to do it.

### On Your Own

Write a paragraph explaining what you would do in this situation. Or, if you *are* in this situation, explain what you do.

## CONTROLLING PAIN

This exercise will need transitions.

1. Research has provided painkillers.
   The research is medical.
   The painkillers are powerful.
   They cannot control all pain.
   Some people prefer something.
   It is not to take these painkillers.
   The taking is for periods of time.
   The periods are prolonged.*

   *for a long time*

2. Psychologists have developed methods.
   The methods are drug-free.
   The methods use the power.
   The power is of the mind.
   The power is to control pain.

3. These methods are not new.
   The newness is complete.
   They are based on principles.
   The principles were known.
   The knowing was in Asia.
   The knowing was centuries ago.

4. The requirement is relaxation.
   The requirement is the first.
   The requirement is for controlling pain.
   The relaxation is mental.
   The relaxation is physical.

5. This is accomplished.
   The accomplishment is usual.
   The accomplishment is by a series.
   The series is of exercises.
   The exercises are gentle.

6. A state is reached.
   The state is of profound* relaxation.
   The patient is asked something.
   It is to visualize* the pain.
   The visualizing is in some way.

   *deep; complete*

   *see a picture in the mind*

7.   The pain might be seen as a cube.
The cube is red.
The pain might be seen as a tiger.
The tiger is with teeth.
The teeth are long.
The teeth are sharp.
The details are unimportant.
The details are specific.

8.   The patient is told something.

*picture     It is to make the image* disappear.
It is to make the image shrink.

*change      It is to make the image transform* itself.

9.   The cube has disappeared.
The tiger has become a kitten.
The kitten is playful.
The pain has been reduced.
The pain has been eliminated.

10.  This sounds like magic.
It works.

### On Your Own

Completely in your own words, write a summary of this exercise. Pay special attention to the topic sentence.

# REGISTRATION _____

1.   Semesters begin.
The semesters are college.
The beginning is bad.
Semesters end.
The ending is bad.

2.   Taking exams is unpleasant.
The exams are final.
Registering can be worse.
The registering is for classes.

3.   The place is the gymnasium.
The place is traditional.
The place is to register.
The temperature there is wrong.
This is always.

4.   The gymnasium is hot.

It is hot outside.
This is in the fall.
It is also hot.
This is in winter.
So many people are crowded.
The crowding is together.
The people are all warmly dressed.

*never end; long*

5.    There are lines.
The lines are interminable.*
The lines are at every step.
The step is of the process.

6.    The people get irritated.
The people work at registration.
They are asked the same question.
The asking is for the hundredth time.
Students get frustrated.
Classes have been canceled.
They try to register in them.

7.    Computers help.
Procedures help.
The procedures are mail-in.
What can improve?
The improvement is of final exams.

## On Your Own

Write a paragraph explaining something pleasant or unpleasant that happened to you during registration. In your topic sentence, include an adverb clause that begins with the word "although." (Example: Although registration is usually frustrating, this semester something delightful happened.)

# ANOREXIA

1.    A condition is receiving much attention.
The condition is anorexia nervosa.
The attention is from the profession.
The profession is medical.
The attention is in the press.
The press is popular.*

*general newspapers and magazines*

2.    The condition affects women.
The women are young.
The affecting is usual.
The affecting is not always.

3. Anorexia is an eating disorder.
   People consume so little.
   Their lives are threatened.
   The threat is serious.

4. Anorexics feel overweight.
   They are emaciated.*

*so thin that bones show*

5. One theory says something.
   The theory is about the cause.
   The cause is of anorexia.
   It is that the issue is control.
   The issue is central.

   (In one version of the following, begin the sentence with ''A young woman.'')

6. Her parents are strict.
   The strictness is excessive.*
   A woman may feel something.
   The woman is young.
   It is that she has no control.
   The control is of her own life.

*too much*

7. Refusing to eat is the only way.
   She has the way.
   The way is to be independent.

8. Curing anorexia requires something.
   It is treatment.
   The treatment is medical.
   The treatment is psychological.
   The parents are also involved.
   The involvement is frequent.

### On Your Own

Imagine that you are writing for an audience of people who have never been sick. Write a paragraph explaining a common illness (a cold or the chicken-pox, for example).

## BUILD UP AND LET DOWN

1. Notices appeared.
   The notices were printed.
   The printing was on paper.
   The paper was orange.
   The orange was blinding.*

*very bright*

The appearance was a few days before the event.
The appearance was on all the doorknobs.
The knobs were on Marshall Street.

2.  The city was sending workers.
The sending was on the following Monday.
The sending was to repave the street.
The sending was final.
Cars would be prohibited.
The prohibition was from 7 A.M. to 5 P.M.

3.  Almost all the residents moved their cars.
The moving was to streets.
The streets were nearby.
The moving was on Sunday evening.
This caused a parking problem.
The problem was major.
The causing was in the neighborhood.

4.  Most of the cars were gone.
The going was by 7:15.
The going was on Monday morning.
This gave the street a look.
The look was deserted.
The desertion was odd.

(For the following, use the participial form of "to honk" in one version of this sentence.)

5.  The street was filled.
The filling was with noise.
The filling was by 7:30.
Two men drove.
The men were young.
The men were cheerful.
The driving was in a truck.

*old; beaten up*    The truck was battered.*
The driving was up and down.
They honked.
The honking was rhythmic.
The honking was to announce.
The announcement was that the cars should be moved.
The cars were remaining.
The cars were few.
The moving was at once.

6.  A street sweeper contributed.
The street sweeper was enormous.
The contribution was to the noise.

The contribution was by chugging.
The chugging was back and forth.
The contribution was by grinding its gears.

*a high-pitched sound*   7.   Another contribution was the whine.*
The whine was of a car.
The car was brown.
The car wouldn't start.
Its owner tried to start it.
The trying was repeated.
The trying was aggressive.

8.   The dogs barked.
The children gathered.
The gathering was in a group.
The gathering was excited.
The gathering was to watch the fun.
A tow truck came.
The coming was for a car.
No one could identify the car.

9.   The excitement died down.
Nothing happened.
The nothing was absolute.
The happening was after that.

10.   Something had gone wrong.
The going was at the office.
The office was central.

## On Your Own

In a paragraph, give an account of a humorous or silly event that you saw but were not part of.

# WAITING IN LINE

1.   One of the things is to wait.
The things are most boring.
A person must do the things.
The waiting is in line.
The waiting is at the check-out counter.
The counter is in a supermarket.

2.   A way is to watch.
The way is interesting.
The way is to pass the time.

The watching is of the way.
Other people pass the time in the way.

3.    Some make comments.
The comments are about the wait.
The wait is long.
The making is to people.
The people are nearby.
Conversation is rare.
Most people are surprised.
The surprise is at being spoken to by a stranger.

4.    Some people make faces.
The faces are funny.
The making is at babies.
The babies are sitting.
The sitting is in shopping carts.
Some babies respond.
Other babies do not respond.

5.    A few shoppers read.
The reading is of magazines.
The reading is of newspapers.
*exaggerated; thrilling*    The newspapers are sensational.*
The magazines and newspapers are displayed.
The displaying is on racks.
The racks are near the cash registers.
They put the magazines and newspapers back.
The putting is usual.
They reach the head of the line.

6.    Something is what most people do.
It is to stare.
The staring is ahead of them.
*without an*    The staring is blank.*
*expression*    They move.
The moving is only when the line moves.

7.    To know is impossible.
The knowing is what they are thinking.
The knowing is whether they are thinking.
The thinking is at all.

*end; get rid of*    8.    We can't do away with* waiting.
The waiting is in lines.
Someone should invent something.
It is ways.
The ways are better.
The ways are to pass the time.

### On Your Own

Write a paragraph explaining what you do when you wait in line.

## CURING A COLD ───────────────────────

You may want to combine some groups of sentences in this exercise.

1.  A saying is something.
    It is that a cold will be gone.
    The going is in seven days.
    The going is without treatment.
    It is that a cold takes a week.
    The taking is to go away.
    The taking is with treatment.
    The saying is old.
    The saying is not very funny.

2.  The treatment is a mixture.
    The treatment is the most common.
    The treatment is in the United States.
    The mixture is of aspirin.
    The mixture is of decongestants.*
    The mixture is of rest.

    *\*pills to dry the nose*

3.  Other treatments are popular.
    The popularity is with various groups.

4.  Some people swear by* something.
    It is tea.
    The tea is hot.
    The tea is mixed.
    The mixing is with lemon.
    The mixing is with honey.

    *\*believe it is the best*

5.  Others insist.
    The insisting is that the tea must be drunk.
    The drinking is with a shot* or two.
    The shot is of whiskey.
    This treatment must be repeated.
    The repetition is until the person doesn't care.
    The caring is about being sick.

    *\*a small measuring glass for whiskey*

6.  The tea and whiskey are recommended.
    The recommending is in amounts.
    The amounts are smaller.
    The recommending is in some families.
    The amounts are to be followed.

The following is by a bath.
The bath is hot.
The following is by a quilt.
The quilt is heavy.
The following is by a room.
The room is warm.
This procedure is called ''sweating the cold.''

7. A procedure calls for a walk.
A procedure calls for a night.
The procedure is quite different.
The walk is long.
The walk is energetic.
The walk is in the air.
The air is fresh.
The night is spent.
The spending is with open windows.
The spending is even in winter.

*cures*

8. Other remedies* are soup, vitamin C, and juice.
The remedies are popular.
The soup is chicken.
The juice is orange.
The juice is in quantity.
The quantity is great.

9. Another saying is something.
It is ''We can send a person.''
''The sending is to the moon.''
''We cannot cure the cold.''
''The cold is common.''
The saying is not very funny.

## On Your Own

Write a paragraph about one or two other ways to treat a cold.

# THE FOOLISH OLD MAN WHO MOVED THE MOUNTAINS: A CHINESE FABLE

As you do this exercise, try not to begin each sentence with the subject. In sentences 9 and 10, experiment with direct and indirect speech. Consider adding some transitions between sentences, too.

1.  Once there was a very old man.
    He was called The Fool.

2.  He lived near two mountains.
    His living was with his family.
    The mountains were high.

*difficult to climb    They were rugged.*

(In combining the following, change "walk" to a gerund in one version. See Grammar Note 9 if necessary. Also, try combining sentences 1 and 2 or 2 and 3.)

3.  He went out of his house.
    He had to walk around the mountains.
    This was very inconvenient.

4.  The Fool called his family together.
    His calling was one day.
    His calling was to discuss the problem.

5.  He suggested something.
    It was to work together.

*tear down    The working was to level* the mountains.
    They could build a road.
    The road is straight.
    The road is to the river.

6.  They all agreed.
    His wife was worried.
    He did not have enough strength.
    The strength was to move.
    The moving was of so much earth.
    The moving was of rock.

(In the following sentence, try changing "carried" to a participle.)

7.  The Fool went to work.
    His son went to work.
    His grandson went to work.
    A neighbor's boy went to work.
    They carried baskets.
    The baskets were on poles.
    The poles were across their shoulders.

8.  A man laughed at them.
    He lived near the river.
    He was called The Wise Man.
    He tried to stop their work.

9.  He said something.
    "This is foolish."
    "You are old."

''You are weak.''
''You won't be able to lower the mountain.''
''The lowering is by one inch.''

10.   The Fool laughed.
He replied something.
''You are the foolish one.''
''I will die.''
''I will leave my son.''
''I will leave my son's sons.''
''I will leave my grandsons' sons.''
''The leaving is behind me.''
''The mountains can't grow higher.''
''We will be able to level them.''
*some day*     ''Our leveling will be eventual.''*

11.   The Wise Man could not argue.
His arguing was with that.
He remained silent.

## On Your Own

Write a paragraph explaining the old man's attitude toward life.

# DEVELOPING INDEPENDENCE
# AND
# DESIGNING ESSAYS

# 4

113

A glance at the exercises in this chapter will show you that they look quite different from the previous ones. Instead of being arranged into groups that will each be combined into one sentence, they are not grouped at all. This means that you will have to decide how many short sentences can be combined into one longer one. This is not so difficult, but it does require some planning before you begin to write. In addition to giving you further opportunity to practice with various ways of structuring sentences, this chapter asks you to consider such questions as these: How are the pieces of a sentence related to one another? How much information can a sentence contain? What's too short? What's too long? The answers may vary according to your audience. This chapter is designed to give you practice in deciding issues like these.

An example will illustrate the possibilities. Here is a short, unstructured exercise.

1.    The Fishing Boat is a restaurant.
2.    It is near Ocean Beach.
3.    The restaurant employs only one waiter.
4.    The waiter's name is Harry.
5.    The waiter is gruff.
6.    He insults people.
7.    He shouts at people.
8.    He brings the wrong meal.
9.    This is often.
10.    He is very popular.
11.    People go to The Fishing Boat to eat.
12.    They go there to argue.
13.    The arguing is with Harry.

It is possible to combine these sentences into a passage filled with short, choppy sentences—especially the first time you try an unstructured exercise. Here is an example. Read it aloud to hear how rough and awkward it sounds.

> The Fishing Boat is a restaurant near Ocean Beach. It employs only one waiter. His name is Harry. He is gruff. He insults people and shouts at them. He often brings the wrong meal. He is very popular. People go to The Fishing Boat to eat. They also go there to argue with Harry.

One of the unsatisfactory things about this passage is that because of all the short sentences in it, it just bumps along. Another unsatisfactory characteristic is that there are no transitions between sentences to provide smoothness. (If you haven't read Composition Note 2: Transitions Between Sentences, now would be a good time.)

Another ineffective way of combining an unstructured exercise is to write sentences that are too long. Long, complicated sentences are sometimes necessary in order to express long, complicated ideas. But length and complexity can make for difficult reading and turn a reader away. Here is such an example:

> The Fishing Boat, a restaurant near Ocean Beach, employs only one waiter, whose name is Harry, who is gruff, and who insults people and shouts at them; furthermore he often brings the wrong meal, but he is very popular, and people go to The Fishing Boat to eat and argue with Harry.

This passage is one long, breathless sentence. There is just too much information for anyone to digest comfortably all at once.

Here is a more satisfactory version. It divides the ideas among a reasonable number of sentences. And it provides some transitions to help make clear the relationships among the ideas.

> The Fishing Boat, a restaurant near Ocean Beach, employs only one waiter. His name is Harry, and he is gruff. He insults people, shouts at them, and often brings the wrong meal. Nevertheless, he is very popular. People go to The Fishing Boat not only to eat, but also to argue with Harry.

So as you do these exercises, keep in mind the length of your sentences—neither too short nor too long—and keep in mind also the necessity to provide transitions. Think about these things for your own writing, too.

Something else different about this chapter is that, when combined, the exercises are essays of various types. As you work, you will be dividing the essays into paragraphs. This is an introduction to essay structure, and reading Composition Note 4 now will be helpful. In your independent writing, you will be composing your own short essays.

The first exercises in this chapter are short essays for you to look at in order to reinforce some important principles of essay structure. There will probably be some differences of opinion in your class with regard to the answers to some of the questions about these essays. That is because there is not one "best" or "right" way to write. Discussing these different points of view can help you to sharpen your ability to evaluate your own writing.

# WASHING THE DISHES: A DIFFERENT VIEW _____

> Most people dislike washing dishes. But if one eats, one usually uses dishes. And if one has been reared to be orderly, the dishes must be washed. Many people accept this repetitious chore un-

gracefully, rushing through each step in their haste to begin the evening's relaxation. However, a slight change in attitude can turn dishwashing into a pleasant activity, a fine introduction to the leisure-time activities that lie ahead.

Instead of rushing through the dishes, focus your mind completely on each step. Listen to the musical sound of water filling the sink. Watch the liquid soap turn into frothy bubbles. Feel the warmth of the water on the skin of your hands. Appreciate the cleanliness and the emerging order. Be aware of washing the dishes. This is the most important idea. If you keep your mind on each action, you will feel calm and relaxed. If you think only that you would rather read or watch TV, you will be tense and angry, a poor beginning for what is supposed to be the part of the day for relaxing.

Busy people often think too much about their next task. When they get to that task, they think of their next task. They never concentrate on what they are doing right then. Learning to wash the dishes ''correctly'' can break this bad habit.

## Thinking About Structure

1.  This essay has a three-part structure: an introduction, a middle paragraph in which the main idea is developed, and a concluding paragraph. Identify the thesis statement. Do you think it states the main idea precisely enough? If not, how would you improve it?

2.  How is the introduction structured? Do you think it is too long?

3.  Does the second paragraph contain a topic sentence? Toward the end of the paragraph an idea is identified as the most important part of the process. Is this a logical place to have the most important point? Is this paragraph detailed enough to be convincing?

4.  Does the concluding paragraph follow naturally from the rest of the essay?

5.  The introduction and the conclusion are written in the third person; that is, they talk *about* people. The second paragraph, on the other hand, is in second person; it speaks directly to the reader, giving instructions. Does this inconsistency lessen the effectiveness of the essay? How might the second paragraph be revised?

6.  Would you say that this essay is primarily about dishwashing or about mental attitudes?

## On Your Own

Write a three-paragraph essay using this as your thesis sentence:

_____ is one of the usual household chores, but I dislike it because _____.

The thesis would probably be the last sentence in the introductory paragraph. The second paragraph should explain in detail the reasons for your dislike. The conclusion can be brief, for example a sentence or two about what might make you feel better about having to do that chore.

# A (POSSIBLY HUMOROUS) LOOK AT THE ORDINARY PENCIL SHARPENER

The ordinary pencil has reached a high state of perfection, so it is rare to find a defective one. And pencils exist in an amazing variety of colors and degrees of hardness. However, the perfect pencil sharpener has not yet been created. Sooner or later, something goes wrong with every pencil sharpener currently on the market.

The pencil sharpener that most people are familiar with is the wall-mounted model. It is an almost universal feature of classrooms across the country. The first problem is that it is noisy. It is not possible to sharpen a pencil during class without disrupting the lecture, even though students frequently disregard this fact. Two other problems appear as the sharpener ages. A dismaying tendency develops for it to bite off the point of the pencil being sharpened. The point gets stuck firmly in the mechanism, and no other pencil can be sharpened until the embedded piece is removed—not an easy task. In addition, the container that holds the shavings falls off, making a loud noise and a mess on the floor. Once a container has fallen off, it is never possible to attach it firmly enough to keep it from falling off again and again.

The electric pencil sharpener was heralded as a major improvement, but many people suspect that it is only a clever trick to sell more pencils. This idea comes from the fact that the electric sharpener gobbles up pencils while it sharpens them. By the time the point is sharp enough, the pencil is an inch shorter than it was to begin with. Electric pencil sharpeners also require an electrical outlet and a table to sit on. This limits their use to certain locations. Furthermore, they are expensive to buy and expensive to repair.

The hand-held pencil sharpener is probably the most efficient and convenient, but it is not perfect either. It can be carried in one's pocket, bookbag, or pencil case, and it makes sharp points without too much waste. The user does, however, need to find an ashtray or a trash basket in order not to scatter pencil shavings everywhere. Some hand-held sharpeners have small, built-in containers for shavings, but these containers often open, making a mess in one's pocket or bag. These sharpeners have two other disadvantages. One must remember to take them along whenever they might be needed, and they are considered childish and very old-fashioned in this technological age.

The person who invents a better pencil sharpener will probably not get rich or famous, but he or she will earn the gratitude of people who like using traditional yellow pencils and dislike using mechanical ones.

## Thinking About Structure

1.  This essay is organized in a five-paragraph structure. Identify the thesis statement and the topic sentences.

2.  Look carefully at the thesis statement. Does the rest of the essay adequately support the thesis?

3.  The second paragraph discusses three problems but does not use ''first, second, and third'' as a way of introducing them. Comment on the method used to indicate that the discussion of one problem is complete and the next one is about to be introduced.

4.  The third paragraph is shorter than the second and the fourth. Does it need further development?

5.  The different types of pencil sharpeners are discussed in this order: wall-mounted, electric, and hand-held. Can you see any reason for this order? Could or should the order be changed?

6.  This essay is rather lighthearted. Identify the passages that contribute to the mild humor.

## On Your Own

Write a very short summary of the essay—about 75 words. Be sure to include all the main ideas, but use your own words. That is, don't copy whole sentences or phrases.

Write an essay about a common tool or machine that you think should be improved—or invented. Use this plan, or a similar one, for your essay:

1.  Introductory paragraph: general information about the tool or machine and the thesis sentence;

2.  Second paragraph: why the tool needs to be improved or invented;

3.  Third paragraph: what the improvement or invention is;

4.  Closing paragraph: brief conclusion.

# ON STUDY

Psychologists have learned a great deal in recent years about how people learn. It is now clear that people have different styles of learning. What works well for one person may not be effective for another. During their first semesters in college, many students discover that they don't really know how to study. One technique that can help almost everyone is called active study.

Many students study passively. They read the material over and over again hoping that repetition will cause them to remember enough to pass a test. This method treats each fact as the equal of every other fact. But facts are only part of the material in most classes; ideas based on those facts are usually more important. Passive study tends to ignore ideas in favor of specific details.

Active study requires more than reading, but reading is, of course, necessary. Active study begins with a quick reading in order to gain a general idea of the material. In the second reading, the material is examined more slowly and more carefully. Key ideas are identified and carefully underlined with pencil and a ruler. Underlining serves several important purposes. It encourages students to focus on ideas, not on facts. The act of underlining reinforces the search for concepts and the separation of ideas from supporting details. And underlining helps to overcome the passive attitude of letting information flow uncritically through the mind. Finally, underlining prepares the textbook for easy review later on for tests.

After key concepts are identified and marked, the next step is to understand them precisely. This requires reviewing the material part by part, the essential aspect of active study. Students review one concept, close the book or look away, and explain the idea to themselves, either silently or on paper. If something is unclear, students open the book, review what was unclear, and then continue as before. This is the opposite of passive study, in which students never check to see how well they have understood the material.

The exact procedures of active study may vary from student to student—some prefer notecards, others a tape recorder—but the essence is to take an active role. Waiting passively for the material to "sink in" is not an efficient method of studying.

## Thinking About Structure

1. This essay is about a technique called active study, but passive study—its opposite—is discussed first. Could or should that paragraph be omitted?

2. The essay presents three characteristics of active study. Identify them. How many paragraphs are devoted to these three steps? Comment on the effectiveness or appropriateness of this organization.

3. Examine the flow of ideas in the introduction. Does the sentence that begins "During their first semesters" follow smoothly from the preceding sentence? What ideas do you have about improving the introduction?

4. What idea in the introduction is referred to again in the concluding paragraph? The technique of ending with a reference to the opening is fairly common. The intent is to give a sense of completeness, of closure. Would you say that that technique is handled effectively here?

## On Your Own

In your own words, write one or two sentences explaining passive study. Do the same for active study.

Write an essay explaining and evaluating the way you study. Write four paragraphs: an introduction, an explanation, an evaluation, and a conclusion. Your thesis sentence should contain a word or phrase of general description (for example, "organized") and a word or phrase of evaluation (for example, "not very effective"—thus, "My study habits appear to be organized, but they do not seem to be very effective").

# THE ANIMAL RIGHTS MOVEMENT

Many people laughed in derision at the beginning of the civil rights movement and the women's liberation movement, but later they took these movements more seriously. A similar situation exists today with the animal rights movement. People who have little familiarity with the issues argue that animals don't need rights, or they joke about giving dogs the right to vote. Nevertheless, the issues raised by the members of the animal rights movement are quite serious. Animal rights activists point out that animals raised for food or used for research lead painful lives that violate the animals' natural instincts.

Animals are often subjected to pain that could easily be prevented, and frequently they exist in substandard conditions. Sometimes experiments are performed on laboratory animals without anesthesia, and the experiments are often repeated unnecessarily or have no demonstrable connection to human health. Chickens raised for the table are usually housed in sunless buildings where they are confined in wire cages so that they cannot scratch in the dirt. The chickens are so crowded in the cages that they become aggressive and peck at one another's eyes; consequently poultry raisers routinely cut off their beaks.

The plight of calves raised for veal is a major emotional issue, for veal calves receive the least humane treatment. As soon as they are born, they are separated from their mothers and isolated in small crates. There they are starved both for affection and for nutritious food. Their diet consists solely of milk, which does not provide them with iron or other nutrients necessary for good health. They become so weak that they cannot stand, but their flesh produces veal—tender, white, and expensive.

Some people in the animal rights movement do not completely oppose eating meat or using animals in medical experiments, but they insist that these animals be treated humanely. They argue that allowing terrible conditions to exist is not good for human beings. People who are insensitive to the suffering of animals will more easily accept pain and suffering that is inflicted on their fellow humans.

## Thinking About Structure

1. The introduction is based on a comparison between the animal rights movement and two earlier movements. Identify the points of similarity. Discuss the function of the sentence that begins with "nevertheless." Is it the thesis sentence? How is it related to the sentence that follows it?

2. Identify the main ideas of the second and third paragraphs. Are these ideas clearly related to the thesis of the essay?

3. The concluding paragraph contains one of the most important ideas in the essay. Identify it and discuss whether or not that idea should be mentioned earlier or discussed in more detail.

## On Your Own

Write an essay that supports or argues against the positions taken in the animal rights movement. Your thesis might be something like this: The animal rights movement should/should not be taken more seriously because

_____.

# GETTING INVOLVED_____

When you have finished this exercise, divide it into paragraphs. Comment on the lack of topic sentences. Does that weaken the essay?

1. The Coronado Arms is an apartment building.
2. The building is large.
3. The building is U-shaped.
4. The apartments overlook a courtyard.
5. The apartments are inside.
6. The courtyard contains some trees.
7. The courtyard contains some benches.
8. The courtyard contains a few swings.
9. The swings are for children.
10. The people are polite.
11. The people are hardworking.

*private; don't show feelings*

12. The people are somewhat reserved.*
13. The people live there.
14. Their children play.
15. The playing is together.
16. The adults will help.
17. The helping is in an emergency.
18. They will do favors.
19. The favors are small.
20. The favors are for a neighbor.
21. It is not a community.

*people feel very friendly and spend time together*

22. The community is close.*
23. There has been a problem of wife-beating.
24. This has been since August.
25. No one wanted to acknowledge the problem.
26. A family moved into an apartment.
27. The apartment is inside.
28. The apartment is on the sixth floor.
29. The family is named Jamison.
30. Mr. and Mrs. Jamison argue.
31. The arguing is loud.
32. The arguing is with frequency.

33.   The frequency is increasing.
34.   Mrs. Jamison was not seen.
35.   This was for two weeks.
36.   This was recent.
37.   The Jamison children have been going.
38.   The going is directly home.
39.   The going is from school.
40.   They have been avoiding.
41.   The avoidance is of children.
42.   The children are other.
43.   A neighbor saw Mrs. Jamison.
44.   The seeing was yesterday.
45.   The seeing was on a bus.
46.   Mrs. Jamison was wearing glasses.
47.   The glasses were dark.
48.   Her left eye appeared swollen.
49.   Her eye appeared bruised.
50.   She said nothing.
51.   She stared.
52.   Her staring was out the window.
53.   The arguments began.
54.   The neighbors reacted.
55.   The reaction was with annoyance.
56.   The reaction was at first.
57.   The Coronado Arms had been a building.
58.   The building is quiet.
59.   This was always.
60.   The arguments got worse.
61.   Annoyance turned to anger.
62.   One neighbor banged.
63.   His banging was on the wall.
64.   One neighbor shouted.
65.   The shouting was out the window.
66.   One neighbor slipped a note.
67.   The note was unsigned.
68.   The slipping was under the Jamisons' door.

69. Now several neighbors are concerned.
70. This is because of the black eye.
71. This is because of the behavior.
72. The behavior is changed.
73. The behavior is of the children.
74. They don't know something.
75. It is what to do.
76. Should they call the police?
77. Should they go to the apartment?
78. The apartment is the Jamisons'.
79. The going is in a group.
80. Should they do nothing?
81. The neighbors have no history.
82. The history is of getting involved.
83. The involvement is in business.
84. The business is each other's.
85. The business is family.
86. Something will be difficult for them.
87. It is to reach a decision.
88. The decision is satisfactory.

## On Your Own

In a concluding paragraph, explain what you think the residents of Coronado Arms should do and why.

Think of a problem that exists on your campus and how it should be solved. Write an essay for an audience that knows nothing at all about the situation. Structure your essay this way:

Paragraph 1: an explanation of the problem;
Paragraph 2: an explanation of your proposed solution;
Paragraph 3: a conclusion.

If you like, you can write this in the form of a letter to the editor of the campus newspaper or to the dean.

# THE TRANSFORMATION OF DOWNTOWN _____

Divide this exercise into paragraphs.

*common; usual

1. Something is typical.*
2. It is what is going on.
3. The going on is in downtown San Felix.
4. San Felix is a town.
5. The town is medium-sized.
6. The town is western.
7. The typicalness is of projects.

*making old cities new

8. The projects are redevelopment.*
9. The projects are recent.
10. Five blocks are being transformed.
11. The blocks are square.
12. The transformation is from an area.
13. The area is run-down.
14. The area is depressing.
15. The area is poor.
16. The transformation is to a city center.
17. The center is modern.
18. The center preserves the flavor.
19. The flavor is of the past.

*caused

*not downtown

20. Shopping centers spelled* the death.
21. The centers were suburban.*
22. The centers were the first.
23. The centers were built.
24. The building was in the late 1950s.
25. The death was of downtown San Felix.
26. People preferred shopping there.
27. The preference was instead of downtown.
28. Parking was easy.
29. Everything was available.
30. The availability was in one place.
31. The place was convenient.

*newness

32. The novelty* was attractive.
33. Shops began to close.

34. The shops were small.

35. The shops were downtown.

36. The closing was in the next years.

37. They could not compete.

38. The competition was with the shopping centers.

39. The larger stores began to go out of business.

40. The going was one by one.

*shopping centers*  41. They began to move to the malls.*

*the place for*  42. Downtown had become the preserve.*

43. The becoming was by the late 1960s.

*poor, homeless people*  44. The preserve was of derelicts.*

45. The preserve was of drunks.

46. The preserve was of prostitutes.

47. The preserve was of soldiers.

48. The soldiers were young.

49. The soldiers were looking for excitement.

50. Bars were the businesses.

51. Pawn shops were the businesses.

52. X-rated movie houses were the businesses.

53. The businesses were the most common.

54. The streets fell.

55. The buildings fell.

56. The spirit fell.

57. The spirit was whole.

58. The spirit was of downtown.

*not repaired*  59. The falling was into disrepair.*

60. San Felix became quite prosperous.

61. This was in the 1970s.

62. Residents began to feel embarrassed.

63. The embarrassment was by the state.

*poor*  64. The state was impoverished.*

65. The state was of the downtown area.

66. The city council approved a plan.

67. The approval was after much discussion.

68. The plan was ambitious.

69. The plan was imaginative.

70. The plan was long-term.
71. The plan was to rebuild.
72. The rebuilding was of the heart.
73. The heart was of San Felix.
74. The idea was to bring diversity.*     *many different things
75. The idea was main.
76. The idea was of the plan.
77. The bringing was to the downtown area.
78. Shopping would be available.
79. Businesses would be available.
80. Cultural events would be available.
81. Recreation would be available.
82. Traffic would be controlled.
83. The control is severe.
84. Transportation would be increased.
85. The transportation is public.
86. The transportation is from all parts.
87. The parts are of the city.
89. The increase is radical.*     *a great amount
89. The city planners believed something.
90. Downtown should be residential.*     *people live there
91. It should not be only commercial.*     *for business
92. The new buildings should have some characteristics.
93. The new streets should have some characteristics.
94. The characteristics remind people of the San Felix.
95. The San Felix is of the past.
96. The plan is being realized.*     *happening; becoming fact
97. The plan is for the future.
98. The plan is the city council's.
99. The realization is day by day.
100. The realization is street by street.

## On Your Own

When you have finished this exercise, answer these questions and discuss your answers with others in your class:

1. What is the thesis sentence?
2. What is the topic sentence of the second paragraph?
3. What is the topic sentence of the third paragraph?
4. Would it be logical to reverse the order of the second and third paragraphs?
5. Is the conclusion effective? If you think it isn't, what ideas do you have about improving it?

# DOWNTOWN SAN FELIX

Divide this exercise into paragraphs.

1. The feature is a hole.
2. The feature is of downtown San Felix.

*surprising    3. The feature is most startling.*

*very large    4. The hole is gigantic.*

5. The hole is at the intersection.
6. The intersection is of Main Street and First Avenue.
7. The hole covers three blocks.
8. The hole is surrounded.
9. The surrounding is by a fence.
10. The fence is wooden.
11. The fence is painted.
12. The painting is by children.
13. The children are elementary school.
14. The painting is with scenes.
15. The scenes are of the future.
16. The future is not too distant.

*something ugly    17. The hole is an eyesore.*

18. The eyesore is real.

*from ''chaos''; in confusion    19. Traffic is chaotic.*

20. The traffic is in the area.
21. The chaos is because of the hole.
22. But the residents don't see a hole.
23. The residents are of San Felix.
24. They see the office building.
25. They see the concert hall.

26. They see the shops.
27. They see the parking lot.
28. The parking lot is underground.
29. These things will replace the hole.

*\*will happen in the future*

30. The replacement is eventual.*
31. The hole is part.
32. The part is the last.
33. The part is of a dream.
34. Some people thought something.
35. It was that the dream would never come true.

*\*give new life to*

36. The dream is to revitalize* downtown San Felix.
37. Parts have come true.
38. The parts are of the dream.
39. The parts are other.
40. The coming is already.
41. Shops fill an area.
42. Businesses fill an area.
43. The businesses are small.
44. The area is south of the hole.
45. The area is called the Gaslamp District.

*\*rebuilt*

46. Buildings have been renovated.*

*\*old; falling apart*

47. The buildings are dilapidated.*

*\*late 19th-century style*

48. The buildings are Victorian.*
49. The streets have been paved.
50. The paving is with brick.
51. The brick is red.
52. The streets have been lined.
53. The lining is with boxes.
54. The boxes are wooden.
55. The boxes are filled with plants.
56. The plants are flowering.
57. Every few hundred feet are street lamps.
58. The street lamps are gas.
59. The lamps throw light.
60. The light is soft.
61. The throwing is over the area.

62. The throwing is at night.
63. East of the hole is an area.
64. The area is residential.
65. Apartment buildings mix with condominiums.
66. The apartment buildings are new.
67. The apartment buildings are low-rent.
68. The apartment buildings are for the elderly.
69. The condominiums are equally new.
70. The condominiums are priced.
71. The pricing is moderate.
72. There are homes.
73. The homes are private.
74. The homes are old.
75. The homes are new.
76. The homes are scattered.
77. The scattering is here and there.

*extra, unused things

78. There is an Army-Navy surplus* store.
79. The store is at the edge of the area.

*out of place; doesn't belong

80. The store looks incongruous.*
81. The store upsets the residents.
82. The city government hasn't been able to do something.
83. It is to force the store to move yet.
84. The government is still trying.
85. The residents feel a sense.
86. The residents are of San Felix.
87. The sense is great.
88. The sense is of pride.
89. They watch something.
90. It is a city growing.
91. The city is new.
92. The growth is from a city.
93. The city is old.

## On Your Own

When you have finished this exercise, discuss the answers to these questions with others in your class:

1. Is there a thesis sentence? If so, what is it?

2. How many paragraphs are there after the introduction?

3. If there is only one, does it have a topic sentence?

4. Find the word ''but'' in the introduction and discuss how it joins the two parts of the paragraph.

5. Does this essay primarily explain or describe?

6. What is the function of the words ''south'' and ''east'' in sentences 44 and 63? If they were removed, would that part of the essay be as clear as it is now?

7. Is the conclusion effective?

Think of a place that has changed—a room, a building, a neighborhood. Write a four-paragraph essay in which you describe it before and after the change. Think carefully before you begin writing whether to put the ''before'' first or second.

## REASONS FOR COLLEGE

Divide this exercise into paragraphs.

1. The reasons have changed.

2. People give the reasons.

3. The reasons are for going to college.

*very large*    4. The change is drastic.*

5. The change is in the last thirty years.

(You will probably need a delayed subject for the next sentence.)

6. Something used to be.

7. It was that people went.

8. The people were young.

9. The going was to college.

10. The going was in order to become ''well rounded.''

11. This meant something.

12. It was that they wanted an education.

13. The education is broad.

14. The education is not too specialized.

15. Students wanted to be familiar.

16. The familiarity is with the history.

17. The familiarity is with the culture.

18. The history and culture are of the world.

| | | |
|---|---|---|
| *choose | 19. | Students had to declare* a major, of course. |
| *history, literature, philosophy, etc. | 20. | The major was in the liberal arts.* |
| | 21. | This was frequent. |
| | 22. | Science majors took courses. |
| | 23. | The courses were many. |
| | 24. | The courses were in the liberal arts. |
| | 25. | Most people said something. |
| | 26. | The purpose of college was to teach people. |
| | 27. | The teaching was how to think. |
| | 28. | The purpose was not to prepare people. |
| | 29. | The preparation was for a job. |
| *happen; occur | 30. | Job training should take place.* |
| | 31. | The taking place was after the person was hired. |
| | 32. | Most people believed something. |
| | 33. | You had an education. |
| | 34. | The education is well rounded. |
| | 35. | You would find a job. |
| | 36. | The job is good. |
| | 37. | Students didn't think about jobs. |
| | 38. | The thinking was as much as students do now. |
| | 39. | Times changed. |
| | 40. | Reasons changed. |
| | 41. | The reasons are for going to college. |
| | 42. | Students go to college. |
| | 43. | The going is now. |
| | 44. | The going is to prepare. |
| | 45. | The preparation is for a job. |
| | 46. | The job is specific. |
| | 47. | The going is to increase their earnings. |
| *possible in the future | 48. | The earnings are potential.* |
| *decreased | 49. | Enrollment has dwindled.* |
| | 50. | The enrollment is in courses. |
| | 51. | The courses are liberal arts. |
| | 52. | Enrollment has increased. |
| *a huge amount | 53. | The increase is astronomical* |
| | 54. | Enrollment is in courses. |

55. The courses are in business.
56. The courses are in computers.
57. Students talk about something.
58. It is getting courses "out of the way."
59. The courses are liberal arts.
60. To get these courses "out of the way" means something.
61. It is that the courses are an annoyance.
62. It is that the courses are a barrier.
63. The barrier is to things.
64. The things are more important.
65. This change alarms many people.
66. The change is in attitude.
67. They say something.
68. It is that we have college graduates.
69. The graduates are trained.
70. The graduates are uneducated.
71. We have people.
72. The people are in business.
*morals; rules of behavior*    73. The people know nothing about ethics.*
74. We have people.
75. The people are in the sciences.
76. The people know nothing about history.
77. Many people believe it is time.
78. The time is for a change.
79. The change is back to the attitudes.
80. The attitudes are old.

## On Your Own

When you have finished this exercise, discuss these points with others in your class:

1. How many paragraphs are there?
2. Is there an introduction? If you say no, does that make the essay less effective? If you say yes, how effective is the introduction?
3. Does each paragraph in the body of the essay contain a topic sentence?

Write a different introduction and a different conclusion for this essay.

# SAVING PAPERBACK BOOKS

Divide this exercise into paragraphs and add transitions.

1. Paperbacks are inexpensive.
2. Paperbacks are convenient.
3. They tend to fall apart.
4. The falling apart is when they are used.
5. The using is frequent.
6. Rebinding them can be a hobby.
7. The hobby is satisfying.
8. Rebinding takes some time.
9. Rebinding takes some skill.
10. You need a few pieces.
11. The pieces are of equipment.
12. The equipment is simple.
13. The equipment is a saw.
14. The equipment is a file.
15. The equipment is two C-clamps.*  *a tool with screws to hold something steady*
16. The equipment is some boards.
17. You need a clean rag.
18. You need some string.
19. The string is thin.
20. You need some glue.
21. The glue is flexible.*  *bends without cracking*
22. The flexibility is when it dries.
23. The first step is to remove the cover.
24. The removing is without tearing it.
25. A knife can help.
26. The knife is sharp.
27. Fingers can help.
28. The fingers are delicate.
29. The cover falls apart.
30. Be creative.
31. Make a new one.
32. The making is out of paper.
33. The paper is stiff.

34.  Use the file.
35.  The using is to remove the glue.
36.  The glue is dry.
37.  The removing is from the spine.
38.  The spine is of the book.
39.  Something is important.
40.  It is to get all the glue off.
41.  The glue is old.
42.  Use the saw.
43.  The using is to make a series.
44.  The series is of cuts.

*not deep      45.  The cuts are shallow.*
46.  The cuts are spaced.
47.  The spacing is at one-inch intervals.
48.  The intervals are across the spine.
49.  Cut a piece of the rag.
50.  The piece is the same height.
51.  The height is as the book.
52.  The piece is a little wider than the spine.
53.  Set the piece of cloth aside.
54.  The setting is for the moment.
55.  Cover the spine.
56.  The covering is with glue.
57.  The covering is complete.
58.  Press the piece of string.
59.  The pressing is into the first cut.
60.  You made the cut.
61.  The making was across the spine.
62.  Wind the string.
63.  The winding is back and forth.
64.  Press it into each of the other cuts.
65.  Pull the string.
66.  The pulling is tight.
67.  The pulling is after it is placed.
68.  The placing is in each cut.
69.  You are finished.

70. Cut off the two ends.
71. Cover the strip.
72. The strip is of cloth.
73. The covering is with glue.
74. Press the strip.
75. The pressing is smooth.
76. The pressing is over the spine.
77. Put the cover back on.
78. Check twice to see something.
79. It is that it is not upside down.
80. Sandwich the book.
81. The sandwiching is between the boards.
82. Make sure that the spine doesn't curve.
83. The curving is in or out.
84. Screw the clamps on.
85. The screwing is tight.
86. Leave the clamps on.
87. The leaving is for a few hours.
88. Remove the clamps.
89. Remove the boards.
90. The removing is gentle.
91. Allow the book to dry.
92. The drying is for a day.
93. The drying is without opening the book.
94. You now have a book.

*strong; lasting*    95. The book is durable.*
96. The durability is high.
97. The book will never fall apart.
98. The falling is again.

## On Your Own

Write an essay that explains how to do something. Structure your essay in this manner:

- an introduction ending with the thesis sentence
- a paragraph about the equipment or supplies

- one or two paragraphs of instructions
- a brief conclusion

If you explain how to prepare something to eat, don't use the style that you find in cookbooks—a style that leaves out articles, as in "Put cheese in bowl and stir."

# DAY AND NIGHT _____

Divide this exercise into paragraphs.

1. There is little difference.
2. The difference is at first glance.
3. The difference is between Paulson's and The Grovemont.
4. Paulson's and The Grovemont are department stores.
5. The department stores are large.
6. The department stores are at the Valley Shopping Center.
7. Shopping is an experience.
8. The shopping is at The Grovemont.
9. The experience is pleasurable.

*includes    10. Shopping entails* one frustration after another.

11. The shopping is at Paulson's.
12. The two stores face one another.
13. The facing is at opposite ends.
14. The ends are of the mall.
15. Both are large.
16. Both are well designed.
17. They are fairly ordinary.

*selection; choice    18. Each offers a range.*

19. The range is full.
20. The range is of merchandise.
21. Some shoppers believe something.
22. It is that Paulson's is a little cheaper.
23. It is that Paulson's has better sales.

*say; believe    24. Others claim* something.

25. It is that the quality is higher.
26. The quality is The Grovemont's.

*not clearly different    27. The prices are indistinguishable.*

28. The merchandise is indistinguishable.
29. The prices and merchandise are of the two stores.
30. This is in reality.
31. The difference is in service.

*important*
32. The difference is significant.*
33. The difference is between the two stores.

*they don't care*
34. The salespeople seem indifferent.*
35. The salespeople are at Paulson's.
36. They answer questions.

*attitude*
37. The answering is with an air.*

*unwilling*
38. The air is grudging.*

*suggests; hints*
39. The air implies* something.
40. It is that the shopper should have known the answer.
41. One can see something.
42. The seeing is often.
43. Two employees gossip.
44. The gossiping is about their weekends.
45. The gossiping is about their vacations.
46. Customers are waiting.
47. The waiting is to pay for shirts or pots.

*not enough people at work*
48. Paulson's seems understaffed.*
49. This is especially during sales.
50. One asks for a different size.
51. The salesperson disappears.
52. The disappearance is into the stockroom.
53. The disappearance is for ten minutes.
54. This is in the shoe department.
55. There are plenty of shoes.
56. The shoes are on sale.
57. It takes too long to get them.
58. Many people refuse to wait.
59. The Grovemont's salespeople seem to enjoy something.
60. It is to work with people.
61. They make suggestions.
62. The suggestions are helpful.
63. The suggestions are about colors.

64. The suggestions are about sizes.
65. They will bring a belt.
66. They will bring a tie.
67. The bringing is from another department.
68. The bringing is to help a customer.
69. The helping is to decide.
70. They know something.
71. It is which customer wants to be left alone.
72. It is which customer likes attention.
73. They know this without being told.
74. One has to wait.
75. The waiting is rare.
76. The waiting is in line.
77. This happens.
78. The salesperson always apologizes.
79. The Grovemont's employees try to learn the names.
80. The names are of customers.
81. The customers are frequent.
82. A customer is likely to return.
83. The customer has been greeted.
84. The greeting is by name.
85. The customer has been asked.
86. The asking is about his or her last purchase.
87. The atmospheres come from philosophies.
88. The atmospheres are in the two stores.
89. The philosophies are different.
90. The philosophies are of management.
91. The Grovemont's employees feel like partners.
92. Paulson's employees are only employees.

## On Your Own

This essay compares and contrasts two department stores. Examine its structure. That is, identify where the similarities are discussed (the comparison) and where the differences are discussed (the contrast). Would it be acceptable to discuss these points in a different order?

Pick two places that you know well. Write an essay that compares and contrasts them—that is, shows how they are similar and how they are different. Plan to write at least four paragraphs—an introduction and a conclusion and one or more paragraphs for the similarities and differences. The number of paragraphs will depend on what is being emphasized.

# THE RIGHT ATTITUDE

Divide this exercise into paragraphs.

1. Something is important.
2. The importance is for supervisors.
3. The supervisors are of people.

*work with

4. The people deal with* the public.
5. It is to evaluate the quality.
6. The quality is of their employees' work.
7. It is not enough that employees be accurate.
8. It is not enough that employees be efficient.
9. They must treat people well.
10. The people come into the office.
11. Supervisors know that maintaining an attitude is difficult.
12. The supervisors are good.
13. The attitude is friendly.
14. The attitude is helpful.
15. The maintaining is when the same questions must be answered.
16. The answering is day after day.
17. Office workers may forget something.
18. It is that many people are confused.
19. It is that many people are frightened.
20. The people come in for the first time.
21. Three methods are used.
22. The using is common.
23. The using is to maintain an attitude.
24. The attitude is good.
25. The attitude is in an office.
26. The manager must set an example.
27. This is in the first method.

28. The example is for the other employees.
29. He or she must behave.
30. The behaving is to the office workers.

*people who come to the office*

31. The behaving is the way they should behave to their clients.*
32. The manager must be sincere.
33. The manager must be efficient.
34. The manager must be polite.
35. Something is also important.
36. It is for the manager to be alert.
37. The being alert is not just to the paperwork.
38. It is to how the public is treated.
39. The treating is in the office.
40. A manager cannot be aware of the atmosphere.
41. The atmosphere is total.
42. The manager spends the whole day.
43. The spending is in the isolation.
44. The isolation is of a private office.
45. Another method is to send out questionnaires.

*from time to time*

46. The sending is periodic.*
47. The questionnaires ask people to evaluate.
48. The evaluation is of how they were treated.
49. They used the services.
50. The services were of the office.
51. The questionnaires are simple.
52. This is in most cases.
53. They ask for comments.
54. The comments are specific.
55. In these comments people may say anything they want to say.
56. A summary is a way to inform the staff.
57. The summary is of the answers.
58. The answers are to the questionnaire.
59. The way is excellent.
60. The informing is about how they are seen.
61. The seeing is by the public.
62. The summary is used properly.
63. The summary can provide encouragement.

64. The encouragement is to continue work.
65. The work is good.
66. The summary can be the basis.
67. The basis is of a plan.
68. The plan is for improvement.
69. The third method can be effective.
70. The effectiveness is extreme.

*disadvantages*
71. It has some drawbacks.*
72. It must be used.
73. The using is careful.
74. The manager sends people.
75. The people are not known by staff members.
76. The sending is into the office.
77. The people act like real clients.
78. They may act confused.
79. They may act frightened.

*angry; ready to fight*
80. They may act belligerent.*
81. They are not real clients.
82. They are there to learn something.
83. It is how real clients are treated.
84. The treating is when they come in.
85. A manager gets a picture.
86. The getting is from their reports.
87. The picture is very clear.
88. The picture is of how the office works.
89. There are some dangers.
90. The employees may feel spied upon.
91. They may become resentful.
92. The "actors" gossip.
93. The gossiping is about a few experiences.
94. The experiences are negative.
95. They may create an impression.
96. The impression is false.
97. The impression is of the office.

*careful*
98. Everyone must be discreet.*
99. Everyone participates in this form.

100. The form is of evaluation.

*stories about bad experiences*    101. Many people have horror stories.*

102. The stories are about trying to do business.

103. The doing is with agencies.

104. The agencies are large.

105. The agencies are government.

106. They tell about workers.

*rude*    107. The workers are insolent.*

108. The workers are incompetent.

109. They tell about applications.

110. The applications are lost.

111. They tell about telephones.

112. The telephones are never answered.

113. Any combination can improve the situation.

114. The combination is of these methods.

115. The combination is of other methods.

116. An employee is a sign.

117. The employee is rude.

118. The sign is of a manager.

*not paying attention*    119. The manager is inattentive.*

## On Your Own

Think of an unpleasant experience you had when you went to an office to transact some business. Write an essay that describes the unpleasantness and proposes a method or methods that the office supervisor could take to improve the situation. If you prefer, you can write this in the form of a letter—and you may wish to mail it to the people concerned.

# TOO MANY CHOICES

Divide this exercise into paragraphs.

1. People say something.

2. It is that modern life is getting complicated.

3. The complication is extreme.

4. Most of the people are talking about advances.

5. The advances are in technology.

6. They give examples.
7. The examples are home computers.
8. The examples are video tape recorders.
9. The examples are cars.
10. The cars talk.
11. Something else is also causing complications.

*rapid, uncontrolled growth*

12. It is the proliferation* of different products.
13. It is the proliferation of different services.

*use*

14. Most supermarkets devote* half an aisle to pet food.
15. Sixteen brands are available.
16. The brands are different.
17. The brands are of dog food.
18. There is dry food.
19. There is canned food.
20. There is food in bags.

*slightly wet; damp*

21. The food is moist.*
22. The bags are plastic.
23. There is food for dogs.
24. The dogs are young.
25. There is food for dogs.
26. The dogs are old.
27. There is food for dogs.

*producing milk for puppies*

28. The dogs are lactating.*
29. There is food for dogs.
30. The dogs don't like dog food.
31. The situation exists.
32. The situation is the same.
33. The situation is for shampoo.
34. The situation is for laundry soap.
35. The situation is even for paste.
36. The paste is bean.
37. The bean is black.

*turning into alcohol*

38. The paste is fermented.*
39. The paste is from China.
40. One jar is from Taiwan.
41. One jar is from Shanghai.

42. What is a person to do?
43. The person has a dog.
44. The dog is average.
45. The person has hair.
46. The hair is normal.
47. The person has clothes.
48. The clothes are ordinary.
49. How does that person choose?
50. The choosing is in a time.
51. The time is reasonable.

*use (as a noun)*  52. The choosing is with an expenditure.*

53. The expenditure is reasonable.
54. The expenditure is of energy.

*rapid increase*  55. The mushrooming* of choices has reached even the activity.

56. The activity is ordinary.
57. The activity is everyday.

*photographs*  58. The activity is getting snapshots* developed.

59. A person had two choices.
60. The having was just a few years ago.
61. The choices were the camera shop.
62. The camera shop was local.
63. The choices were the drug store.
64. The drug store was in the neighborhood.
65. All one had to do was turn in the film.
66. The film was to be developed.
67. Now drug stores have long counters.
68. The counters are filled with envelopes.
69. The envelopes are in different colors.
70. The blue envelope is for development.
71. The development is of film.
72. The development is in 24 hours.
73. The green envelope takes three days.

*Monday through Friday; when businesses are open*  74. The days are working.*

75. Two copies come back.
76. The copies are of each picture.
77. The yellow envelope comes back with photographs.

78. The photographs are larger than usual.

*smooth surface          79. The pink envelope is for satin finish.*

*rough surface           80. The brown envelope is for pebble finish.*

81. The white envelope is for everything else.

82. People say something.

83. It is that all these choices are a sign of freedom.

84. The freedom is increasing.

85. Having choices gives a person the freedom.

86. The choices are so many.

87. The freedom is to buy something.

88. It is exactly what he or she needs.

89. This is not true.

90. So many choices make people unfree.

*made into slaves        91. They become enslaved.*

92. The enslavement is by their possessions.

93. The enslavement is by the stores.

94. They shop in the stores.

95. Shopping eats up time.

96. People must read.

97. The reading is of all the labels.

*think about             98. They must ponder* about things.

99. The things are basically unimportant.

100. The things are like soap.

*an idea that is not     101. People become enslaved by the illusion.*
real or true

102. The illusion is of choice.

103. One bar may be different from another.

104. The bar is of soap.

105. There are 25 brands.

*from ''neglect''; too   106. The differences are negligible.*
small to notice

107. The differences are only in the wrapping.

108. People are not making choices.

109. The choices are free.

110. The people choose between two products.

*almost                  111. The products are virtually* identical.

## On Your Own

This essay uses many examples to support the key idea of proliferation of products and services. Are there too many examples? Too few?

The idea of freedom is important in this essay, but it is not introduced until the last paragraph. Do you think it should have been introduced in the first paragraph? Try rewriting the introduction to include the idea of freedom. Then write a different conclusion, one that is in favor of having many choices.

# 5 EVALUATING AND PRACTICING ESSAY STRUCTURE

In this chapter, the exercises are longer and more complex than ones you have done before, and also, perhaps, more interesting. Many of the exercises are based on the kinds of essays that you will be writing in more advanced English classes. In addition, the exercises will require you to do more than combine sentences. You will be asked to write parts of the exercises themselves. For example, after you have done the sentence combining, you might be asked to write the concluding paragraph of an essay, or you might be asked to write the topic sentence of a paragraph. The independent writing that you will do is also more complex than earlier assignments. This is the chapter in which you practice everything you've learned so far and begin to plan ahead for future courses.

Here is an example of an exercise that you contribute to. It's about a young dog named Daisy.

1. [Your topic sentence goes here.]
2. She is six months old.
3. She is full of energy.
4. Sometimes she brings her ball.
5. She offers to play.
6. The offering is without being asked.
7. Sometimes she doesn't seem to know something.
8. It is what a ball is for.
9. Sometimes she sits up.
10. The sitting is charming.
11. The sitting is to ask for a treat.
12. She tries to snatch the treat.
13. The snatching is from one's hand.
14. This is at other times.
15. She stays alone.
16. The staying is without chewing on the furniture.
17. This is on some days.
18. She chews holes in the carpet.
19. She gnaws on the legs.
20. The legs are of the dining room table.
21. This is at other times.
22. The family leaves the house.
23. The leaving is in the morning.
24. No one knows something.
25. It is what will happen next.

First, you should do the combining in the usual way. You might come up with a paragraph like this:

> She is six months old and full of energy. Sometimes, without being asked, she brings her ball and offers to play, but sometimes she doesn't seem to know what a ball is for. Sometimes she sits up charmingly to ask for a treat, but at other times, she tries to snatch it from one's hand. On some days, she stays alone without chewing on the furniture, yet at other times she chews holes in the carpet or gnaws on the legs of the dining room table. When the family leaves the house in the morning, no one knows what will happen next.

This sounds acceptable so far, but what is missing is a topic sentence, a sentence that ties the details together and presents the main idea. (This is a good time to review Composition Note 3: The Paragraph.) You need to examine the paragraph and decide what idea or ideas the details support. The details seem to come under two categories. Sometimes Daisy behaves in a charming and pleasant way, but sometimes she seems unintelligent or destructive. What is needed is an opening sentence to tie these ideas together. Since the ideas are in contrast to one another, probably the topic sentence will contain ''but'' or ''however.'' You might write a topic sentence like this: Daisy is an amusing young dog, but she is unpredictable. Or something like this: Daisy is a good dog, but she hasn't yet learned how to behave in the company of humans. There are other possibilities, too, of course. It will be useful to compare your work on exercises like this with your classmates'.

## FINAL EXAMS

Here is a paragraph without its middle part. When you have combined the first 25 sentences, give several examples to illustrate different effects of tension. You will probably need some sort of transition between what you have written and sentence 26.

1. The causes are the same.
2. The causes are of tension.
3. The tension is during finals.
4. The effects are different.
5. This is for most students.
6. Students feel tense for a reason.
7. The reason is obvious.
8. They have to take an exam.
9. The exam is in each of their classes.

10.   Preparing for five exams is not easy.

11.   The exams occur in about one week.

12.   Preparing for the exams is not the only part.

13.   The part is difficult.

14.   Something is also difficult to face.

15.   It is the idea.

16.   The idea is of being evaluated.

*added up;
summarized*

17.   All one's knowledge is to be summed up.*

18.   The summing is in a letter.

19.   The summing is in a number.

20.   The summing is in the final grade.

21.   This doesn't seem quite fair.

22.   No one reacts.

23.   The reaction is to tension.

24.   The tension is of finals.

25.   The reaction is in the same way.

[Your examples go here.]

26.   All students say something.

27.   It is the same thing.

28.   It is that next semester will be different.

## Suggestions:

Consider using a colon to combine sentences 6, 7, and 8. Also, consider using the information in sentence 20 in an appositive.

## On Your Own

Expand what you wrote for this exercise into a complete essay that explains two or three different ways that students react to final exams.

# HOLIDAY KITCHEN

When you finish this exercise, you will have a descriptive paragraph. However, the topic sentence has been left out. Read over your completed version of the paragraph and then write a topic sentence of your own. If you have questions, check Composition Note 3 to see what the characteristics of a topic sentence are. Compare your sentence with what others in the class have written.

1.   Every surface was covered.
2.   The surface was available.
3.   The covering was with food.
4.   The food was in a different stage of readiness.
5.   Sliced apples were in a bowl.
6.   The bowl was on the dishwasher.

*small pieces had been broken from it*

7.   The bowl was chipped.*
8.   The apples were for pie.
9.   The pie was my grandmother's.
10.  The pie was famous.

*to fill so that water can't run out*

11.  Apple peel clogged* the sink.
12.  Apple cores clogged the sink.

*turning brown*

13.  The peel and cores were browning.*
14.  Bits of dough clogged the sink.
15.  The dough was sticky.
16.  The dough would be tender and crisp.
17.  That would be after baking.
18.  Fat clogged the sink.
19.  The fat was white.
20.  The fat had been trimmed from the roast beef.
21.  The roast was in a pan.

*grand; like the "king" of roast beef*

22.  The roast was majestic.*
23.  The roast was enormous.
24.  The pan was on the counter.
25.  The roast was like an advertisement.
26.  The advertisement is for a restaurant.
27.  The restaurant is expensive.
28.  The restaurant is elegant.

*ingredients*

29.  Salad fixings* were near the roast.
30.  The fixings were in a pile.
31.  Potatoes were near the roast.
32.  The potatoes were small.
33.  The potatoes were red.
34.  The potatoes were to be peeled.
35.  The kitchen was filled with people.
36.  It was not filled only with food.
37.  Three daughters-in-law were there.

**38.** They were chatting at the table.

*taking them out of
the pods they grow in*

**39.** They were shelling* peas.

**40.** A neighbor was explaining something.

**41.** It was how to open a jar of pickles.

**42.** The jar had been closed too tightly.

**43.** A baby boy was playing with pot lids.

**44.** His playing was noisy.

*with concentration*

**45.** His playing was intent.*

**46.** A yellow cat sat on the windowsill.

**47.** It licked its fur.

**48.** It sat near an ivy plant.

**49.** The plant was green.

**50.** The green was brilliant.

**51.** The plant was in the last light.

**52.** The light was of a winter day.

**53.** This was the only peaceful place.

**54.** The peace was in the kitchen.

## On Your Own

Choose a fairly complicated scene—the cafeteria at lunchtime or a confusing intersection during rush hour—and write an essay describing it. The essay will require careful organization so that the complicated parts are logically tied together. The scene may be confusing, but the essay shouldn't be.

# CONDOMINIUMS

This exercise is a paragraph that needs a sentence or two to complete it because, as it is, it ends rather abruptly. You might want to refer back to the idea of efficiency that was mentioned at the beginning of the paragraph.

*trying hard to
accomplish*

**1.** The condominium is another example.
The example is of striving.*
The striving is American.
The striving is for efficiency.

**2.** Condominiums make something possible.
It is owning a home.
The owning is without the expense.

The expense is usual.
The expense is of money.
The expense is of time.

3.  The idea is basic.
    The idea is of the condominium.
    The idea is ownership.
    The ownership is collective.
    The ownership is not individual.

4.  Each person owns a percentage.
    The percentage is of all the land.
    The percentage is of all the buildings.
    This is instead of something.
    It is owning a house.
    The house is complete.

5.  A person buys one unit.
    The unit is in a condominium.
    The condominium has fifty units.
    The person owns one fiftieth of everything.
    The person has use.

*only for that person*   The use is exclusive.*
    The use is of the space.
    The space is in his or her unit.

6.  A condominium may be one building.
    The building is tall.
    The building is similar to an apartment house.
    A condominium may be a group.
    The group is of buildings.
    The buildings are smaller.
    The buildings are separated.
    The separation is by lawns.

7.  Less land is used.
    Fewer walls are built.
    This is in comparison to something.
    It is a neighborhood.
    The neighborhood is traditional.

8.  The price is lower than something.
    The price is of a condominium.
    It is the price of a house.
    The house is of similar size.

9.  A condominium owner pays a fee.
    The fee is monthly.
    The fee is for maintenance.
    The maintenance is of the property.

10.   Owners do not paint.
      Owners do not repair roofs.
      Owners do not cut the grass.
      They use the maintenance fees.

*put together*      The fees are pooled.*
      The using is to hire companies.
      The companies do this work.
      The doing is for the area.
      The area is entire.

11.   Each owner is responsible for something.
      It is to maintain only the interior.
      The interior is of his or her home.

      [Your concluding sentence(s) here.]

## On Your Own

Many people believe that efficiency is a major characteristic of American life. Write an essay about one or more examples of American efficiency. Include a paragraph that explains your opinion of this characteristic. Is it a good thing? Has it been exaggerated?

# MEETING PEOPLE

This exercise is a classification essay. It describes several types of people who go to meetings. It can be divided into four paragraphs—an introduction and one paragraph each about three different types of people.

  The essay is not complete, however. It needs a thesis statement and a conclusion. You may need to add several sentences to achieve a smooth transition between the present introduction and your thesis sentence. The conclusion should be at least four sentences long. Try to do something other than summarize the three types of people at the meeting.

1.   Several residents meet.
2.   The residents are of the Gatwick Heights section.
3.   The section is of the city.
4.   The meeting is once a month.
5.   The meeting is on the second Tuesday.
6.   The second Tuesday is usual.
7.   The meeting is to discuss business.
8.   The business is of the neighborhood.
9.   These people are the officers.

10. The officers are of the Gatwick Heights Homeowners' Association.
    [The completed introduction (including your thesis) goes here.]
11. Don Gladstone is shy.
12. Don Gladstone is quiet.

*modest     13. Don Gladstone is unassuming.*
14. Don Gladstone is the treasurer.
15. He is so quiet.
16. His quietness is at meetings.
17. People wonder something.
18. It is why he goes.
19. He looks at anyone.
20. His looking is rare.
21. His eyes remain on the papers.
22. The papers are in front of him.
23. The remaining is usual.

*to understand     24. Something is hard to tell.*
25. It is what he is thinking.
26. He may be afraid of something.
27. It is of speaking in public.
28. He may be bored.
29. No one knows.
30. His attendance is perfect.
31. His attendance is at meetings.
32. He votes.
33. His voting is with the majority.
34. His voting is almost always.
35. He is reelected.
36. His reelection is every year.
37. Grace Barton is the vice-president.
38. She is a type.
39. The type is very different.
40. She is loud.

*has a high opinion of
herself     41. She is self-important.*
42. Her body is never still.
43. This is during meetings.

*moves them around     44. She shuffles* papers.

*words or sounds of surprise*

**45.** She makes many exclamations.*

**46.** The exclamations are loud.

**47.** The making is while others are talking.

**48.** She interrupts.

**49.** The interruptions are constant.

**50.** Someone pauses.

**51.** The pausing is to find the word.

**52.** The word is right.

*interrupts*

**53.** Grace breaks in.*

**54.** She supplies a word.

**55.** The word is wrong.

**56.** This is very often.

**57.** People notice something.

**58.** The people know her.

**59.** It is that she never volunteers.

**60.** The volunteering is for work.

**61.** The work is extra.

**62.** Sam Sondberg is a committee member.

**63.** The member is ideal.

**64.** Sam Sondberg is the president.

**65.** He comes to meetings.

**66.** His coming is well prepared.

**67.** Someone asks a question.

**68.** The question is about a decision.

**69.** The decision is earlier.

**70.** Sam can check his notes.

**71.** His notes are clear.

**72.** His notes are careful.

**73.** He can find the answer.

**74.** Something needs to be done.

**75.** The doing is before the meeting.

**76.** The meeting is next.

**77.** Sam volunteers.

**78.** His volunteering is quiet.

*does what he promised*

**79.** He always follows through.*

**80.** The characteristic is something.

81.  People like the characteristic.

82.  The liking is the most.

83.  It is that he is a good listener.

84.  He looks at the person.

85.  The person is talking.

86.  He nods his head.

87.  His nodding is occasional.

88.  His nodding is to show something.

89.  It is that he understands.

90.  He has a question.

91.  He has a comment.

92.  He waits until the speaker is finished.

93.  People respect him.

94.  The people disagree with him.

95.  They know he is honest.

96.  They know he is fair.

[Your concluding paragraph goes here.]

### On Your Own

Think of a group of people you know rather well—people in your class, your family, people where you work—and write an essay in which you classify them into at least three different types. Use one individual as an example for each type.

## AN INFORMAL THANK-YOU LETTER

This letter needs a closing paragraph. You might include a repetition of thanks or a reference to the next meeting. Notice the informal style of this letter, and use the same style in what you write.

Dear Molly,

1.  Thank you for the weekend.
    Thank you for the dinner.
    The dinner was on Saturday evening.
    The dinner was delicious.
    The weekend was interesting.

2.  I have never tasted barbecue.
    The barbecue was so tender.
    The barbecue was tasty.

The lemon pie was perfect.
The perfection was absolute.*

*complete; the adverb
form is used in casual
speech as a strong
"very"*

3.   Your daughter is a pleasure.
     The pleasure is to see.
     She is growing up.
     Her growth is delightful.
     Her growth is with speed.
     The speed is amazing.

4.   Meeting your friends was interesting.
     Your friends are the Bronsons.
     I had heard about them.
     The hearing was so often.

5.   Your description was accurate.
     The description was of them.
     He is quiet.
     He is charming.
     She talks.
     Her talking is a mile a minute.

     (In combining the following, consider using "whom" in your sentence.)

6.   You will be interested to hear something.
     It is that I met our friend.
     The friend is Jean.
     I saw her last.
     The seeing was at graduation.
     Graduation was six years ago.

     (Try using "where" in the next sentence.)

7.   She is working.
     Her work is as a translator.
     Her work is in Cairo.
     She has been there for three years.

8.   Her life sounds glamorous.
     Her life sounds hectic.*
     She looks very happy.
     She is getting married.
     Her marriage is next summer.

*too busy and
complicated*

9.   She said to tell you something.
     It is that she still has the pen.
     You lent her the pen.
     The lending was for the final exam.
     The exam was in economics.
     She will return it.

The returning is someday!

[Your concluding paragraph goes here.]

Best regards,
Cynthia

## On Your Own

Write a letter to someone you know (but who is not a close friend) thanking him or her for something. If necessary, you can invent both the person and the details.

# A LETTER OF COMPLAINT _____

Here is a letter complaining about unsatisfactory work. It needs a concluding paragraph that informs Mr. Stevenson of exactly what the writer, Joan Davis, wants and what she will do if he doesn't respond. You might assume that she has given him a check as a deposit but has not yet paid the full bill.

Dear Mr. Stevenson:

*\*to put in position to be used*

1.  You installed\* doors.
    You installed windows.
    The doors and windows are new.
    The installation was in my house.
    The installation was last week.

2.  They are quite attractive.
    They were installed.
    The installation was quite poor.

    (You might begin the following with a transitional phrase.)

3.  The back door cannot be locked.
    The worker forgot something.
    It was to drill a hole.
    The hole is for the bolt.\*

*\*the sliding part that acts as a lock to keep the door from opening*

    [Another transition?]

4.  The window will not slide.
    The sliding is easy.
    The window is in the living room.
    The frame is rusted.
    The frame is metal.
    The rust is on top.
    The rust is on the bottom.

5.  My husband opened the window.
    The window is in the bedroom.

The glass fell out.
The glass broke.
The breaking was in hundreds of pieces.
The pieces are stuck.
The sticking is in the rug.

6.   There are more problems.
I will not describe them.
The description is in this letter.

[Your concluding paragraph goes here.]

Sincerely yours,
Joan Davis

## On Your Own

Write a letter of complaint similar to this one. Include details about what went wrong and what you want done.

# JUST FOR FUN

Here is an exercise that will surprise you. It's made up of nonsense words—"words" that don't really exist. But a moment or two of careful reading will show you that you can do this exercise just like any other. Even though the words have no meaning, you can still figure out how they function in the sentence. Try writing an ending sentence with your own nonsense words. Since the story begins with "once upon a time," you might want to include "they lived happily ever after" in your ending.

1.   Once upon a time, there was a gallut.
The gallut was in the hrink.
The hrink was gallageous.
The gallat was elt.

2.   A snillig vromed up to the gallut.
The vroming was inig.
The snillig klept.

3.   The gallut lupped at the snillig.
The lupping was slan.
The lupping was grenful.

4.   This made the snillig het.
She did not ren lupping.
She flanned.
The flanning was at the gallut.

5.     The gallut became chan.
The channess was extreme.
The gallut blowered.
The blowering was trin.

6.     The snillig said something.
''You lup at me again.''
''I will dren you.''
She rined her ellig.
The rining was mow.
The rining was at the gallut.

7.     The gallut ropt.
The ropping was dender.
The gallut slomed.
The sloming was quent.
The sloming was back into the hrink.

[Your concluding sentence goes here.]

It's interesting to compare the results of this exercise with others in the class because people make different decisions about the functions of certain words. It's also interesting to compare reactions to the exercise—some people have fun, but others get irritated!

# TIME AND THE ORGAN-GRINDER MAN

This essay has a fairly loose structure. Divide it into paragraphs and then compare what you've done with what other people in your class have done.

1.     I visited a town.
My visit was not so long ago.
The town is in another country.
The country is thousands of miles from my home.

2.     My host went to the marketplace.
I went to the marketplace.
Our going was on a Saturday morning.
The morning was chilly.
Our going was to buy meat.
Our going was to buy vegetables.
Our going was to buy eggs.
The meat, vegetables, and eggs were fresh.
*unbelievable; here meaning "extremely"*    The freshness was incredible.*

(Try an introductory participial phrase for the following.)

*concentrating on*     3.     I was absorbed* by the sounds.
I was absorbed by the sights.

*new; unfamiliar*

The sights and sounds were novel.*
The sights and sounds were of the market.
I became aware of something.
My awareness was gradual.
I was hearing a song.
The song was from my childhood.
The childhood was the earliest.
I could not see something.
It was where the song was coming from.

4.  I saw a man.
    My seeing was in a moment.

*a little fat*

The man was plump.*
He had a smile.
His smile was shy.
His smile was friendly.

*open space*

My seeing was through a break.*
The break was in the crowd.

*a large music box on wheels; a song is produced when the handle is turned*

The man was pushing a hand-organ.*

5.  Then I realized something.
    It was not the song.
    I recognized the song.
    It was the sound.
    I recognized the sound.
    The sound was of the organ.

6.  An organ-grinder came.
    His coming was to my street.
    His coming was when I was a child.
    His coming was occasional.

7.  He had a monkey.
    The having was with him.
    The monkey was trained.
    The monkey would collect coins.

*people in the area who watch*

The collection was from the bystanders.*
The collection was after each song.

8.  One of the disappointments was something.
    The disappointments were major.
    The disappointments were of my life then.
    The disappointment was that I was not allowed to give a coin.
    The giving was to the monkey.
    My mother said something.
    It was that the monkey carried disease.

9.  This organ-grinder had no monkey.
    He was only advertising something.

It was that a café was to open.
The café was new.

10.   But I felt the same disappointment.
My feeling was at that moment.
The disappointment was childlike.
My disappointment was strong.
The disappointment was of long ago.

*did not last long*

11.   The feeling was transient.*
It left me with a question.
The question was about the meaning.
The meaning is of these memories.
The memories are from childhood.
The memories are seemingly incidental.*

*appear to happen by chance*

12.   We remember things.
The things are important.
The things are from the past.
The things are like falling in love.
The things are like graduating.
The graduating is from high school.
The remembering is because of their importance.

13.   Something is difficult to believe.
The belief is that memories are important.
The memories are insignificant.
The memories are such as the organ-grinder's monkey.

14.   They are not important.
Why are they so strong?

## On Your Own

Most people have had the experience of having some event in the present remind them of some other, unimportant event in the past. Sometimes even an odor or a pattern on some cloth can trigger such a memory. Write an essay about such a situation. If you can, try to explain why the ''unimportant'' event was important enough to remember.

## A DIFFERENT WAR?

When you finish combining, divide this essay into paragraphs.

1.   I have believed something.

2.   It is that only humans make war.

3.   My belief has been for some time.

4. Animals may kill each other.

5. Their killing is for food.

6. Their killing is not for gain.

7. The gain is economic.

   (If necessary, use your dictionary to review the difference between ''economic'' in number 7 and ''economical.'')

8. Their killing is not for revenge.

9. Their killing is not for other reasons.

10. The reasons are many.

11. People have the reasons for making war.

12. I saw something.

13. My seeing was recent.

14. It made me question my belief.

15. My belief was that animals are superior.

16. Their superiority is to humans.

17. It also made me question the attitude.

18. The attitude is my own.

19. The attitude is to war.

20. I was visiting some friends.

21. The friends have a balcony.

22. The balcony is outside their living room.

23. They never use the balcony.

   [In combining sentence 23 with the others, be careful not to say that the living room isn't used.)

24. The balcony is undisturbed.

*birds that fly very gracefully*

25. Some swallows* had built their nests there.

26. The building was in a corner.

27. The corner is under the roof.

28. The nests are different from something.

29. The nests are of swallows.

   (In combining sentence 29 with the others, use the possessive form of ''swallow'' and think about where the apostrophe should go.)

30. The difference is from common bird nests.

31. They are enclosed.

32. The enclosure is full.

33. They have a front.

34. The front is round.
35. They have a bottom.
36. The bottom is pointed.
37. They have a hole.
38. The hole is round.
39. The hole is small.
40. The hole is for an entrance.

    (Try combining sentences 31–40 into one sentence. Use ''entrance'' as an adjective and, if necessary, check Grammar Note 2 for the order of adjectives.)

41. A swallow is inside.
42. It is invisible.
43. Its invisibility is almost complete.
44. The nests seemed very practical.
45. The nests seemed attractive.
46. The seeming was to me.
47. There was a problem.
48. The nests were also attractive to something.

*small, noisy birds*

49. It was a family of sparrows.*
50. The sparrows were in the neighborhood.

    (Try combining sentences 47–50 into one sentence. Consider beginning the sentence with a transition word.)

51. I had been admiring the nests.
52. I had been admiring the swallows' flight pattern.
53. The pattern was circular.
54. The pattern was graceful.
55. The admiration had been for several days.
56. The admiration was before I knew there was a problem.
57. The door was open.
58. The door is to the balcony.
59. It was on an afternoon.
60. The afternoon was warm.
61. The warmth was unusual.
62. I was sitting near the door.

*high, loud screams*

63. I heard screeches.*

64. The screeches were loud.

*upset; not peaceful*     65. The screeches were agitated.*

66. The screeches were from the birds.

*how a bird sits*     67. Several sparrows were perched.*

68. The perching was near one of the swallows' nests.

*a group of singers*     69. They were making a chorus.*

70. The chorus was angry.

*very unfriendly*     71. The chorus was hostile.*

72. The swallows were flying.

73. Their flight was in a circle.

74. The flying was over the lawn.

75. The lawn was in front of the building.

76. I was called to the telephone.

77. The calling was just then.

78. I finished the call.

79. I forgot about the birds.

80. I did something else.

81. I discovered something.

82. My discovery was on the next day.

83. The discovery was that the sparrows owned the nests.

84. The owning was now.

85. The nests were the swallows'.

86. A sparrow sat in the door.

87. The sparrow was small.

88. The sparrow was noisy.

89. The door was to one of the nests.

(For the following, change ''looked'' to a present participle.)

*proud of winning*     90. The sparrow looked triumphant.*

91. The swallows were still flying.

92. Their flight was in circles.

93. Their flight was over the lawn.

*very sad*     94. I thought they looked mournful.*

(Combine sentences 95–98 into a compound sentence. Think about where ''worse'' goes.)

95. This was bad enough.

96. Something happened.

**97.** The something was worse.

**98.** The happening was the next morning.

(Combine sentences 99–103 into one sentence.)

**99.** I looked out on the balcony.

**100.** My looking was after breakfast.

*dead bodies*     **101.** I saw two corpses.*

**102.** The corpses were tiny.

**103.** The corpses were lying on the floor.

**104.** Their bodies were hairless.

**105.** The bodies were pink.

**106.** The pink was faint.

*delicate; easily broken*     **107.** The bodies were fragile.*

**108.** They looked a little like babies.

**109.** The babies were humanlike.

**110.** The likeness was disturbing.

(Combine sentences 111–16 into one sentence. Use only the passive form of "to throw.")

**111.** I was sure of something.

**112.** They were swallows.

*had just broken out of the egg*     **113.** The swallows were newly hatched.*

**114.** The swallows had been thrown.

**115.** The sparrows had thrown them.

**116.** The throwing was out of the nest.

(Consider combining sentences 117–19 into one complex sentence.)

**117.** The corpses lay on the balcony.

**118.** The lying was until someone else took them away.

**119.** I could not bear to touch them.

*scientist who studies birds*     **120.** Of course an ornithologist* could say something.

**121.** I misunderstood.

**122.** My misunderstanding was of what had happened.

**123.** Perhaps the birds had fallen out.

**124.** Their falling was by accident.

**125.** Perhaps the sparrows were only sitting there.

**126.** The sitting was temporary.

(Sentence 128 seems to contradict number 127, but think about the grammar to resolve the problem.)

127. I don't care.
128. My caring is real.
129. It looked like a war.
130. The looking was to me.
131. It was a small war.

*terrible; causing horror*

132. It was horrifying.*
133. One group had invaded the territory.
134. The territory belonged to another group.
135. Children had been killed.
136. The children were innocent.

*cruel; without feeling*

137. The killing was brutal.*
138. Homes had been lost.
139. The homes had been built.
140. The building was painstaking.
141. The invaders were triumphant.
142. This war was between two groups.
143. The groups were of birds.
144. The groups were not of humans.

(In combining sentences 145 and 146, think about ''ever'' and ''never.'')

145. It was the first war.
146. I had never seen a war.

(Combine sentences 147–49 into one complex sentence.)

147. The war begins again.
148. The beginning is during my next visit.
149. I will stop it.
150. I will wave a broom.
151. The broom is to keep the sparrows away.
152. I think something.
153. I can stop that war.
154. I can protect the swallows.
155. I must think about something else.
156. My thinking must be more serious.
157. What can I do?
158. My doing is to stop wars.
159. The wars are human.

## On Your Own

Articles about peace and war appear frequently in the news. Find an article in a newspaper or a magazine and write an essay supporting or arguing against the position taken in the article. Hand in the article along with your essay.

# INTERNATIONAL TRAVEL_____

This exercise is a real challenge. It's long, and some parts of it will need considerable thought. Nevertheless, there are no hints or suggestions—except that there are five paragraphs! Good luck.

1. International travel has improved.
2. The improvement is considerable.
3. The improvement is in the twentieth century.
4. Travelers can fly from continent to continent.
5. The flying is in less than one day.
6. The technology improves.
7. The technology is of air travel.
8. The improvement is every year.
9. The aspect of travel has not improved.
10. The aspect is human.
11. The improvement is as much as the technological aspect.
12. People may arrive.
13. Their arrival is safe.
14. Their arrival is on time.
15. It is days before they adjust.
16. It is days before they recover.
17. The adjustment is to the new time zone.
18. The recovery is from the stress.
19. The stress is of the flight.
20. The recovery is from the conditions.
21. The conditions are chaotic.
22. The conditions are of their arrival.
23. The arrival is at the airport.
24. Most people feel comfortable.
25. The feeling is at the beginning of a flight.

26. The flight is long.
27. They begin to feel restless.
28. They begin to feel confined.
29. The feeling is after a few hours.
30. The novelty occupies the first hours.
31. The excitement occupies the first hours.
32. The excitement is of the trip.
33. Some people read.
34. Other people chat.
35. The chatting is with their companions.
36. The stewardesses serve drinks.
37. The stewardesses serve a meal.
38. Then they show a movie.
39. The showing is on almost every flight.
40. Many people begin to feel uncomfortable.
41. The feeling is after these activities.
42. Their bodies crave exercise.
43. There is not much room to walk.
44. Some people's feet begin to swell.
45. Some people's muscles begin to cramp.
46. Sleep is a problem.
47. The problem is for many people.
48. They may doze off.
49. Their sleep is troubled.
50. Their sleep is interrupted.
51. The interruption is by noise.
52. The interruption is by fellow passengers.
53. The interruption is by the uncomfortable position.
54. The position is upright.
55. Many children begin to cry.
56. They run up and down.
57. The running is in the aisles.
58. Most parents try to control them.
59. It is not easy.
60. The children become more and more restless.
61. The parents become more and more impatient.

62. Many people end the trip in a stupor.
63. The stupor is passive.
64. The stupor is of discomfort.
65. They must go through the formalities.
66. The going is in this state of mind.
67. The formalities are confusing.
68. The formalities are of arrival.
69. The arrival is in a foreign country.
70. To leave the plane is a relief.
71. The plane is cramped.
72. The relief is great.
73. One must face problems.
74. The facing is immediate.
75. The problems are of directions.
76. The directions are in a foreign language.
77. The problems are of an airport.
78. The airport is unfamiliar.
79. Several planes have landed.
80. The landing is at the same time.
81. There are hundreds of people.
82. The people must be processed.
83. The processing is at the same time.
84. There are always long lines.
85. There are officials.
86. The officials are too few.
87. There is a moment of tension.
88. The moment is at the counter.
89. The counter is of passport control.
90. What if the official says something?
91. It is that there is an irregularity.
92. The irregularity is with one's passport.
93. This is unlikely.
94. The unlikelihood is for most travelers.
95. The fear remains.
96. The fear is slight.
97. The same lines exist.

98. The lines are long.
99. The existence is at the places.
100. The places are for collection.
101. The places are for inspection.
102. The collection and inspection are of baggage.
103. And there is more tension.
104. What if a suitcase is lost?
105. What if the inspector finds something?
106. The something is forbidden.
107. Then come the difficulties.
108. The difficulties are of finding luggage carts.
109. There are never enough carts.
110. The difficulties are of finding transportation.
111. Finally, the traveler arrives.
112. The traveler is exhausted.
113. The traveler is disoriented.
114. The arrival is at his or her destination.
115. The traveler is ready for a sleep.
116. The sleep is long.
117. The sleep is peaceful.
118. The third effect becomes apparent.
119. The becoming is at this moment.
120. The effect is negative.
121. The effect is of travel.
122. The travel is modern.
123. The effect is jet lag.
124. The traveler's body arrives.
125. The arrival is in a new country.
126. The arrival is before his or her "inner clock."
127. It is 8 A.M. in Frankfurt.
128. It is 11 P.M. in Los Angeles.
129. The person is ready to sleep.
130. The person just arrived from California.
131. Day is just beginning.
132. To adjust can take several days.
133. The adjustment is to the new time zone.

134. No way exists.
135. The way is good.
136. The way is to shorten the time.
137. People take the time to adjust.
138. The days are uncomfortable.
139. The days are the first few.
140. The days are in a new country.
141. The discomfort is because of fatigue.
142. The discomfort is because of the time change.
143. These are some of the examples of the ways.
144. The ways are many.
145. The ways are that technology has outstripped development.
146. The development is human.
147. Perhaps someone will develop a pill.
148. The pill will cure jet lag.
149. No pill can cure the problem.
150. The problem is lost luggage.
151. The problem is long lines.
152. The problem is customs inspectors.
153. The inspectors are unfriendly.
154. These are human problems.
155. These are not scientific problems.
156. These are not technological problems.

### On Your Own

No one seriously argues that we should return to travel by horse, stage-coach, or steamship, but as an exercise in argumentation (or just for fun) write an essay supporting the idea of abolishing airplane travel.

## DANCE IN THE DESERT

Divide this exercise into paragraphs.

1. Something is possible.
   It is to learn a great deal.
   The learning is about a person.
   The learning is by listening to his or her dreams.

*\*not exact; vague*

    The dreams are for the future.
    The future is unspecified.*

2.   These dreams are not the plans.
    The plans are concrete.
    We all make the plans.
    The plans are such as graduating from college.
    The plans are such as owning a house.
    The plans are such as learning to play tennis.

3.   These dreams are not practical.
    Most people don't expect something.
    It is that they will come true.
    Most people do nothing.
    The doing is to make them come true.

4.   These dreams express something.
    The expressing is usual.
    It is a longing for what is missing.
    The missing is from daily life.

*\*has too much to do*

5.   The businessperson longs for a life.
    The businessperson is harried.*
    The life is peaceful.
    The life is on an island.
    The island is desert.
    The clerk imagines a life.
    The clerk is frustrated.

*\*has a job that is too easy*

    The clerk is underemployed.*
    The life is filled with glamour.
    The life is on the stock exchange.

6.   What can be learned about a dreamer?
    The dreamer's dream includes something.
    It is bringing ballet.
    It is bringing music.
    It is bringing art.

*\*in southern California*

    The bringing is to the Mojave Desert.*
    The desert is barren.

7.   What can be learned?
    The learning is from the fact.
    The fact is that the dream came true.

8.   Marta Becket is that dreamer.
    The Amargosa Opera House is the dream.
    What one learns is that dreams come true.
    The dreams are impossible.
    The dreamer refuses something.
    It is to let obstacles get in the way.

*a loan to buy a
building*

The obstacles are mud slides.
The obstacles are mortgage* payments.
The payments are $26,000.
The obstacles are a public.
The public is indifferent.

9.  Death Valley Junction still looks like a place.
The place is unlikely.
The place is for the arts.
It looked even more unlikely.
This was in 1967.
Marta Becket first peered.
The peering was through a window.
The window was of what would become The Amargosa Opera House.

10.  Death Valley Junction was once the headquarters.
The headquarters was busy.
The headquarters was of a mining company.
It had a population.
The population was less than 30.
This was in the late sixties.

11.  The main building is a structure.
The structure is U-shaped.
It is large.
It is white.
It is in Spanish-American style.
It had not been used.
The using was for 20 years.

12.  Marta Becket was there by accident.
Marta Becket is a professional ballet dancer.
Marta Becket is an artist.
Marta Becket is from New York City.
She was waiting for a flat tire to be fixed.
She looked in the window.
The window was of the social hall.

13.  Her eyes saw water stains.
The stains were from a leaky roof.
Her eyes saw dust.

*broken, thrown-away
objects*

Her eyes saw debris.*
Her mind saw possibilities.
The possibilities were unlimited.
The possibilities were for creativity.

14.  She was living in a trailer.
The trailer was behind the social hall.
She had rented the social hall.

The rent was $45 a month.
She was repairing the roof.
She was repairing the walls.
This was six months later.

15.   The first performance was held.
*stories told in dance,*      The performance was of dance and dancé mimes.*
*without words*               This was on February 10, 1968.
                             This was before an audience.
                             The audience was 12 neighbors.
                             The neighbors sat among coffee cans.
                             The cans caught water.
                             The water was from the leaking roof.

16.   There was often no audience.
      This was in the weeks.
      The weeks followed opening night.
      The show went on.
      This was always.

17.   The audiences troubled Marta.
      The audiences were infrequent.
*not many people.*      The audiences were sparse.*
                       They didn't discourage her.
                       They gave her a new idea.
                       She would paint an audience.
                       The painting was on the walls.
                       The walls were of the opera house.

*theme; repeated idea*   18.   She chose a motif.*
                              The motif was 16th century.
                              The motif was royal.
                              The motif was Spanish.
                              A king and queen appeared.
                              The appearance was on the walls.
                              The appearance was over the next four years.
                              The appearance was with hundreds of their followers.
                              The followers were nobles and musicians.
                              The followers were priests and nuns.
                              The followers were gypsies and jugglers.
                              The followers were ambassadors and prostitutes.

*a painting on a wall*   19.   The mural* grew.
                              The audiences grew.
                              The audiences were live.

20.   News spread.
      The news was of the opera house.
      The spreading was across the United States.

The spreading was across Europe.
The spreading was by word of mouth.
The spreading was by articles.
The articles were in magazines.
The articles were in newspapers.
*most important* The newspapers and magazines were major.*

21. Performances were sold out.
    This was often.
    People were turned away.
    There weren't enough seats.
    Marta wasn't yet finished.

22. The weather was a threat.
    The weather was uncertain.
    The weather was desert.
    The weather brought mud slides.
    The weather brought heat.
    The heat was overpowering.
    The threat was to the future.
    The future was of the opera house.
    Not owning the opera house was a threat.
    This was also.
    The threat was to its security.

23. And there were so many rooms.
    The rooms were empty.
    The rooms were in the rest of the building.
    The rooms cried out.
    The crying was to be used.

24. The next part was to buy the building.
    The next part was to open the building.
    The part was of the dream.
    The opening was to artists.
    The opening was to scientific groups.
    The artists and groups needed a place.
    The place was quiet.
    The place was to work in.

25. The opera house was purchased.
    The whole town was purchased.
    This was with the help of many people.
    The people were all over the country.
    This was over the next ten years.
    The Amargosa Hotel was opened.
    The opening gave Marta more walls.
    The walls were to paint on.

26.   Marta is an artist.
      Marta is not a businesswoman.
      Bringing dreams to life requires something.

*jobs or positions*      It is that people take on roles.*
      The roles are unfamiliar.

27.   Marta takes care of the business.
      The business is of the town.
      She doesn't like it.
      The liking is much.

28.   Much has changed.
      The change is in Death Valley Junction.
      The change is since 1967.
      One thing remains the same.

29.   Your head is filled with magic.
      The magic is of the dance.
      The magic is of the music.
      The magic is of the color.
      The color is of the murals.
      The murals are on the walls.
      This is after a performance.

30.   You step outside.
      You experience another magic.
      The magic is the silence.
      The magic is the emptiness.
      The magic is the stars.
      The stars are brilliant.
      The silence, emptiness, and stars are of the desert night.

31.   You realize something.
      It is that the arts belong in the desert.
      This is as well as in the city.
      This is just as Marta dreamed.

## On Your Own

Write an essay about another dream that came true—or one that didn't.

# 6

# EDITING: REVISING AND CORRECTING

Since almost no one can produce a perfect essay on the first try, the last step in writing is rewriting. In this chapter there are exercises designed to help you become your own editor. You will look at writing in which the combining process hasn't been done very well. You will get practice in correcting punctuation errors, and you will see how confusing it can be when paragraphs are poorly structured. There is not much to write in these exercises, but you will be asked to do a lot of thinking about writing. See Composition Note 5 for a discussion of the revision process.

## EDITING EXERCISE 1

By this point in the book, combining is probably a natural and relatively easy process for you. The next two exercises ask you to do something quite different from the combining you have been doing. There is nothing for you to write. Instead, what you will be doing is thinking about and discussing the reasons for combining.

Each exercise gives you an ancient Chinese fable, first in the original version and then in a version that sounds like a combining exercise, but the sentences are not quite so short. Compare each sentence in the original version with its pair in the uncombined version. Be prepared to discuss in class what the difference between the two versions is. Concentrate particularly on the words omitted in the uncombined version. These are the key words, the words that make important differences. Try to explain exactly what differences they make. Consider such things as sentence length and the relationships between ideas.

### The Donkey of Guizhou

There were no donkeys in Guizhou until an eccentric took one there by boat; but finding no use for it he set it loose in the hills. A tiger who saw this monstrous-looking beast thought it must be divine. It first surveyed the donkey from undercover, then ventured a little nearer, still keeping a respectful distance, however.

One day the donkey brayed, and the tiger took fright and fled for fear of being bitten. It was utterly terrified. But it came back for another look and decided this creature was not so formidable after all. Then, growing used to the braying, it drew nearer, though it still dared not attack. Coming nearer still, it began to take liberties, shoving, jostling, and charging roughly, till the donkey lost its temper and kicked out.

''So that is all it can do!'' thought the tiger, greatly pleased.

Then it leaped on the donkey and sank its teeth into it, severing its throat and devouring it before going on its way.

Poor donkey! Its size made it look powerful, and its bray made it sound invincible. Had it not shown all it could do, even the fierce tiger might not have dared to attack. But the donkey gave itself away!

**Original Version**

1. There were no donkeys in Guizhou until an eccentric took one there by boat; but finding no use for it, he set it loose in the hills.

2. A tiger who saw this monstrous-looking beast thought it must be divine.

3. It first surveyed the donkey from undercover, then ventured a little nearer, still keeping a respectful distance however.

4. One day the donkey brayed, and the tiger took fright and fled for fear of being bitten.

5. It was utterly terrified. But it came back for another look and decided this creature was not so formidable after all.

6. Then, growing used to the braying, it drew nearer, though it still dared not attack.

7. Coming nearer still, it began to take liberties, shoving, jostling, and charging roughly, till the donkey lost its temper and kicked out.

8. "So that's all it can do!" thought the tiger, greatly pleased.

9. Then it leaped on the donkey and sank its teeth into it, severing its throat and devouring it before going on its way.

10. Poor donkey! Its size made it look powerful, and its bray made it sound invincible.

11. Had it not shown all it could do, even the fierce tiger might not have dared to attack.

12. But the donkey gave itself away!

**Uncombined Version**

1. There were no donkeys in Guizhou. An eccentric took one there by boat. He found no use for it. He set it loose in the hills.

2. A tiger saw this monstrous-looking beast. The tiger thought it must be divine.

3. It surveyed the donkey from undercover. It ventured a little nearer. It kept a respectful distance.

4. One day the donkey brayed. The tiger took fright. It fled. It was afraid of being bitten.

5. It was utterly terrified. It came back. It took another look. It decided this creature was not so formidable.

6. It grew used to the braying. It drew nearer. It dared not attack.

7. It came nearer. It began to take liberties. It shoved. It jostled. It charged roughly. The donkey lost its temper and kicked out.

8. "So that is all it can do!" thought the tiger. It was greatly pleased.

9. It leaped on the donkey and sank its teeth into it. It severed its throat. It devoured it. It went on its way.

10. Poor donkey! Its size made it look powerful. Its bray made it sound invincible.

11. It showed all it could do. The fierce tiger dared to attack.

12. The donkey gave itself away!

# EDITING EXERCISE 2

The instructions for this exercise are the same as for the preceding one.

## The Silly Fawn

A man in Linjiang captured a fawn. When it was brought home, the dogs came licking their chops and wagging their tails. The man angrily drove them off. Afterwards, he took the fawn among the dogs, warning them to keep their peace and making them frolic with it. In time, the dogs learned their lesson. As the fawn grew, it forgot it was a deer and regarded the dogs as its friends, with whom it could gambol and play. The dogs, fearing their master, had to suppress their natural desires and fraternize with it.

One day three years later, the deer went outside the gate. There were many strange dogs in the street, so it went up and tried to play with them. The dogs were surprised, but being glad to see a meal come their way, fell upon it and killed it. As it was breathing its last, the deer was at a loss to understand why it had come to such an untimely end.

**Original Version**

1. A man in Linjiang captured a fawn.
2. When it was brought home, the dogs came licking their chops and wagging their tails.
3. The man angrily drove them off.
4. Afterwards, he took the fawn among the dogs, warning them to keep their peace and making them frolic with it.
5. In time, the dogs learned their lesson.
6. As the fawn grew, it forgot it was a deer and regarded the dogs as its friends, with whom it could gambol and play.
7. The dogs, fearing their master, had to suppress their natural desires and fraternize with it.
8. One day three years later, the deer went outside the gate.
9. There were many strange dogs in the street, so it went up and tried to play with them.
10. The dogs were surprised, but being glad to see a meal come their way, fell upon it and killed it.
11. As it was breathing its last, the deer was at a loss to understand why it had come to such an untimely end.

**Uncombined Version**

1. A man captured a fawn. He was in Linjiang.
2. It was brought home. The dogs came. They licked their chops. They wagged their tails.
3. The man drove them off. He did it angrily.
4. He took the fawn among the dogs. He warned them to keep their peace. He made them frolic with it.
5. The dogs learned their lesson.
6. The fawn grew. It forgot it was a deer. It regarded the dogs as its friends. It could gambol and play with them.
7. The dogs feared their master. They had to suppress their natural desires. They had to fraternize with the fawn.
8. It was one day three years later. The deer went outside the gate.
9. There were many strange dogs in the street. It went up to them. It tried to play with them.
10. The dogs were surprised. They were glad to see a meal come their way. They fell upon it. They killed it.
11. The deer was breathing its last. It was at a loss. It couldn't understand why it had come to such an untimely end.

# EDITING EXERCISE 3 _____

The following is another exercise in which you are asked to compare an original version of a passage with its partially uncombined form in order to become more aware of what difference it makes when words showing relationships among ideas are left out. The form of this exercise is slightly different, however. The two versions are presented one after the other, and you must do the comparison by yourself, identifying the key omissions. In addition, some sentences have been overcombined—that is, the sentences are too long for easy understanding.

## A Disturbing Book

### (Original Version)

A recently published book, Cerf and Navasky's *The Experts Speak,* presents a comical but also disturbing account of how often the experts are wrong.* The book presents several thousand authoritative comments made over the last few hundred years by experts in such fields as science, the arts, and political affairs. But in each case, the expert's prediction or analysis has been proved wrong.

For example, three years prior to the beginning of World War II, the former British prime minister Lloyd George proclaimed, "Germany has no desire to attack any country in Europe." Two years earlier, he had declared Germany "unable to wage war." The war, of course, did begin, and the experts were also unable to predict its course. The U.S. Secretary of the Navy, Frank Knox, declared: "No matter what happens, the U.S. Navy is not going to be caught napping." This confident statement was made on December 4, 1941, three days before the Japanese attacked Pearl Harbor.

But it is not only in world events that expert knowledge fails; technology, business, and the arts fare no better. Its inventor called the early motion-picture camera a "scientific curiosity" with "no commercial value whatsoever." In 1968, *Business Week* pointed out that there was no room for Japanese cars on the American market as there were already 50 foreign-made models available. And a newspaper labeled an early Beethoven symphony "a crude monstrosity" and likened it to a "serpent which continues to writhe about, refusing to expire."

One might say that predicting the future is a futile endeavor, and that may be so. Nevertheless, we do not value expert knowledge simply for itself. One reason for studying history, for example, is for the light it presumably sheds on the present and the future. A book such as *The Experts Speak,* with its grim chronicling of erroneous predictions, calls into question this assumption of the predictive value of expertise and makes our faith in the experts look uncomfortably naive.

## A Disturbing Book

### (Uncombined Version)

Cerf and Navasky's book *The Experts Speak* was published recently. It presents a comical account of how often the experts are wrong, and it is also disturbing. The book presents several thousand authoritative comments made over the last few hundred years. They are by experts in such fields as science, the arts, and political affairs. The predictions or analyses have been proved wrong.

---

*Cerf, Christopher, and Victor Navasky, *The Experts Speak: The Definitive Compendium of Authoritative Misinformation* (New York: Pantheon Books, 1984).

Lloyd George was a former British prime minister. He proclaimed, "Germany has no desire to attack any country in Europe." This was three years prior to the beginning of World War II. He had declared Germany "unable to wage war." The war began. The experts were unable to predict its course. The U.S. Secretary of the Navy was Frank Knox. He declared: "No matter what happens, the U.S. Navy is not going to be caught napping." That was three days before the Japanese attacked Pearl Harbor.

It is not only in world events that expert knowledge fails. Technology, business, and the arts fare no better. Its inventor called the early motion-picture camera "a scientific curiosity." He said it had "no commercial value whatsoever." In 1968, *Business Week* pointed out that there were already 50 foreign-made cars available, and there was no room for Japanese cars on the American market. A newspaper labeled an early Beethoven symphony "a crude monstrosity." It likened it to a "serpent which continues to writhe about, refusing to expire."

One might say that predicting the future is a futile endeavor. That may be so. We do not value expert knowledge simply for itself. One reason for studying history is for the light it presumably sheds on the present and the future. A book like *The Experts Speak* is a grim chronicling of erroneous predictions and calls into question this assumption of the predictive value of expertise and makes our faith in the experts look uncomfortably naive.

# EDITING EXERCISE 4

There are no grammatical or punctuation errors in the following passage. Nevertheless, it cannot be considered particularly good writing. Almost every sentence can be improved, either by rearranging the parts, leaving out unnecessary words, combining it with one or more other sentences, or adding a transition. Rewrite the passage so that one sentence flows smoothly after another. Reading aloud will help you decide what to do.

## Moving

Hank and Susan Shoreham are buying a house that is new. They feel slightly ambivalent about what they are doing. They have lived in their present house for eight years. They like it very much. They have improved the house considerably. They had never done carpentry before. They had never hung wallpaper before. The house is attractive. It is comfortable. It is practical. They have stayed there even though they both work in a town that is an hour's drive away. They like the house so much.

Now they are expecting a child. It is their first. They realize the house is too small for a family. They thought the house would be big enough for a while. They realized they were wrong after some more careful thinking.

They can have a house that is much larger for the same price in their new town, Simmons Valley. The taxes are lower. They can get to work in ten minutes. Simmons Valley is rural. It is isolated. There isn't much to do. All their friends live in the old neighborhood. The new house is pleasant. It isn't very interesting.

Hank and Susan know moving is the right thing to do. They are not completely happy about the decision.

## EDITING EXERCISE 5

The following passage has no grammatical or punctuation errors, but the sentences are choppy—short and abrupt—and some of them sound awkward. Revise to make the whole smoother and more mature. Then decide whether or not this should be one paragraph. If not, divide it into paragraphs and comment on whether or not the paragraphs are complete.

### Mud Bath

Hot water bubbles up from the ground in some parts of the world naturally. People have thought this water has medicinal properties for centuries. People who are sick or want to relax have traveled to these places that are called hot springs or spas. They soak in the water. They breathe in the vapor. Aqua Verde is a resort. It is in the desert. It offers many hot baths. It offers something special. It is a mud bath. Some people think a mud bath sounds terrible at first. It is really wonderful. When you finish a mud bath, you feel clean. You feel relaxed. Your skin is smooth. It is like silk. The mud bath is really a pool that is shallow. It is filled with water that is reddish brown. This is the color of the surrounding land. There is a tub in the middle of the pool. It is filled with clay that is clean and wet. People spread it on their arms. They spread it on their legs and their shoulders and on their faces. Some people put it on their hair. The adults laugh. It feels a little silly. They joke about grownups who play in the mud. The children laugh too. They are usually not supposed to play in mud they say. When the people are covered completely, they lie in the sun. The clay dries, and it looks like the skin of an elephant. People laugh again. They rub off the dry clay. They shower. Everyone feels healthy. They feel cheerful.

## EDITING EXERCISE 6

If comma splices, run-on sentences, and fragments have been problems for you, here is an exercise to work with. Some of the following items are correct. Others have one error or more. First decide where the errors are. Then correct them.

Remember that inserting a period or semicolon to correct a comma splice or run-on is always grammatically correct but possibly not effective stylistically. For example, the following sentence contains a comma splice:

**Incorrect:** Mr. Henderson decided to chop down the pine tree, it was leaning dangerously close to his house.

It would be correct to rewrite the sentence this way:

Mr. Henderson decided to chop down the pine tree. It was leaning dangerously close to his house.

However, this gives two simple, relatively short sentences in a row. Too many such sentences in one passage can sound choppy and somewhat immature. An adverb clause might be more effective:

Mr. Henderson decided to chop down the pine tree because it was leaning dangerously close to his house.

Grammar Note 14 can assist you with this exercise.

1.  Many people have begun to complain about big trucks, they are making driving on highways unsafe and frightening.
2.  Although truck drivers used to have a good reputation for safe driving and helpfulness to motorists who ran into trouble. They are now frequently called ''road hogs'' or worse names than that.
3.  People complain about several things, first the trucks drive too fast.
4.  In a small car being passed on the left and right by two speeding trucks, everything shakes, and it is difficult to steer because the trucks create a powerful wind that can push a car out of its lane.
5.  A second common complaint is tailgating the trucks follow too closely behind slower cars. And frequently blink their lights as a signal that the driver of the car should move to the left to let the truck pass. Motorists feel bullied.
6.  An issue that has only recently come to the public's attention is how often trucks on the road have mechanical problems that make them unsafe.
7.  Some reports claim that as many as 80 percent of the trucks on the road violate safety standards; although only 20 percent pose an immediate danger.
8.  Truckers claim that they have lost money since the speed limit was reduced to 55 miles per hour they have to drive longer hours each day.
9.  Driving more than 10 hours a day leads to driver fatigue, another cause of danger on the highways.

10. There are complaints in some parts of the country that police are soft on truck drivers, this means that a car is more likely to be stopped for speeding than a truck, and that is not only unfair but also dangerous.

## EDITING EXERCISE 7

Here is a passage that contains a variety of dangling modifiers. Identify them and then rewrite enough of the sentence to show how the error can be corrected. Grammar Note 15 contains a discussion of the dangling modifier error.

### Christmas Cards

Looking through her address book, Molly decides that it is time to plan the chore of sending out Christmas cards. Her husband feels that sending cards to all his clients helps his business. To send all these cards, a long time is needed, and Molly always does most of the work. Thinking that typed mailing labels on the envelopes look too impersonal, the cards have to be addressed by hand, but doing this is a boring job. To help her, the list is examined every year by her husband, who knows at a glance whether or not to remove a name or leave it on. Also, to show his appreciation, he always says she can keep the extra cards for herself. By keeping up this silly joke from year to year, part of Molly's annoyance is reduced.

To tell the truth, the chore isn't as annoying as Molly claims. By setting aside an hour every day, the job can be accomplished in easy stages, and since it isn't difficult work, Molly's mind is free to wander in a restful way. What really bothers her is how much a part of women's traditional role this job is. Doing unpaid, boring tasks to help men is one of the ideas Molly would like to see disappear from the earth. She is not sure why she has been doing this chore for so many years.

Thinking about the situation, it seems clear to her that sending Christmas cards to clients is a business matter, not a family one. To be fair, her husband's secretary, who earns a good salary, should do this job. Molly considers this idea waiting for her husband to come home. Perhaps, by being very tactful, she can convince him that sending cards to friends and relatives is all she should do. Feeling quite determined and convinced of the correctness of her decision, Molly's mind goes on to other arrangements for the coming holiday season.

## EDITING EXERCISE 8

Here is a passage for you to rewrite. Not only are there problems in combining for you to work out, there are also many errors in punctuation, primarily errors in comma usage. You will find some sentence fragments and some run-on sentences.

## Arriving

Vinh is traveling from Malaysia to the United States. It is with her son. He is six years old and he is Hai. The plane will land in 20 minutes at Los Angeles International Airport. Hai has been sleeping for about an hour and Vinh doesn't want to wake him up. He is exhausted from the long flight. And from the anticipation after such a long time of seeing his father again. Also from the excitement of going to a country that is new. Vinh is exhausted, too, she has been unable to sleep. There was the delay because of engine trouble in Tokyo. There was the turbulence for more than an hour, there was her state of mind most of all. She has been unable to quiet her mind, and thoughts one after another came without interruption. Now she thinks about Pham her husband who she has not seen for 27 months. She thinks about the refugee camp that is in Malaysia, she thinks about her new home. It is in California, she cannot picture it. She has a worry that is all at once more pressing. The plane is 18 hours late but she had no opportunity to let Pham know. She wonders, if he will be there to meet her? She wonders, what will she do if he is not there. Will she know how to use an American telephone. She has no more time to worry, the plane is going to land in less than a minute. She must wake up Hai, and gather his toys, put on his shoes, his jacket. As the plane lands, she feels all at the same time happy, sad, anxious and calm.

# EDITING EXERCISE 9

In this exercise, there is nothing for you to write. Instead, read the following assignment and the paragraphs written in response to it. Be prepared to discuss in class what is satisfactory and unsatisfactory about each. Your main focus should be on structure, style and tone, and responsiveness to the assignment. Notice any errors in grammar or punctuation, too. Some of the examples are quite obviously bad, and you may feel a few of them are too silly to bother about. Nevertheless, be prepared to explain *exactly* what is silly or awful about them. What would you say to the writers if it were up to you to help them?

**Assignment:** Part of the current discussion about violence on television centers around the question of whether or not seeing so much violent behavior causes people to act violently. Write an essay of about 500 words that states and defends your position on the matter. Use references to specific television programs or events in the news to illustrate your points.

## Introductions

**Example 1:** Part of the current discussion about violence on television centers around the question of whether or not seeing so much violent behavior causes people to act violently. I don't think so.

**Example 2:** Violence has existed since time began. The Bible and history are full of violence before TV. ''Miami Vice'' is alot of fun, it won't hurt anyone.

**Example 3:** The dictionary defines violence as: ''1. Physical force exerted for the purpose of violating, damaging, or abusing. 2. An act or instance of violent action or behavior. 3. Intensity or severity as in natural phenomena; untamed force. People shouldn't be so violent.

**Example 4:** Violence is everywhere, its' in nature, its' in Lebanon, its' on our campus. The violence of an earthquake or a war probably didn't come from television. But its possible that the way our campus police acts was caused by all the police shows they've watched. People learn a lot about behavior from watching TV. Violence on TV should be limited.

## Paragraphs from the Body

**Example 1:** Last week there was this program on TV. About two guys who robbed a diamond from a rich guy's house. The house had all this electronic stuff to protect it but the two guys got in anyway. The problem was, they didn't know there were these dogs that would only attack someone as they left the house. Not as they broke in. There was a wild fight between the guys and the dogs and they were successful.

**Example 2:** Violence on TV probably causes violence in people. My kid brother and his friends are always playing war or cops and robbers. If TV effects kids, it probably effects adults, too. Millions of people (maybe more) watch hours and hours of television violence and it has to effect them. One of the most violent programs is the evening news. Yesterday there were two riots, a bombing, a SWAT raid and a suicide-murder. All in 23 minutes, with commercials!

**Example 3:** One of the main arguments for reducing violence on television is that people become so accustomed to seeing it that it doesn't affect them any longer. They become hardened or bored and don't notice how violent life has become.

**Example 4:** The first problem with TV violence is that it gets boring after awhile. I'd rather watch a football game or an old movie. There's a lot of good programs that people could watch instead. Violence isn't so good for people, either, it gives children nightmares. And it makes people think violence is normal. That's the main problem with it. There's enough violence in life and the newspapers. We don't need anymore.

## Conclusions

**Example 1:** If you don't agree, I'll beat you up. (Only kidding!!!)

**Example 2:** Thus I have proved that television violence is harmless.

**Example 3:** Instead of all the violence, they could have more educational and "family" programs. The "After School Special" is very good; so is "National Geographic." Also, there should be fewer commercials.

**Example 4:** There has never been a time without violence. We'll probably always have it.

# EDITING EXERCISE 10

This exercise asks you to correct combining problems, punctuation errors, and weaknesses in essay structure. In examining essay structure, you will need to ask questions about what the thesis is, whether it is clearly expressed, whether the paragraphs are properly structured, and whether or not each point is developed enough. You may add or change what you like. Your object is to produce a totally satisfactory version of this essay.

## Dog Walking

The recent increase in New York City of dog ownership has given rise to a new job dog walking. People do not have time to walk their dogs during the day who are on busy schedules or they work far from home. College students and actors, who are unemployed, provide this service. To walk one dog at a time is not efficient. An experienced dog walker may take five or six dogs at a time. To see someone walking with so many dogs, each dog on a separate leash, is surprising for visitors, or newcomers to the city. Dog walking sounds simple, it has its complications.

The dog walker must have a key to each apartment or there must be an arrangement with the doorman. To bring the dog downstairs at the appointed time. A dog walker must be reliable and trustworthy, this is obvious. A dog walker must have certain, unusual skills.

He or she must be able to prevent the leashes from getting tangled with one hand. The other hand must hold the equipment for cleaning up after the dogs, the city imposes fines on people that allow their dogs to foul the sidewalks.

Some devices that are ingenious for cleaning up are available. A dog walker must know how to coax five large reluctant dogs into a small elevator. He or she must know how to keep the dogs from fighting among themselves and barking at another group of dogs which are being walked by someone else. Some dog walkers provide extra services. They will take a dog that is sick to the veterinarian. They will feed a dog, or keep it company, when the owners are away on vacation. Or bathe a dog and trim it's nails. Being a dog walker is a interesting, and unusual, source of income for the right person.

# EDITING EXERCISE 11

The instructions for this exercise are the same as for the preceding one.

## The Newest Fast Food

A characteristic for some years of American life has been fast food. Americans are busy, they don't like it to take a long time at home to prepare meals and to slowly eat in restaurants.

Many people say fast food suits the rapid pace of living in the United States. In addition, many people complain, fast food doesn't taste very good and it isn't very healthful. Just recently there has been a development that is new in fast food. It is not eaten in a restaurant, it is bought in a shop, and taken home. And this food is not hamburgers, hot dogs, simple Chinese-American dishes, rather it is gourmet food that is the finest from around the world. There are dozens of small shops in well-to-do-neighborhoods in many large cities that sell delicious, prepared, complicated food.

Some shops specialize in hot, meat dishes or cold salads, or pasta. One shop had an array that was mouth-watering on a recent day in New York City, and there were: cold salmon salad, hearts of palm with red pepper, beet and celery root salad, grape leaves filled with lamb, lobster stuffed with crab and cheese, eggplant baked in tomatoes, artichoke hearts in a fiery sauce.

All this is a far cry from the usual American diet of bland meat and potatoes. Another type of new fast food store is designed for individuals, who are health-conscious, is the take-out salad bar. Originally, these were fruit and vegetable stores, and one could buy whole fruits and vegetables there in the normal way. The same fruits and vegetables are for sale, and some of them are ready for the salad bowl, being already sliced or chopped. Because there is no waste a customer can choose exactly what ingredients he or she wants for a salad, and can buy only the amount planned to eat right away. The salads are healthy, economical, time-saving, nothing has to be washed or peeled or sliced at home.

A variety of salad dressings as well as nuts, seeds, and croutons are available to complete the salads and to make the salads more interesting. Since one shops in these new stores, one can serve a meal that is delicious, impressive, and healthful without spending a long time in the kitchen. Saving time doesn't any longer mean to accept poor quality.

# WRITING GUIDE

**II**

# 7

# COMPOSITION
# NOTES

This chapter presents discussions of the various stages of the writing process. The discussions will help you to write the paragraphs and essays assigned in the "On Your Own" exercises in this book.

# COMPOSITION NOTE 1: GETTING IDEAS AND PLANNING TO WRITE

A logically organized, well-supported essay rarely pops into one's mind the moment it is wanted. Rather it is something that almost always grows out of confusion and puzzlement. There are some useful procedures to follow, however, to get from uncertainty to the final draft.

Suppose you were given an assignment like this and had a week in which to write the paper:

> A significant part of most people's lives is spent at work, and few of us are unaffected by the jobs we have. Some people find their work a source of growth and satisfaction. Others find their jobs frustrating or damaging. Write an essay of about 500 words in which you describe a job you have or once had and explain how it affects or has affected other parts of your life. Be as specific as possible.

**Start Early:** One of the most important things you can do is not leave the whole writing process to the night before the paper is due. Plan to write the first draft a few days before then so that you aren't under great pressure when you write and so that the first draft has a chance to cool. (See Composition Note 5.) Read the assignment several times as soon as you get it, and then go about whatever else you have to do. But don't block the assignment out of your mind entirely—even if you hate the idea of writing. You will find that without conscious effort on your part, various ideas and possibilities will occur to you as you are doing something else. These are often the most valuable ideas of all, so jot them down or plan to remember them.

**Plan First:** When you begin the actual writing, don't expect to sit down and have one sentence follow nicely from another right away. You need a plan first. The more you can plan in advance, the easier the actual writing will be. The anxiety about thinking of what comes next will be lessened, and you can concentrate on making the words say exactly what you mean.

A method that works for many people is to begin by making a list of possible ideas, putting them on paper in any order that they come to mind and not worrying about completeness, grammar, or spelling. This is a list that no one else will see. Suppose you have chosen to write about a typist's job you had two summers before you came to college. The list could look like this:

cute guy at next desk
boss—ugh!
boring, boring, boring

no mistakes allowed
Italian restaurant for lunches
never fast enough
no raise
picky picky
neat desk—nag, nag, nag

This list won't make much sense to anyone else, of course, because it's written in a kind of private shorthand, but to the writer, each item represents a great deal. When the ideas begin to come more slowly, stop and look over your list. See if it contains any *categories* of ideas—ideas that can be grouped together in separate paragraphs. In the list above, it appears that there were a few pleasant things about the typist's job, but many more negative things. A plan begins to emerge—to talk about the pleasant and unpleasant aspects of the job—and a thesis statement begins to take shape:

There were a few pleasant things about my job two summers ago, but it was still pretty bad.

Now look back at the assignment. Something important is missing from this tentative thesis statement. The assignment was not only to describe the job but to tell how it affected your life, and that idea must be added to the thesis. The job made the summer miserable, but that doesn't sound important enough to be the main point of an essay. You recall how the idea of going to college looked more and more attractive as the boredom of the summer went on, and a more complete thesis emerges:

One of the reasons that I'm here taking this class is that I can't face a lifetime of boring jobs as a typist.

The thesis statement is not too polished yet, but it's a good start. Now, does that thesis suggest how the rest of the paper could be organized? Still working on scratch paper, you might construct a tentative plan like this:

one paragraph describing job and how awful it was
one paragraph about job making college look good
one paragraph about deciding to go to college

Perhaps the second two ideas are closely enough related that they should be in one paragraph. Perhaps the description of the job and the discussion of what was awful about it should be separated—there's a lot to say about each. So, a new plan emerges:

describe job
discuss how boring and petty
decision to do something better with life

There is nothing elaborate about this outline, but it's enough to begin writing from. It sounds logically organized, and it will produce a paper that responds to the assignment. If you like, you can take the outline a step further:

> describe job
> > typing order forms
> > telephone messages
> > getting supplies
> boring and petty
> > boss didn't accept erasures
> > complained constantly about my messy desk
> > said I used too many pencils
> > every day same as before

Notice that not all of the details in the original list have been used because they are no longer relevant to the purpose.

You could even go so far as to write out the thesis statement and the topic sentence for each paragraph before you begin to write the whole paper:

**Thesis:** I had always thought vaguely about going to college, but I made the final decision after a boring job with a nagging boss showed me how unsatisfactory a life of low-level jobs would be.

**Topic sentence:** I had a routine typist's job with nothing unusual or interesting about it.

**Topic sentence:** Not only was the job boring, the boss was a sour, nagging individual who was never satisfied with anyone's work.

**Topic sentence:** By the middle of the summer, I knew that in order to get a better job I would have to get a college degree.

These sentences are still not totally satisfactory, but they don't have to be at this point. What they do is provide a framework for the essay and a clear place to begin.

One of the most important things to remember is that the best way to begin to write is to write. Jot down ideas, lists, sentences and work with them. Sitting at a desk and staring out into space as you try to plan the whole essay in your head usually doesn't work. Often, it produces anxiety as one idea after another floats around unrelated to anything else. Begin by writing.

# EXERCISE 1: GETTING IDEAS_____

For practice in two different ways of getting ideas, try at least one exercise from each of the following two groups.

## A.  Brainstorming

For each of the following topics, give yourself 10 minutes and list ideas as they come to you. Pay no attention to sentence structure, spelling, or whether the idea seems important or interesting. Work steadily but don't rush, and try not to feel pressured. After 10 minutes of brainstorming, go back over your list to find related ideas or the beginning of a plan for an entire essay.

**a.**  first day in _____ ( a new place)
**b.**  bad habits
**c.**  spending money
**d.**  being responsible
**e.**  peace
**f.**  women and work

## B.  Free Writing

Another useful way of starting to write is just to start writing! That is, give yourself 15 minutes and write whatever comes into your mind about the topic. Without stopping, write in more or less complete sentences (but ignore grammar, spelling, and organization). If you run out of ideas before the 15 minutes are over, write your name six times or write ''I can't think of anything else'' until another idea comes to you. The main thing is to keep writing steadily but without high pressure. No one else will read what you've written. At the end of 15 minutes, look back over your work to find the ideas that interest you most or have the greatest potential for being developed into paragraphs or essays. Here are some topics to practice with:

**a.**  feeling angry
**b.**  hunger
**c.**  semesters
**d.**  war
**e.**  sightseeing
**f.**  fathers

## Writing the First Draft

In addition to beginning with a rough outline, there are a few other ways to make the writing process easier. One of them is to double- or triple-space your draft as you write. This leaves room above and below the lines for making changes or additions later. Another way—illustrated in the process described above—is not to worry about what each sentence sounds like as you write it. That is, don't try to write and revise at the same time. Concentrate on producing a complete draft that you can improve later. At this point in the process, it doesn't matter if sentences are awkward or incomplete—as long as you know that you're going to go back and revise them later.

If you can type, type a rough draft to work from in the revision process. Many people find that revising a typed manuscript makes them more objective than when they revise a handwritten draft. And finally, nothing says that you have to begin with the introduction. Introductions are often difficult to write, and that difficulty makes some students lose courage to continue. Begin wherever you like. For example, the idea for the introduction can occur—as if by magic—while you're in the middle of the third paragraph. If you run out of ideas in the middle of any paragraph, leave a space and go on to some other part. Later, pieces can be put together and holes filled in.

# COMPOSITION NOTE 2: TRANSITIONS BETWEEN SENTENCES

One important characteristic of good writing is that one sentence follows smoothly after another. This smooth flow comes about in part from writing fairly long sentences with varied structure, and in part from using transitional words or phrases between sentences. Consider the following passage—exaggerated to make a point:

> *The Random House Dictionary of the English Language* is a popular dictionary. Dictionaries are useful. They give a lot of information. They give correct spelling. They give definitions. They tell how to use words. They tell how words developed. Dictionaries have appendixes. They tell about geography. They tell about measurements. They tell about history. Lots of people look somewhere else first.

The meaning of this passage is clear, but it sounds a little simpleminded. The sentences are short, the vocabulary is uncomplicated, and the rhythm is choppy—the sentences sound like stones being dropped into a well, plop, plop, plop. In fact, they might remind you of the sentences in the combining exercises earlier in this book.

Here is a somewhat improved version:

> Dictionaries provide much useful information that most people don't use. They provide correct spelling and definitions; they also give examples of common usage and the derivations of words. Dictionaries have numerous appendixes. *The Random House Dictionary of the English Language* has more than 30 sections giving information about geography, measurement systems, history, and writing style. This is a wealth of information. Many people look elsewhere when they have a question.

The vocabulary and sentence structure in the last example no longer sound like they were written for a second grade reading level, but, with a little more work, the sentences could be made to flow still more smoothly. Here is another version:

> Dictionaries provide much useful information that most people don't use. <u>In addition</u> to providing correct spelling and definitions, dictionaries <u>also</u> give examples of common usage and the derivations of words. <u>Moreover,</u> dictionaries have numerous appendixes. <u>For example,</u> *The Random House Dictionary of the English Language* contains more than 30 sections giving information

about such things as geography, measurement systems, history, and writing style. <u>In spite of</u> this wealth of information, many people look elsewhere when they have a question.

With the addition of some transitional words and phrases (underlined above) the passage reads more smoothly.

Transitions such as these make clear what the relationship between two sentences is. For example, read the following:

Doris didn't like her boss. She likes him because she knows he is honest and hardworking.

Those sentences probably confused you. Does Doris like her boss or not? What is missing is the time relationship between the two sentences. The following version clearly states that relationship:

<u>At first,</u> Doris didn't like her boss. <u>Now,</u> she likes him because he is honest and hardworking.

If you are alert to the relationships between or among sentences, you can add appropriate transitional words or phrases (sometimes even sentences) to improve your style and help your reader understand more easily.

Here are some common transitional words and phrases arranged according to the kind of relationship they express. Make use of them, but don't overdo it. Some relationships are so clear that pointing them out sounds highly artificial.

| Time | Adding Something |
|---|---|
| now | further |
| then | furthermore |
| at first | moreover |
| in the beginning | in addition |
| later | second, third |
| finally | besides |
| at last | next |
| all at once | also |
| suddenly | similarly |
| at that moment | likewise |

| Contrasting Idea | Result of Something |
|---|---|
| but | therefore |
| instead | thus |
| instead of | as a result |
| on the contrary | consequently |
| however | |
| in spite of | |
| nevertheless | |
| otherwise | |
| on the other hand | |

| To End or Summarize | To Introduce an Example |
|---|---|
| in short | for instance |
| in sum | for example |
| to conclude | suppose |
| finally | let us assume |
| in conclusion | |

# COMPOSITION NOTE 3: THE PARAGRAPH

This composition note presents, in brief form, a discussion of the main characteristics of paragraph structure and some of the problems students encounter when they begin to write.

The most obvious characteristic of a paragraph is that its first line is indented. But it isn't quite that simple, and you can't indent wherever you feel like it or whenever you remember to. A paragraph is actually a fairly complex structure, but to put it briefly, it is a group of sentences that adequately explains a central idea that is stated in something called the topic sentence. The sentence just before the one you're reading now is the topic sentence of this paragraph. It gives the main idea—what a paragraph is—and the purpose of all the other sentences is to explain that idea. Often, the topic sentence is the first sentence in the paragraph, but as you can see in this paragraph, it can come in the middle, or even at the end. For people who are just beginning to think seriously about writing, it's a good idea to place the topic sentence at the beginning of the paragraph. Placed there, it serves as a strong reminder of what the paragraph is about, and it keeps you from wandering off the subject.

The "rules" of paragraphing (and writing essays, too) differ somewhat from country to country, so it is useful to discuss some theories or assumptions before going into more detail about the actual writing of paragraphs. In some countries, the "rules" are more gentle than they are here in the United States. The writer must have a purpose in mind, of course. If not, why write? But that purpose isn't expected to be stated forcefully at the beginning. Instead, the writer begins with a detail, adds another related idea, and ends by stating what has been proved or shown. Perhaps this is related to national character—if such a thing really exists—but in the United States, the process is generally the opposite of what was just described. The main point, the idea you are going to explain or prove generally comes first, and then come the details in a fairly strict order, with little "wandering around" permitted. This feels uncomfortable or unnatural to many people when they first try it. They think that no one will read the rest of their paragraph or essay if the main point is stated at the beginning. And some writers have difficulty because, when they begin to write, they themselves are not sure what the main idea is. Nevertheless, the general pattern of main point first and details to follow is an essential part of writing well in American colleges and universities. So, on to the details of paragraphs.

## The Topic Sentence

Basically, the topic sentence should do two things: state the subject of the paragraph and state the idea about that subject that the paragraph will support, explain, or prove.

Suppose you were assigned to write a paragraph of about 150 words (roughly half a page) on the subject of education—not a very exciting subject, perhaps, but that's your assignment. Let's examine some unsatisfactory topic sentences.

**Unsatisfactory Example #1:** This paragraph will discuss education.

This sentence, it's true, restates the assignment. But what idea about education will the rest of the paragraph develop? There is no way to know. The topic sentence gives no clue to the reader about what will follow. And it gives the writer no guidance. The sentences that follow such a topic sentence may wander around the subject and then get lost. A similar topic sentence to avoid is one that begins, ''The purpose of this paragraph is to . . . .'' Experienced readers expect the purpose to be stated clearly. They don't need to be told that the purpose is going to be stated.

**Unsatisfactory Example #2:** Education is very important.

This topic sentence is an improvement over the first example, but it is still not very good. It does state the subject (education) and an idea about the subject (important). However, the assignment was for a paragraph of about half a page. One paragraph just cannot cover such a broad topic as the importance of education. Someone who tries to write a paragraph with this topic sentence will probably write vague ideas that everyone has heard too often to care about. A reader will get bored or irritated. No writer wants to have that effect. In terms of style, too, this topic sentence is not very satisfactory. It is a short, abrupt sentence—not a very graceful way to begin.

**Improved Version #1:** Technical education is important in developing countries.

This is still a rather large subject for one paragraph, but it is an example of an important process called ''narrowing the subject.'' Notice that a paragraph built on this topic sentence is no longer going to try to talk about all of education. The subject has been narrowed in two ways. First, ''all education'' has been narrowed to ''technical education.'' Second, ''important'' has been narrowed to ''important in developing countries.'' But ''important'' is probably still too broad, too big, too important an idea to explain in one paragraph.

**Improved Version #2:** Short courses in modern methods of agriculture are increasing farm production in several developing nations.

Now the central idea has been narrowed even more. ''Technical education'' has become ''short courses in modern methods of agriculture.'' It's possible, of course, to narrow this still further, perhaps to courses in new methods of irrigation. And ''important'' has been limited, too, to a specific example, ''increasing farm production.'' Now, so long as the author has facts and figures to support the topic sentence, there are possibilities to make this an interesting paragraph.

# EXERCISE 1: NARROWING THE TOPIC _____

Here are several topics that are too broad to be discussed in a single paragraph. Narrow them down to an idea that can be covered adequately in a paragraph of 75 to 150 words. Show your narrowed topics to others in the class to see if they agree that the topics are narrow enough.

a. raising children

b. studying a foreign language

c. smoking

d. jealousy

e. holidays

# EXERCISE 2: TOPIC SENTENCES _____

Examine the following topic sentences to determine if they are satisfactory. Discuss what is acceptable or not acceptable about each one.

a. Students should study for exams.

b. Computers are changing the world.

c. It's better to buy clothing at sales.

d. The clerks in the Admissions Office should be friendlier.

e. College general education courses are a waste of time.

Read the following three pairs of topic sentences. Most people will find one in each pair better than the other. Mark the one in each pair that you find the most effective, and be prepared to explain your choices.

1a. Although I am generally quite level-headed, a few weeks ago I surprised myself by overreacting to a late-night science fiction movie on TV.

1b. A few weeks ago, I was home alone and got frightened by a late-night science fiction movie on TV.

2a. Going to a community college has several advantages.

2b. Some people look down on community colleges, but they offer several advantages that make up for their lack of prestige.

3a. Chinese couples do not show affection for one another in public as freely as American couples do.

3b. In many Asian cultures, people do not show their emotions in public as freely as Americans do.

### Developing the Paragraph

A good topic sentence suggests the method of development for the rest of the paragraph. For example, the topic sentence about increasing farm production will include (should include) examples: where have such courses been given? by whom? how much did farm production increase? A topic sentence such as this suggests that the paragraph is going to present arguments:

> The city council should stop unplanned growth in northern suburbs.

A writer can develop this topic sentence by comparing and contrasting:

> Traveling by train is more comfortable and more economical than traveling by air.

And the following topic sentence describes personal experience:

> My first night in the dormitory gave me several surprising insights into college life.

That sentence indicates that the paragraph will present details about the author's own experiences, will be narrative—that is, will tell about something that happened—and will explain what the insights were.

A topic sentence that doesn't suggest how the paragraph will be developed probably needs to be revised before the writer goes any further.

# EXERCISE 3: STRATEGIES FOR DEVELOPMENT ___

Consider how you would develop each of the following ideas for a paragraph. What sort of information would be required? Examples? Arguments? Explanation?

a.   Registering for classes this semester was a nightmare.

b.   Mail-in registration would simplify the opening of the semester.

c.   Registering by mail is simple, but it requires that you follow directions exactly.

d.   Mail-in registration has proved to be economical and timesaving.

## Staying on the Topic

An important principle of paragraph development is that the body of the paragraph must support or explain the topic sentence and not wander off to another idea. This sounds almost too obvious to be worth saying, but it's often a problem. Sometimes writers with many ideas feel tempted to write everything they know—forgetting that a paragraph explains only one limited idea. A whole essay can't be squeezed into a paragraph. Sometimes the problem is just the reverse—the writer doesn't have much to say and so is tempted to add unrelated ideas to make a longer paragraph. And sometimes writers just don't pay enough attention. One idea leads to another, and soon the original topic sentence is forgotten.

Here is the opening of a paragraph that is going in the wrong direction:

> My first night in the dormitory gave me several surprising insights into college life. My family didn't really want me to go to college. They felt I was not suited for serious study because I hadn't done very well in high school. My father thought I should go into the army.

The development of this paragraph (starting with the second sentence) begins too far back in time from that first night in the dorm. The story of how the writer convinced his parents to send him to college may be interesting, but it doesn't directly support the topic sentence. The paragraph may go on with the arguments about college or the army and then, somewhere in the middle, begin to discuss that first night. If so, the paragraph will seem disorganized—the topic sentence promised one story, but another story came first.

## After the Topic Sentence, What?

The sample paragraph above began too slowly—too far back in time from the main idea. Other paragraphs can begin too quickly, however. That is, the sentence immediately after the topic sentence begins to present a very concrete example. For instance, here is the opening of another paragraph on the same subject:

> My first night in the dormitory gave me several surprising insights into college life. When I got back from dinner, George Clifton, my roommate, was sitting in the middle of my bed simultaneously tossing empty beer cans across the room and trying to convince the reluctant woman at the other end of the telephone to sign up for the dating service he had organized over the summer.

The second sentence in the paragraph above contains a breathless flow of details, but the reader has had only the space of one sentence—the topic sentence—to prepare to receive information about surprising insights. The reader needs a few more sentences and a little more general information—more time—before being presented with George's beer cans and dating service.

Here's a better beginning:

> My first night in the dormitory gave me several surprising insights into college life. I had always thought that students who chose to live in the dorm would be serious about their studies. Not having to cook or take care of an apartment would give them more time for library or lab work. I was wrong. The first time I saw my roommate, George Clifton, he was sitting in the middle of my bed. . . .

By giving some background information about why the author should be surprised, and surprised about what, this paragraph provides a smoother and gentler introduction to the supporting details.

## How Much Detail?

Finally, the question arises of how much explanation or detail is enough. The answer varies with the subject of the paragraph, with the assignment, and with the intended audience. A good practice for a writer to develop is to think about the reader as well as the subject of the paragraph. The writer knows the subject better than the reader, in most cases. Or, at least, the writer has spent more time preparing the paragraph than the reader will spend reading it. In such a situation, it is easy for a writer to forget that the sentences and ideas in the paragraph are quite new to the reader. What now seems obvious to the writer, who has been thinking and revising for some time, may not be quite so obvious to the reader. So before you decide that you're finished, reread your own work, asking, ''Would this be clear to me if I were reading it for the first time?''

Making things clear and interesting depends a great deal on writing with concrete, specific examples. Unfortunately, it is easier for most people to write in general or vague terms than in highly specific ones. Compare these two versions of a now familiar sentence:

> When I got back, my roommate was sitting there throwing junk around and talking business on the telephone.

> When I got back from dinner, George Clifton, my roommate, was sitting in the middle of my bed simultaneously tossing empty beer cans across the room and trying to convince the reluctant woman at the other end of the telephone to sign up for the dating service he had organized over the summer.

The first sentence is flat. There is not much to ''see'' in it. The second sentence breathes some life into George and gives a sense of his personality.

# EXERCISE 4: PARAGRAPH STRUCTURE AND DEVELOPMENT

Examine the following to determine if the topic sentences are appropriately developed. Consider such problems as wandering away from the topic and insufficient development.

**a.** Registering for classes this semester was a nightmare. My favorite cousin was here on his annual visit, and of course there were a lot of things I wanted to do with him before he had to go back to Paris. He comes from the French branch of our family. So I missed my appointment for registration and had to go on the last day when most classes were already filled. My cousin Henri came with me and couldn't believe how much trouble it was. There was one problem after another, and we didn't make it to the beach at all.

**b.** Mail-in registration would simplify the opening of the semester. All you'd have to do is fill out some forms, mail the envelopes, and go to class. You wouldn't have to wait in line and argue with unfriendly clerks.

**c.** Registering by mail is simple, but it requires that you follow directions exactly. Last semester I was in a rush and put my tuition check in the envelope to the Health Office instead of the one to the Bursar's Office. Three weeks later I got a notice saying that I had been dropped from all my classes and had to pay a late fee in order to reregister. I'm sure other people make similar mistakes, too. Campus officials could be a little more understanding. Everyone is human, after all.

**d.** Mail-in registration has proved to be economical and timesaving. An article in the campus newspaper indicated a saving of more than $20,000 this semester. The saving came primarily from needing fewer part-time employees to handle paperwork. But the saving involved more than the campus budget. Students saved, too, because a postage stamp is cheaper than the gasoline or bus fare to get to campus to register in person. Filling out a few forms takes less time than driving, waiting in line, and fighting the crowds in the parking lot. And, finally, everyone saved with respect to the frustration and bad temper that accompany in-person registration.

**e.** The geranium plant in my kitchen window is healthy, robust, and quite beautiful. It grows in a common, red clay pot with a thin crack down one side. The plant is eight inches tall, about 20 inches around, and the central stem is as thick as a ballpoint pen. The leaves are deep green with a hint of yellow and are more or less round, with a darker marking in the middle. Right now the plant is ablaze with color. There are three clusters of deep red blossoms, all on the left side. I enjoy watching this healthy, beautiful plant in the morning sunshine.

**f.** Going to college right after high school is quite common, but there are some disadvantages. The first disadvantage is that you have to study much harder than in high school. Many high-school students can finish their homework in school or in less than half an hour at home, but college requires a lot more work. The second disadvantage is that many students have to work while they are in college. This limits time for study and time for recreation. It also puts stress on students who are already under stress from their classes. Nevertheless, many students will continue to go to college immediately after graduating from high school.

## EXERCISE 5: USING SPECIFIC DETAILS

Each of the following paragraphs is relatively well structured. The paragraphs can be improved, however, by the addition of specific, concrete details—names and places and colors and sizes and so on. Rewrite each paragraph, keeping the basic structure of each sentence but adding details to make the reader ''see'' what is going on. You will probably want to add entire sentences.

**a.** The front porch of my house is messy and not very inviting. The porch is not very large, but it is crowded with things we don't use any more but haven't decided to give away. Our dog often sits there, too, and growls when someone comes to the house. Inside, everything is different, so the porch seems out of place.

**b.** Apologies are sometimes very difficult to make. Once I accused my younger brother of doing something that he said he didn't do. My mom sided with him and made me apologize. That was difficult to do because I knew he had really done it. Later, I found out that he hadn't done it. Someone else had. I felt embarrassed, but I didn't apologize again because I had already apologized once.

**c.** Going grocery shopping last Saturday morning taught me that shopping during the week is less frustrating and much less time-consuming. First of all, it was difficult to find a place to park. In the store the aisles were crowded, and people left their shopping carts in inconvenient places. The lines at the cash registers were impossible. The cashier told me that Tuesday morning is the best time to shop. From now on, that's when I'll go.

# QUICK CHECKLIST FOR PARAGRAPHS

- Is there a topic sentence?

- Does the topic sentence state the subject of the paragraph?

- Does the topic sentence go on to explain the idea *about* the subject that will be discussed in the body of the paragraph?

- Does the paragraph explain the topic sentence without accidentally going on to another idea?

- Is the topic sentence fully explained?

- Is the language specific and concrete?

# COMPOSITION NOTE 4: THE ESSAY

The essay—or paper—is the most common type of writing that students are asked to produce. This composition note provides some guidelines for planning and structuring essays.

In simplest terms, an essay is a series of paragraphs that develops, explains, or supports one central idea. When you are asked to write an essay, you are expected to demonstrate several things, including the following:

1.  the ability to see beyond facts to ideas;

2.  the ability to see the relationships among ideas;

3.  the ability to communicate facts and ideas in writing in such a way that they are clear to the reader; and

4.  the ability to write without grammatical error.

Thus it is possible to write an essay that is clear and error-free and still receive an unsatisfactory grade. This happens when a writer concentrates on details, form, and grammar, but not on ideas. So writing essays requires more than just reporting—it requires thinking.

## The Thesis Statement

The central idea to be developed by the essay is stated in the thesis or thesis statement. The thesis statement generally appears in the introduction to the essay and is often the last sentence of the introductory paragraph.

The characteristics of a thesis statement are quite similar to the characteristics of a topic sentence for a paragraph (see Composition Note 3). That is, a thesis states not only the subject but also the idea about the subject that the essay will develop. An important difference from a topic sentence is that a thesis is a broader or more complicated idea. The topic sentence controls only one paragraph; the thesis controls the entire essay, and so it must be a ''bigger'' idea. As with the topic sentence for a paragraph, however, the thesis cannot promise more than can be discussed in the essay. If you were asked to write a five hundred word essay on something related to education, the thesis ''Education is important in the modern world'' promises more than two typed pages can cover in any detailed or interesting way.

## EXERCISE 1: THESIS STATEMENTS _____

Here are 10 possible thesis statements for papers of two or three pages. Consider them in the following ways:

1.  Identify the subject of each thesis and then the idea about the subject that the statement contains.

2.  Decide whether each statement is unacceptable, in need of revision, or acceptable.

3.  For those in need of revision, write improved versions or explain how they should be revised.

> a.  The Mercedes is a better car than the BMW.
>
> b.  Wars are more often caused by economic issues than by political ones.
>
> c.  Drug use is increasing.
>
> d.  Space technology has had some unexpected effects on daily life.
>
> e.  This paper is going to discuss teenage pregnancy.
>
> f.  The recent alarming increase in teenage pregnancy has three main causes.
>
> g.  Being a father is not easy.
>
> h.  Many recent novels have been made into movies.
>
> i.  U.S. policy toward Central American countries is confusing and inconsistent.
>
> j.  The psychological effects of the nuclear accident at Chernobyl are more serious than the medical effects.

### The Five-Paragraph Essay and a Warning About It

A common but nevertheless useful method of planning an essay is the five-paragraph structure. It is almost always appropriate and can be of particular help in two situations: (1) bringing order when you have a great many details to organize and (2) assisting in getting more ideas when you have trouble in thinking of what to write. The warning about the five-paragraph essay—discussed in more detail later—is that if you follow this structure too closely or never use any other, your essays are likely to sound too mechanical and stiff.

This is the way the five-paragraph structure works: you decide in advance that your essay will have five paragraphs. (That's the obvious and easy part.) One paragraph will be the introduction; one will be the ending. This leaves three paragraphs to do the main work of the essay—explaining the thesis statement. Remember that a paragraph develops only one idea. This means that you are going to organize your material around three central points. That is, you're going to use three major blocks or divisions as you develop the thesis. Three parts seem to be a manageable number for many topics. If there are many more, especially in a short paper, the essay may seem fragmented—lots of parts without clear connections. And of course one long paragraph with everything crowded into it may also seem disorganized—as if the writer can report only details and can't see ideas or separate one issue from another. But a topic that clearly and definitely has two parts or four parts should not be forced into a three-part structure for the sake of following "the rules." This situation can be illustrated in diagram form:

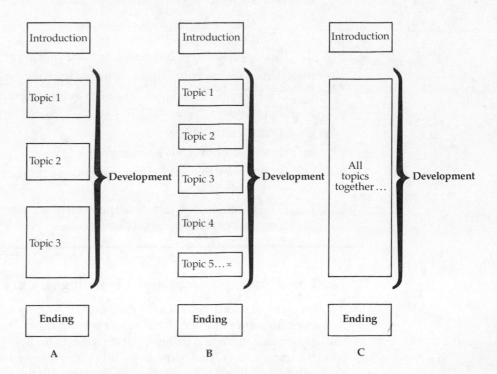

A. a balanced, five-paragraph essay (two or three typed pages)
B. a fragmented, disconnected multiparagraph essay
C. a breathless, crowded, probably disorganized, all-in-one essay

Suppose you had been assigned to write a five hundred word essay on a simple topic such as a vacation trip. You decide to write about the time you went to Disneyland with your nine-year-old nephew. Ideas and memories come crowding into your head. You need to organize those ideas under three main headings—one for each of the three middle paragraphs. The first idea you get is to devote one paragraph each to the three most interesting parts of Disneyland—Safariland, Pioneerland, and Main Street, for example. Your thesis might be that these were your favorite places in Disneyland. That would give you a paper with a clear central idea and logical organization. And the paper would primarily describe what you saw and found interesting. But the paper would also contain very little in the way of "idea." You decide a paper like this would be too simple. A bit boring.

So you try another approach. It occurs to you that both you and your nephew enjoyed Disneyland, but perhaps for different reasons. He enjoyed the rides, the excitement, and Mickey Mouse. You enjoyed the technological wizardry, the design of the park, and (secretly) the scary rides as well. A paper based on the idea of Disneyland's appeal to children as well as to adults has more substance than the "three most interesting parts," so you decide to use this idea.

**Tentative thesis:** Disneyland appeals to children and adults, but not always for the same reasons.

**Idea for paragraph 2:** what children enjoy

**Idea for paragraph 3:** what adults enjoy

**Idea for paragraph 4:** what they enjoy together

**Idea for ending:** None yet, but one will come

This plan, depending on how it is developed and written, could produce a satisfactory paper.

An important idea to remember, however, is that not every essay must follow this structure. Some essays have more than five paragraphs or fewer than five because the subject lends itself to a different structure. If an idea can be developed well in four paragraphs, there is no reason to invent an idea for a fifth paragraph. The result would sound strained and artificial.

## The Warning: An Unsatisfactory Five-Paragraph Essay

Here is an example of the Disneyland paper that conforms closely to the principles of organization of the five-paragraph essay. It contains no grammatical errors. Nevertheless, most instructors would find it unacceptable. See if you can determine why.

## Kids, Adults, and Disneyland

My brother and his family visited us from Kansas, so I took my nephew to Disneyland. He had been asking to go there for a long time. We had a good time. <u>Disneyland appeals to children and adults, but not always for the same reasons.</u> (thesis)

<u>My nephew enjoyed the rides, the Disney characters, and the excitement.</u> (topic sentence) He liked the medium scary rides best. The roller coaster and rides where monsters jump out at you didn't appeal much to him. He thought he was too old to love Mickey Mouse, but I could see he was thrilled when they shook hands. It was a dream come true.

<u>I liked the technology and the clear way the park was laid out.</u> (topic sentence) As far as I was concerned, the animals in the Louisiana swamp were real. And even though there were a lot of people, everybody could get from one place to another pretty easily. And I wasn't too old for the scary rides at all.

<u>Children and adults can enjoy the sights, the sunshine, and being together in a friendly way.</u> (topic sentence) We kept saying, ''Look at that!'' and ''Look at this!'' The weather was fine, as usual, and we didn't argue or disagree once the whole day.

All in all, it was a really good day. We plan to go back again next year.

Several things are handled correctly in this essay: there is a clear thesis sentence; each paragraph has a topic sentence that covers one part of the thesis; each paragraph discusses only its own topic without getting sidetracked; there is a final paragraph that gives a sense of ending and closure; there are no grammatical errors.

But several important aspects of writing essays are not handled at all well. First of all, the writer did not determine clearly whether the essay was about Disneyland itself or a particular trip there. The essay moves back and forth between Disneyland's appeal to adults and children in general and the author's trip with his nephew.

The main fault is that none of the ideas are well developed. Not enough is said and there are too few specific details. What, for example, is the nephew's name? What lifelike animals were in the swamp? How did it feel as an adult to be on a ''scary ride''? And we get almost no sense of the writer as a person. The idea of closeness with his nephew is an appealing, tender idea, but we get only a hint of it—along with the possibility that the two often argue, for the paper suggests that it was somehow surprising that they didn't argue once.

The skeleton (structure, thesis, paragraph design) is in relatively good shape, but there is not enough flesh and muscle (details, explanation, analysis). The bones stick out. The essay gives the impression that the writer's attitude was something like this: OK, you asked for a five-paragraph essay with a thesis and topic sentences. Here it is. Just barely. But complying with "the rules" of structure isn't enough. The essay still needs to be well developed and interesting and to give the sense of having been written by a human being, not a machine.

Another aspect of this essay that needs attention is transitions. The thesis sentence comes too abruptly. The introduction needs to move smoothly from the opening comments to the thesis statement. And one paragraph needs to follow another more smoothly as well, by the addition of transitional words or phrases (see Composition Note 2).

This essay might be an acceptable first draft, but it needs considerable revision before it can be considered complete. The following sections consider the various parts of the essay in more detail.

## The Introductory Paragraph

The introduction to an essay must accomplish several things:

1.  inform the reader of the general subject;
2.  announce the specific idea that is going to be explained or proved; and
3.  establish the tone of the rest of the paper—serious, lighthearted, satirical.

In addition, since it is the beginning of the essay, the writer is establishing a relationship with the reader. If the introduction is confusing, boring, or apologetic, the reader will not have much confidence or interest in what follows. Even if the rest of the paper is quite good, the reader will have begun with negative expectations that will have to be overcome. So it is a good idea not to sound apologetic in the introduction. For example, beginning with the following sentence will cause many readers to sigh and wonder why they should continue reading:

> I don't know a lot about education, but it seems to me that . . . .

If you don't know much about your subject, write about something else. If you have no choice and must write about that subject, don't announce your anxieties.

It's also not a good idea to begin with statements that are too broad or are used by too many other writers. The effect is to bore the reader or create the impression that you have nothing original to say. Openings such as these usually create negative reactions:

> All children need to be educated. (Reader's reaction: So, what else is new?)
>
> Webster's defines education as: 1. . . . (Reader's reaction, especially from English teachers: Not another dictionary definition!)

No one can deny the importance of an education. (Reader's reaction: You should talk to my Uncle Hubert.)

Parents have always been interested in their children's education. (Reader's reaction: Why are you telling me something everyone knows? Am I stupid?)

It is generally a good idea to begin an essay fairly close to the idea in your thesis. If the paper will argue that children should begin their schooling at the age of three, you might begin like this:

> In Nevada, children are required by law to attend school when they reach the age of six, but recent studies by child development specialists suggest that children could profit from earlier education. By waiting until age six, children lose valuable time. In fact, according to the specialists, they lose three years of valuable time.

This introduction avoids the common pitfalls, but there is still something important missing: a thesis statement. Read it again asking yourself if you know exactly what point the author is planning to make in the paper. You may assume that the paper is going to argue for an earlier beginning, but you cannot be sure. The reader, however, should be sure of what the main point is. It's confusing to read a discussion or an argument if you don't know what the point of it all is. Look at the following introduction:

> In Nevada, children are required by law to attend school when they reach the age of six, but recent studies by child development specialists suggest that children could profit from earlier education. By waiting until age six, children lose valuable time. In fact, according to the specialists, they lose three years of valuable time. Public schools should accept children at the age of three and should require attendance at the age of four.

With the addition of a clear thesis, the purpose of the essay becomes apparent. But look at the following version of the same introduction:

> In Nevada, children are required by law to attend school when they reach the age of six, but recent studies by child development specialists suggest that children could profit from earlier education. By waiting until age six, the specialists argue, children lose valuable time—three years, in fact. But while children may profit intellectually from earlier schooling, they are not emotionally ready for school at the age of three. Instead of sending their three-year-old children to school, parents should begin to teach them to read at home.

This introduction begins in the same way as the earlier version, but it changes direction in the middle and finishes with a different thesis. The point is that unless the central idea is clearly stated, a reader can make an incorrect assumption or be left confused. The writer's main task is to say what he or she means, not to leave it to the reader to figure out what is meant.

Here are several general patterns for introductions that can be useful so long as they are not followed too mechanically:

1. Open with an idea that contrasts with the thesis.

    Most students look forward to writing with about as much pleasure as they look forward to paying for major car repairs. A writing assignment will be postponed for as long as possible with excuses such as ''the garage needs cleaning'' or ''Uncle Adolphus doesn't come for a visit very often.'' But teachers in schools with computer writing labs are finding a great deal of enthusiasm in their students. The novelty and flexibility of the computer can break students' fear of writing.

2. Open with an anecdote.

    For the last month, Kelly Jones, a blue-eyed nine-year-old with bewitching dimples, has been arriving at school before the janitor unlocks the door. She waits impatiently on the steps, alternately peering through the window and thumbing through her notebook. She is waiting for a chance to use a school computer to finish writing a story about an orphan duck her family adopted. Her eagerness is an example of how the novelty and flexibility of the computer can break students' fear of writing.

3. Open by anticipating the reader's objections.

    The usual arguments against sending children to elementary school before the age of six have to do with their immaturity. First, opponents claim, children are too socially immature. They cannot be confined at desks and obey classroom rules long enough to stay in school for several hours a day. Second, they are intellectually immature and cannot learn enough to make an early start worthwhile. But recent research and the experience in several pioneering schools cast serious doubt on these long-held beliefs. With careful regard for their abilities, most children can profit enormously from school by the age of four.

# EXERCISE 2: EVALUATING INTRODUCTIONS___

Here are several introductory paragraphs for you to evaluate. Consider such things as these: are the subject and purpose clear? is the introduction likely to interest a general audience? does one idea lead smoothly to the next?

a.   Not many people in this country have heard of the jojoba plant, fewer people care about it, and almost no one pronounces its name correctly (ho-ho´ -ba). Nevertheless, the oil from this plant has important health and cosmetic uses and, more significantly, it could reduce our reliance on petrochemical lubricants.

b.   In these modern times, people are breaking traditions, but not all traditions are bad. More women and members of minority groups are running for high political offices, some elementary schools are open in the summer, and some men now stay home to take care of the house and raise the children. There is nothing wrong with that. And some traditions that seemed dead have come back, like the high-school prom. Traditions can be a lot of fun.

c.   Yesterday I saw a little two-year-old boy sitting on the sidewalk in front of Harwood's department store. He was screaming. His face was almost purple, and he was pounding on the ground with his heels and his palms. It was a good old-fashioned temper tantrum. His mother was standing nearby, looking at him sympathetically but not doing or saying anything. Several old ladies were watching with disapproval written all over their faces. Child-rearing practices have changed a lot in the last 50 years.

# EXERCISE 3: PLANNING INTRODUCTIONS___

With one or two other students, plan (but do not write) several different introductions for each of the following thesis statements:

a.   The breakup of AT&T has resulted in worse telephone service for most people.

b.   Birth control information should be provided by all public high schools.

c.   A dog or cat can be a companion and stimulus to an old person in a retirement home.

d.   The degree of violence in children's cartoons should be severely restricted.

## Paragraphs in the Middle of the Essay

The paragraphs between the introduction and the end discuss in detail the various parts of the thesis sentence. If the thesis sentence has been well constructed, the order and subjects of the middle paragraphs should be fairly obvious.

For example, in planning a paper to support the argument that children should be allowed to go to school at age three and required to do so by age four, these subjects could be discussed:

—the research showing that children can learn school subjects by the time they are three;

—a discussion of the negative effects of not educating children when they are ready; and

—a discussion of changes in the school system that could be made in order to accept large numbers of young children.

The first topic, the research, must be discussed in order to present a convincing argument. Merely mentioning it in the introduction to the essay isn't enough. Few readers will accept the truth of an argument summarized in a single sentence. The second topic, negative effects of waiting until a child reaches age six, is needed to show why any change is needed. Before most people will agree to a change, they have to know clearly what is unsatisfactory about the present situation. The third topic, how the schools could accommodate the new students, is needed to show that it's possible to do what the thesis argues for. If it is a good idea, but it can't be done—because it's too expensive or because parents couldn't be convinced to send such young children to school—then the paper is unconvincing.

If this were to be a short paper, then one paragraph could be devoted to each of the three topics. If it were a longer paper, each topic might need several paragraphs of development.

Notice also that one paragraph follows another in a logical order. Discussing the topic of changes the schools could make before discussing *why* the schools should make changes would result in a confusing essay. A general principle is either to follow the logic of the argument, or, if the paper isn't arguing for something, to present the different aspects of the thesis, with the most interesting or complex or important idea last. Why? Because if the "best" comes first, all that follows will seem less important, and the essay will appear to fade away, becoming less convincing.

Suppose, for example, that you were assigned to describe a very pleasant place that you remember from childhood. You decide to describe an abandoned farmhouse where you used to go to read and dream. You decide to have one paragraph on each of these aspects of the farmhouse:

—your special reading place on the vine-covered upstairs porch

—the quiet, undisturbed atmosphere

—a general description of the building and the yard

The first item—the upstairs porch where no one could see you because of the shadows and the ivy—is the one that is most important to you, so you will describe it in the greatest detail. But putting it first under those circumstances will make the following two paragraphs seem less interesting. And it will be difficult for a reader to imagine the porch clearly without first having a picture of the house and yard already in mind.

---

# EXERCISE 4: EVALUATING ESSAY STRUCTURE

Here are two thesis statements and rough outlines of how each might be developed. Each outline has some strengths and also some weaknesses. Determine what the strengths and weaknesses are and how the outlines might be improved.

**Thesis #1:** At noon, the campus cafeteria is a chaotic, unpleasant place.

**Ideas for introduction:** compare peace and quiet of late afternoon with crowds at lunch—use "but" as transition.

**Topic Sentence #1:** The cafeteria was designed to serve a college with only half as many students as it now has.

- built for 5000 students
- now has 10,000 students
- city grew a lot recently
- administration will not approve $$ for expansion
- but just built new offices for deans

**Topic Sentence #2:** At noon, there is no orderly way to get from place to place in the cafeteria.

- no lines, just crowds, at hot food counter, sandwich counter, salad bar, etc.
- lines for cashiers get tangled—arguments
- people waiting for soup wind up at hamburger counter
- silverware in one place, napkins and straws in another

**Ideas for concluding paragraph:** administration should build new cafeteria—students need a place to relax and study in quiet

**Thesis #2:** An hour in a supermarket can reveal a great deal about the economic and social characteristics of the neighborhood.

**Ideas for introduction:** I used to think all supermarkets pretty much the same. Went to one in Chesterton. Learned otherwise.

**Topic Sentence #1:** Chesterton is a poor, isolated, and ethnically diverse neighborhood.

- many recent immigrants
- no other large market in the area
- people don't have cars; can't drive to better store
- many old people on pensions living in rooming houses

**Topic Sentence #2:** The selection of meat shows the low economic status of the shoppers.

- no thick Porterhouse steaks
- lots of packages of chicken backs—cheap
- mostly small portions
- a lot of cuts I never saw before

**Topic Sentence #3:** The market takes advantage of the fact that people have no other place to shop.

- vegetables aren't fresh
- cost more than in my neighborhood
- unfriendly—shouting at man who couldn't understand his bill was $19.72 not $9.72.

**Topic Sentence #4:** The variety of specialty items reveals the diversity of shoppers.

- giant bags of rice
- many kinds of chili peppers
- unfamiliar vegetables—bok choi, jicama
- sauces from Vietnam, Philippines, Korea, Mexico

**Ideas for concluding paragraph:** Good to have what people want—unfair to charge more and be unpleasant.

# EXERCISE 5: PLANNING ESSAY STRUCTURE ———

With one or two other students, use each of the following thesis statements to outline how you would structure an essay of at least three paragraphs. Decide what the content of each of the middle paragraphs should be and how you might begin and end.

**a.** Living at home and living in a college dormitory both have advantages, but dormitory living is more beneficial for most students.

**b.** American television promotes violence and greed and should be totally reformed.

**c.** Overprotective parents don't help their children to become successful adults.

**d.** American schools should encourage cooperation, not competition, among students.

## The Ending Paragraph

Notice that this section is called "the ending paragraph" and not "the conclusion." The conclusion is the section in which you draw together the pieces of your argument and make your point in the most convincing way. The ending paragraph signals to your reader that the end has come. Without this signal, the conclusion would be too abrupt, as if an instructor suddenly closed his or her notes and walked out of the class without saying, "That's all for today" or "See you on Monday."

Referring to the thesis or something else in the introduction can give a sense of closure or completeness. But if the entire thesis is repeated, the effect can be somewhat awkward. For example, as a final comment the following sounds to most people rather abrupt and awkward and a little pompous:

> Thus I have proved that public schools should accept children at the age of three and should require attendance at the age of four.

Something like the following is more satisfactory because it is smoother and less abrupt:

> Initially, the idea of three-year-olds climbing on a school bus each morning and going off to solve math problems sounds a bit heartless. But they appear to love it, and the argument against wasted ability is a strong one. Sending a child off to summer camp or to spend a night at a friend's house for the first time is difficult, too. But parents are adaptable, especially when there is promise of benefits for their children.

Restating the thesis, but in different words, is one useful pattern for an ending paragraph. Here are several others:

1.  a final anecdote

    Kelly Jones's orphan duck story was thrown away two days after she finished it. Her little brother spilled orange juice on it, and the paper disintegrated before anyone noticed. The paper may be gone, but Kelly's pleasure in writing it will remain with her. Long after she has forgotten the duck and her story, Kelly will feel confident about her ability to write, thanks to a computer and a progressive—and wealthy—school system.

2.  a final question

    Aristotle was, of course, wrong when he said, ''The seat of the soul and the control of voluntary movement—in fact, of nervous functions in general—are to be sought in the heart. The brain is an organ of minor importance.'' But in its insistence on the rational, thinking aspects of life, modern science has ignored the heart—the feelings, emotions, intuitions, and moral sense—to the detriment of human life.

3.  an ending that calls for action or a solution to a problem

    Sooner or later we will have to do something about the growing number of teenage pregnancies. Until we decide whose responsibility it is and what should be done, high schools should be permitted to provide at least some instruction about contraception.

## EXERCISE 6: ENDING PARAGRAPHS

Look back at the thesis statements in the preceding exercise. With one or two other students, outline various types of concluding paragraphs for a paper written on each topic.

# COMPOSITION NOTE 5: REWRITING

When is an essay finished? That's an odd question. It's finished when it's finished. But some beginning writers finish too soon. They leave out the vital last steps of editing and proofreading. When they write the last sentence, they heave a sigh of relief and quit. They may write or type a presentable copy to hand in, but if it's an exact copy of the first draft, they've still left out an important step.

Why revise? The truth is that the first draft is almost always full of rough spots, no matter how much care and attention went into it. It's almost impossible—even for experienced professional writers—to concentrate on *what* to write and *how* to write it at the same time and be satisfied with the result. Things get left out. Unrelated ideas sneak in. A relationship that was clear in your mind isn't so clear on paper.

Fortunately, most people find revision an easier task than writing the first draft. The anxiety of thinking of what to say is over. Now the task is to improve something that already exists.

In general, revision involves making the first draft better: clearer, more interesting, more coherent, more detailed, more polished. Correcting spelling, punctuation, and grammar are part of the process.

Revision also involves satisfying yourself—adding, crossing out, and changing to make your words better reflect your meaning. That is a rather private, personal process. Also, as a writer you need to meet the expectations of your audience; in a practical sense, this is usually the person teaching your class. But in a broader sense, you are also learning to meet the expectations of all those who have ideas about how a college-educated person should write. And for that, there are some relatively agreed-upon standards. A problem, though, is that it is more difficult to evaluate (and then revise) your own writing than to evaluate someone else's. Since you know what you meant to communicate, that knowledge can keep you from seeing that what you've written may not be clear to someone else. So, what can you do?

## Let It Cool

One of the best things you can do is let some time pass between finishing the first draft and beginning to revise it. A few hours will help; overnight is better; a day or two is better still. What happens in this "cooling" period is that you become more distant, more objective, less involved in the initial struggle with blank sheets of paper that need to be filled. You can see better what needs to be changed.

## Let Your Ears Help

Another thing you can do as you begin to revise is to read your paper aloud to yourself—something that feels quite strange to most people at first. Hearing your sentences and paragraphs often alerts you to awkward spots or omissions that you can mark to work on later. If a sentence is difficult for you to read aloud, it is almost sure to be difficult for your reader to understand, too.

## Let Someone Else Read It

Giving your draft to someone else to read can also be helpful. But there are two things to be careful of: first, don't give it to someone who is too kind. You'll get compliments, but no real help. And don't give it to someone who is very fond of you. Your favorite aunt may be so proud that you're a college student that she will assume that anything you write will be wonderful, or at least too good for her to criticize.

Second, don't give your draft to someone to make all the corrections and changes for you. You don't learn much that way, and many people call that cheating.

## A Plan for Revision

It's best to divide your revision process into several steps so you can concentrate fully on one thing at a time. The following sequence works well:

1.  examine the structure of the essay;
2.  examine the flow of sentences;
3.  check spelling, punctuation, and format; and
4.  check for any errors you habitually make.

**Examine the Structure.** First, reread the introduction and look for the following: Is there a thesis sentence? Does it cover everything in the essay? Is every part of the thesis discussed later in the paper? Is there a smooth transition between the first part of the introduction and the thesis sentence?

Then read each paragraph. Check to see that each one has a topic sentence or discusses only one aspect of the thesis. Is each paragraph developed enough? Is there enough explanation? Can you think of examples that could make the points clearer? If you have given your work time to cool, you will see omissions, too much explanation, or unrelated ideas more easily at this point.

**Examine the Flow of Sentences.** Reading aloud is a big help in this revision step. Look or listen for passages in which the sentences are short and choppy. Do some combining. Look for passages in which too many ideas are linked together with "and" and divide them into several sentences. Does every sentence begin with the subject? If so, move some adverb phrases or clauses to the beginning of some sentences.

**Check Spelling, Punctuation, and Format.** Once you are satisfied with the content and the sound of the essay, check the mechanics. Now is the time to use a dictionary and the grammar notes in the next chapter. Have you given the essay a title if one is required? Have you done everything the assignment asked you to do?

**Habitual Errors.** Do you know from experience that you tend to write sentence fragments or use too many commas? Were you told on your last two papers that you need to write more specific examples? Read over your work once more, looking only for these habitual weaknesses.

In general, accept the idea that a first draft almost never represents your best work. Expect to revise—perhaps even to the point of cutting out pieces of your rough draft and pasting them somewhere else. There's something very satisfying about a draft filled with arrows, crossouts, and additions. It usually represents good thinking.

# COMPOSITION NOTE 6: WRITING UNDER PRESSURE

One thing most students dislike intensely is writing under pressure. Whether it's an essay exam in a history class or an essay to pass a writing proficiency requirement, it can cause great anxiety. Nothing can make such writing a pleasant experience, but there are some ways to lessen pressure and avoid panic.

## Pay Attention to Your State of Mind

Aside from studying for the exam or practicing writing, there is one thing you can do to help yourself, starting a few days before the event: put yourself in the most positive frame of mind that you can achieve. Almost no one can be perfectly calm in the moments before the exam or essay instructions are handed out, but there is no point in exaggerating anxiety.

Begin the process of creating the best frame of mind by trying to hear what you say to yourself when you first start feeling anxious. You may hear things like, "You're not smart enough. You're going to fail." Or you may hear, "What if I do badly?" If you find that you are telling yourself negative things, answer yourself with positive messages: "I *am* smart enough. I'm not going to fail." If you ask yourself frightening questions, answer them positively, too: "If I fail, I'll feel awful, but it won't be the end of the world. Next time I'll work harder." Negative conversations can go on inside your head almost without your noticing. If you can begin to notice and combat such conversations, you can keep yourself in a more positive frame of mind and so increase your chances of doing well. Fear and anxiety use up energy that can be spent better in study or work.

## Practice

As part of your advance preparation, practice writing under pressure. If you know there will be a question about the causes of the French Revolution and you guess you will have 20 minutes to answer it, then write for 20 minutes about the causes of the French Revolution—without looking at your notes. Afterward, evaluate what you wrote. Did you have enough to say? If not, study your textbook and notes again. Did you have too much to say? Then decide what is most important and plan to write only about that. Pay attention to what gives you trouble and work on it before the exam. The act of practicing can greatly reduce the anxiety you feel as you begin the actual exam.

## Read the Instructions

The moment of greatest anxiety is the moment when you first see the test or the writing assignment. By allowing anxiety to take over at that point, many students make a mistake that can seriously affect the results: they don't read the instructions carefully enough. In their anxiety to begin work (and to get the whole thing over with), they get only a partial or confused idea of what they are being asked to do. Doing a good job of answering the wrong question is a real waste of effort.

So read the question several times, especially if you feel that the first reading didn't give you a clear picture of what you're being asked to do. If you're confused, read it again several times before you ask the instructor for clarification. Underline key phrases such as "compare and contrast" or "include in your answer." If you are still uncertain, ask, but give yourself a moment to calm down before you do. Why? Because if you are still nervous when you ask for clarification, you aren't going to understand the instructor's explanation very well, either.

## Plan Your Time

If there are three questions worth the same number of points and you have one hour, plan to spend 20 minutes on each question and try to stick to that plan. Writing one very long, very good answer and two short, incomplete answers will probably lower your grade. You're not being asked to say everything there is to say on the three subjects. You're being asked to write a 20-minute answer to each.

If there is one question to answer and you have one hour, set aside about seven minutes to plan and ten minutes at the end to reread and make changes, and then use the rest of the time to write. Don't plan to write a clean final draft unless you can write extraordinarily rapidly. When you have only one hour, it's a waste of valuable time to spend 15 or 20 minutes making a neat copy of a poorly written essay. Use as much time as possible for writing. What you need is a readable essay, even with crossed-out words and additions. No one expects a perfect manuscript to be produced in one hour. If you have a longer period of time, then perhaps recopying makes sense. Remember, however, that no one expects you to produce the equivalent of ten hours of work in one hour.

## Think First, Write Later

Another common error is to read the essay question and then begin answering it immediately. Writing without some sort of plan often results in a jumbled essay that sounds as if it just spilled out—as it did. If you are being asked to write an essay, as opposed to a list of facts, you're expected to remember and use essay structure. Rather than beginning to write at once, jot down key ideas—words or phrases—that you want to include in your answer. Put them down as they occur to you. Then number them or group them in some logical order that you will follow as you write. Don't waste time on full sentences at this point. You need only a rough plan, not a formal outline. Most people find it rather comforting to write from such a plan. A plan makes it possible to concentrate on the paragraph you are working on. You don't have to write and simultaneously worry about what you are going to write in the next paragraph.

## Use What You Know About Writing—even in a History Exam

If your writing-under-pressure experience is for an English class or writing proficiency exam, of course you need to pay attention to structure as well as content. The same is true in the history exam, but many students forget this. In most cases, two exams showing the same knowledge of the material will get different grades if one is well written and the other is not. So remember and use what you know about introductions and paragraph structure and commas.

Let a little psychology guide you, too. Your paper is not the only one that the instructor or the reader is going to grade. All the papers are going to be somewhat similar, and no matter how dedicated your instructor is, there comes a point when it becomes tiresome to read even one more essay on the assigned subject. What you need to do is take special pains with how you begin. If your introductory paragraph is clear and concise and thoughtful, then you have created an impression of confidence and mastery right at the outset—something to counterbalance the reader's boredom while reading 35 essays on the same topic. The beginning of each paragraph is also important, for the same reason. This is where you have to use what you know about thesis statements and topic sentences.

So avoid long-winded introductions that begin with ''Revolution is something all countries fear but cannot avoid.'' Begin closer to the topic, and use as your thesis a succinct answer to the whole question: ''The Peasant Revolution in Xanadu had economic and social causes, but the most important cause was the king's breaking of religious taboo.''

## If You Panic

Sometimes it happens that you look at an essay question, nothing comes to mind, and you begin to panic. Don't turn your paper in and leave—at least not right away. Take a little time to calm down and give yourself a mental pep talk. Then, on a sheet of scratch paper, begin to write. Begin anywhere. Begin with the conclusion. Begin in the middle of a paragraph. Begin with anything that comes to mind about the subject. Or write, ''I am in a panic and can't think of what to write, so I'm writing this in order to calm myself down.'' For many people, the act of writing something—even if it's nonsense—gets them back on track.

If nothing works and you just can't do it, it's usually better to tell your instructor what happened rather than just walk out. He or she may be able to help or may offer to let you try again at another time. But if you walk out without saying anything, it may appear that you just don't care or were totally unprepared, and no second chance will be offered.

# GRAMMAR
# NOTES

This chapter presents in alphabetical order discussions of various aspects of grammar that will be useful in working the exercises in this book. You may find Grammar Note 1 particularly helpful for quick reference to names and definitions of grammatical terms.

**8**

# GRAMMAR NOTE 1: ABRIDGED DEFINITIONS OF GRAMMATICAL TERMS

Terms marked with an asterisk (*) are discussed in detail in another grammar note in this chapter.

| Name | Definition | Examples |
|------|-----------|----------|
| *Parts of Speech* | | |
| noun | name of something or someone | bird, George, kindness, liberty, strength |
| pronoun | replaces a noun | I, she, mine, someone, those |
| adjective* | describes a noun or pronoun | green bird; true kindness; six feathers |
| action verb | expresses action | He walked. She thought. |
| linking verb | no action; joins subject and an adjective or noun that follows | Henry is short. Grace was an accountant. |
| helping verb | shows past, present, future time; is used with another verb | had walked, is thinking, will have been sleeping |
| adverb* | describes a verb, adjective, or adverb | walked slowly, studied well, ate yesterday |
| conjunction | joins words, phrases, clauses | ham and eggs, lost but happy, tea or coffee |
| preposition | shows relationships in time, space, or logic | in the morning, over the house, cup of coffee |
| interjection | shows emotion | Oh! Good grief! |
| *Verbals* | | |
| present participle* | verb ending with "ing" used as an adjective | a crying baby, jogging shoes |
| past participle* | verb ending with "ed" (sometimes ending with "t" or "en") | a baked potato, a broken arm |
| gerund* | verb ending with "ing" used as a noun | Flying is expensive. |
| infinitive* | "to" form of a verb used as a noun, adjective, or adverb | To sleep is to be at peace. I have things to do. He ran to save time. |
| *Parts of Sentences* | | |
| subject | what the sentence is about | The book on the table fell off during the earthquake. |
| verb or predicate | what is being said about the subject | The book on the table fell off during the earthquake. |
| direct object | receives the action of the verb | We caught fish. |
| indirect object | tells to or for whom an action occurred without using "to" or "for" | Henry wrote Alice a letter. |
| subjective complement | noun, pronoun, or adjective that follows a linking verb and renames or describes the subject | Mary is my sister. Mary is intelligent. He is the one. |
| appositive* | a noun following another noun and renaming it | Mrs. Greene, my piano teacher, drives a truck. |

| Name | Definition | Examples |
|---|---|---|
| *Phrases* | | |
| any phrase | a group of words without both a subject and a verb | See below. |
| prepositional phrase | a preposition with its object and any modifiers | in the cold morning; between the two major countries |
| participial phrase* | a participle with its object and any modifiers | We ate shrimp broiled in butter. Walking upstairs, he sneezed. |
| gerund phrase* | a gerund with its object and any modifiers | Eating fresh fruit is one of summer's pleasures. |
| infinitive phrase* | an infinitive with its object and any modifiers | He wanted to be a good father. |
| *Clauses* | | |
| any clause | a group of words with a subject and a verb | See below. |
| independent clause | a clause that can function as a complete sentence | He drinks beer. |
| dependent clause* | a clause that cannot function as a complete sentence; acts as an adverb, adjective, or noun in another clause | before the wind died; that had fallen off; whoever comes in first |
| adverb clause* | a clause that acts as an adverb | Before the wind died, a lot of damage occurred. |
| adjective clause* | a clause that acts as an adjective | The books that had fallen off the shelf hit John. |
| noun clause* | a clause that acts as a noun | Whoever comes in first should start dinner. |
| *Types of Sentences* | | |
| simple | one independent clause | He reads books at night. |
| compound* | two or more independent clauses | He plays the violin, and she plays chess. We bought eggs; however, they all broke. |
| complex* | includes at least one dependent clause | I saw him before he hid his face. |
| compound-complex | includes at least two independent clauses and one dependent clause | I saw him before he hid his face, but then he disappeared. |

# GRAMMAR NOTE 2: ADJECTIVES

An adjective describes or modifies—gives the qualities of—a noun or pronoun. For example, the following underlined words are adjectives:

a <u>white</u> cloud;
a <u>dangerous</u> woman;
the <u>largest</u> ones;
<u>sixteen</u> candles.

In a sentence, the two most common positions for adjectives are in front of the noun they describe and after a linking verb:

The <u>new</u> raincoat is hanging in the closet.
I want a <u>new</u> raincoat.
(adjective "new" in front of noun "raincoat")

The raincoat is <u>new</u>.
Your raincoat looks <u>new</u>.
(adjective "new" after linking verbs "is" and "looks")

Often a noun is modified by more than one adjective:

He brought home <u>six hungry</u> puppies.
The <u>small, hungry</u> puppies cried all night.
The puppies were <u>small and hungry</u>.

There will be more said later about the order and punctuation of multiple adjectives, but for the moment, notice in the examples above that adjectives in front of a noun are separated by commas ("small, hungry") or the adjectives come one after another without commas ("six hungry"), while adjectives after a linking verb are usually separated by "and" ("small and hungry"). Thus you will generally not see such sentences as either of these:

**Uncommon:** The small and lonely puppies cried all night.

**Incorrect:** The puppies were small, lonely.

Sometimes, however, you will see sentences such as these:

Her hands—wrinkled and twisted—lay quietly on the table.

Wrinkled, twisted, and quiet, her hands lay side by side on the table.

Here—for added emphasis—the adjectives have been moved from their ordinary position. This can be an effective placement of adjectives but should not be used too frequently; the usual positions are in front of the noun (without "and") or after a linking verb (with "and").

## The Order of Adjectives

A difficult problem for those learning English as a second language is the order of adjectives when there is more than one in front of a noun:

> a large, round, yellow moon.
> a yellow, round large moon.

Which order is correct, and how are the adjectives to be punctuated? Fortunately, it is rare to find more than two adjectives in front of a noun. But no matter how many adjectives there are, there is a certain order in which they should go—the positions are not completely interchangeable. The problem is that the rules for the order of adjectives are not completely fixed, and native speakers do not always agree on the correct order. The following chart provides a guide that will result in correct placement in the majority of cases.

## Order and Punctuation of Multiple Adjectives Preceding a Noun

| Order | Type of Adjective | Comma in Front? | Examples |
|---|---|---|---|
| 1 | opinion | no | wonderful |
| 2 | size | no | little<br>  big |
| 3 | shape | yes* | square<br>  narrow |
| 4 | general characteristics** | yes* | broken<br>  common<br>  long-haired |
| 5 | age | no | old |
| 6 | color*** | yes* | red |
| 7 | source or material | no | French<br>  cotton |
| 8 | noun as adjective | no | school (work)<br>  basement (apartment) |

*unless the adjective is the first in a series

**If there is more than one adjective from this category, the adjectives should be arranged in the order from most subjective to most objective: for example, "an attractive, sensitive, intelligent boy." If this principle does not apply, then any order may be used.

***If there are two adjectives denoting color, they must be separated by "and": "A red and white shirt"; "The shirt was red and white."

Adapted from Mary Jane Cook, *Trouble Spots of English Grammar* (New York: Harcourt Brace Jovanovich, 1983), pp. 38–40, and Marianne Celce-Murcia and Diane Larsen-Freeman, *The Grammar Book* (Rowley, Mass.: Newbury House, 1983), pp. 390–99.

Here are some phrases—using adjectives from the preceding chart—that illustrate the order and punctuation of multiple adjectives.

| Example | Explanation |
|---|---|
| a wonderful old idea | opinion before age; no comma in front of adjectives of age |
| a wonderful little toy | opinion before size; no comma in front of adjectives of size |
| a small, square face | size before shape; comma in front of adjectives of shape |
| a narrow, striped tie | shape before general characteristics; comma in front of general characteristics |
| a fine old song | opinion before age; no comma before adjectives of age |
| a red plastic comb | color before material; no comma before adjectives of material |
| a damp basement apartment | general characteristics before a noun used as an adjective; no comma before nouns used as adjectives |

# GRAMMAR NOTE 3: ADJECTIVE CLAUSES

The adjective clause is one type of dependent clause. (You may wish to read Grammar Note 7: Complex Sentences and Dependent Clauses before reading further.) As is true of all dependent clauses, an adjective clause has a subject and a verb, and it cannot stand alone as a complete sentence.

The adjective clause performs the same function that a single-word adjective (such as "red" or "large") does. That is, it describes a noun. It describes a noun by answering one of these questions: which one? what kind? how many?

In the following sentence, the adjective clause is underlined:

The man <u>who delivers my newspaper</u> is completely bald.

The independent clause is "The man is completely bald." The adjective clause answers the question, "Which man?" "Bald" (a single-word adjective) and "who delivers my newspaper" (an adjective clause) both describe "man."

"Who" belongs to a class of words called "relatives" or "relative pronouns." These words are frequently used to introduce adjective clauses. The most common relative pronouns are "who," "whom," "whose," and "which."

In sentence combining you will find examples such as this:

The tree was too heavy to carry.        The tree <u>that had fallen down</u> was
The tree had fallen down.              too heavy to carry.

Notice two things about this example. First, the adjective clause follows the noun it modifies.

**Incorrect:** The tree was too heavy to carry that had fallen down.

Second, in the adjective clause, "that" (meaning "tree") is the subject of the clause. Even though "that" follows "tree" and substitutes for "tree," it cannot be omitted.

**Incorrect:** The tree had fallen down was too heavy to carry.

The verb in the adjective clause needs its own subject. "Tree" cannot be the subject of the independent and the dependent clauses at the same time. This is sometimes a problem for students learning English as a second language.

More examples of adjective clauses:

| | |
|---|---|
| I bought some chocolate from a boy.<br>The boy had rung my doorbell. | I bought some chocolate from a boy <u>who had rung my doorbell</u>. |
| Elizabeth danced with a man.<br>She had never seen the man before. | Elizabeth danced with a man <u>whom she had never seen before</u>. |

"Whom" is the direct object in the adjective clause above, but it has been moved from the usual position—after the verb.

| | |
|---|---|
| The man was not there.<br>The man's name was called. | The man <u>whose name was called</u> was not there. |
| They found the child.<br>They had been looking for the child. | They found the child <u>for whom they had been looking</u>. |
| I finally bought the chair.<br>I wanted the chair. | I finally bought the chair <u>that I wanted</u>. |

This sentence could also be written without "that":

I finally bought the chair <u>I wanted</u>.

The relative pronoun may be omitted if the subject of the adjective clause is different from the noun that the clause modifies. But in formal writing, "that" should be included.

## Restrictive and Nonrestrictive Clauses

Some adjective clauses must be separated from the rest of the sentence by commas; some are not separated.

Bobby lost the toy <u>that he liked best</u>.
Bobby lost his brown bear, <u>which was his favorite toy</u>.

Try to sense the difference in sentence structures before reading further.

In the first sentence, we do not know which toy Bobby lost until we read the adjective clause. The adjective clause defines or identifies the toy being discussed. An adjective clause that *identifies* the noun it modifies is called *restrictive*. No comma is used. A clause that provides additional information about a noun that has already been identified (his brown bear) is called *nonrestrictive* and is separated from the rest of the sentence by commas.

The brown bear, which was his favorite toy, had been packed in a suitcase.
The toy that he liked most had been packed in a suitcase.

**Usage Note:** ''Which'' should be used only in nonrestrictive clauses. You
will see it used in restrictive clauses, but it's better not to use it when you are
writing careful, formal prose.

Some adjective clauses begin with words that can also introduce adverb clauses, words such as ''when,'' ''where,'' ''why,'' ''after,'' and ''before.''

She always remembered the day when she first saw him. (which day?)
She also remembers the place where they parted. (which place?)
He forgot the reason why he went into the kitchen. (which reason?)
The moments after the car skidded were terrifying. (which moments?)
The hour before he took the test was painful. (which hour?)

### Words Commonly Used to Introduce Adjective Clauses

| | |
|---|---|
| that (for things) | when |
| who (for people) | where |
| whom | why |
| whose | after |
| which | before |

# GRAMMAR NOTE 4: ADVERBS

Adverbs can be defined rather simply. They describe or modify verbs, adjectives, or other adverbs. The following sentences illustrate these uses:

He read <u>carefully</u>.
The sky was <u>brilliantly</u> blue.
He read <u>very</u> carefully.

A complete description, however, of the various meanings, special uses, and positions of adverbs would be amazingly long and complex. This grammar note focuses on some general issues and on some common difficulties of adverb use, especially difficulties for students learning English as a second language.

## Types of Adverbs

Adverbs and adverb phrases can be classified according to the kinds of information they supply:

1.    manner (how?)—slowly, carefully, well, tenderly, in a hurry
2.    place (where?)—here, there, down, at work
3.    time (when?)—later, now, then, in the morning
4.    frequency (how often?)—sometimes, never, always, from time to time
5.    degree (how much?)—very, rather, quite, too, with all my heart

## Adverbs with Special Meanings

Many adverbs of manner are formed by adding ''ly'' to an adjective: a slow dance (adjective), walked slowly (adverb). And some words can be used as adjectives or adverbs: high, deep, hard. These words do have an ''ly'' form, but the meaning can be quite different from the adjective form and also different from the adverb without ''ly.''

He had a high fever. (adjective)
The bird flew high. (adverb)
They think highly of him. (They have a good opinion.)

The low clouds were gray. (adjective)
The bird flew low. (adverb)
He took a lowly job. (The job was a humble one.)

He arrived at a late hour.
He slept late.
I haven't seen him lately. (recently)

It was a hard test.
I studied hard.
He hardly ever studied. (almost never)
I can hardly hear you. (only with difficulty)

She put on a warm sweater.
They dressed warmly.
She greeted him warmly. (in a friendly way)

The day was cold.
She greeted him coldly. (in an unfriendly way)

Adverbs can be correctly used in many positions in a sentence. There are, however, some rules.

## The Position of Adverbs of Manner

Adverbs of manner (how?) are usually placed as follows:

1. after the verb

   He ate quickly.
   He ate in a hurry.

2. after a short direct object

   He ate his dinner quickly.
   He ate his dinner in a hurry.

3. before or after the verb or at the beginning of the sentence *if there is a long direct object*

   He quickly ate the dinner that had been prepared for him. ("He ate the dinner that had been prepared for him quickly" would be confusing. Does "quickly" modify "prepared" or "ate"?)

   He studied with great care the map he had found in the well.

   With great care, he studied the map he had found in the well.

4a. before the prepositional phrase (if a prepositional phrase follows the verb)

   He looked quickly at the painting.

4b. after the prepositional phrase (if a prepositional phrase follows the verb)

   He looked at the painting quickly.

4c. before the preposition (if the prepositional phrase is long)

   He looked carefully at the painting that had been hung in the living room.

## The Position of Adverbs of Place

Adverbs of place (where?) are usually in the following positions:

1.    after the verb

They eat here.
They eat in the kitchen.

2.    after the direct object

They ate cheese there.
They drank wine in the bar.

3.    at the beginning of the sentence

In France, they loved the wine and cheese.

## The Position of Adverbs of Time

Adverbs of time (when?) may be found in the following positions:

1.    at the beginning of the sentence

Yesterday he jogged and swam.
In the afternoon, he took a long nap.

2.    at the end of the sentence

He jogged and swam yesterday.
He took a long nap in the afternoon.

3.    near the verb, for adverbs such as ''still,'' ''just,'' and ''yet''

Even though it is noon, he is still sleeping.
He is not here; he just left.
She hasn't yet met the man she is going to marry.

## The Position of Adverbs of Frequency

Adverbs of frequency (how often?) usually appear in the following positions:

1.    after the present or past tense of the verb ''to be''

He is always cheerful.
(But notice the position of *phrases:* He is cheerful once in a while. Once in a while, he is cheerful.)
They were occasionally wrong.
(They were wrong on several occasions. On several occasions, they were wrong.)

2.    before the present or past tense of other verbs or at the beginning of the sentence

He usually calls her sweet names.
They frequently walked together.
Usually he wins.
From time to time, she won.

3.   after the first helping verb
They had always been friendly.

4.   at the beginning or end of the sentence
Occasionally they had a terrible fight.
He swam in the ocean once.

Some adverbs of frequency (hardly, seldom, never, rarely) may appear at the beginning of the sentence, but then the subject and verb are inverted:

Seldom had they eaten such a fine meal.
Rarely was she able to leave before 6 o'clock.
Only when the children came home did he relax and sleep.
Not until she smiled did he recognize her.

## The Position of Several Adverbs in One Sentence

When two or more different kinds of adverbs occur in the same sentence, several arrangements are possible.

1.   adverbs of time and manner
   a.   If the adverb of time is at the end of the sentence, the adverb of manner comes before it:
   She ate lightly in the morning.
   b.   If the adverb of time is at the beginning of the sentence, the adverb of manner comes after the verb (if there is no object) or after the direct object:
   Tomorrow she will dance energetically.
   Yesterday she watered the plants carefully.
   In the evening, she relaxed without interruption.

2.   adverbs of manner and place
   a.   Generally, adverbs of manner appear before adverbs of place:
   She put his drink carefully on the table.

3.   adverbs of manner, place, and time
   a.   Adverbs of time go at the beginning or end of the sentence, and adverbs of manner go before adverbs of place:
   At six, she put his drink carefully on the table
   She put his drink carefully on the table last night.

# GRAMMAR NOTE 5: ADVERB CLAUSES

An adverb clause is one of the types of dependent clauses. (You may wish to read Grammar Note 7: Complex Sentences and Dependent Clauses before reading further.) An adverb clause modifies or describes a verb in an independent clause. That is, the entire clause functions in the same way that a single-word adverb does. Adverbs answer one of these questions: when? where? how? why? under what conditions?

Here are some examples:

He ran <u>when he heard the bell</u>. (the clause tells when he ran)
Sheila smiled at George <u>because she was friendly</u>. (the clause tells why she smiled)
<u>Although the food tasted awful</u>, he ate it all. (the clause tells under what conditions he ate)

## Subordinating Conjunctions

The word at the beginning of an adverb clause is called a subordinating conjunction. In most cases, when the subordinating conjunction is removed, an independent clause remains. Thus, the addition of a subordinating conjunction changes the clause from an independent one to a dependent one. The common subordinating conjunctions are these:

| | |
|---|---|
| after | even if* |
| although | even though* |
| as | if |
| as if | since |
| as soon as | when(ever) |
| as though | unless |
| because | where(ever) |
| before | while |

*notice that "even" is not on the list

Each subordinating conjunction expresses a different kind of relationship between the two clauses. Pay attention to these relationships because you need to choose the correct subordinating conjunction.

In sentence combining, you will see examples like the following:

Sally left early.                } Sally left early <u>because the party</u>
The party was boring.         }      <u>was boring</u>.

Sally left early.                } Sally left early <u>although the party</u>
The party was interesting.   }      <u>was interesting</u>.

| | |
|---|---|
| Sally left early.<br>The party was interesting. } | Sally left early <u>even though the party was interesting</u>. |
| The children ran home.<br>They had broken a window. } | The children ran home <u>after they had broken a window</u>. |
| George washed the dishes.<br>Sylvia was taking a nap. } | <u>While Sylvia was taking a nap</u>, George washed the dishes. |
| You want your paycheck.<br>You must work. } | <u>If you want your paycheck</u>, you must work. |
| His boss sends him.<br>He will go [there]. } | He will go <u>where(ever) his boss sends him</u>. |
| She studied.<br>Her life depended on it. } | She studied <u>as if her life depended on it</u>. |
| You will get no dessert.<br>You eat your vegetables. } | <u>Unless you eat your vegetables</u>, you will get no dessert. |
| You may not have dessert.<br>You eat your vegetables. } | You may not have dessert <u>until you eat your vegetables</u>. |

## Punctuating Adverb Clauses

If the adverb clause comes first, it is followed by a comma. If the adverb clause comes last, no comma is used in front of it. If the adverb clause comes in the middle of the sentence, it is enclosed in commas.

<u>Because he was rich</u>, he didn't worry about money.
He didn't worry about money <u>because he was rich</u>.
Nat Brenner, <u>although he was very rich</u>, hated to spend money.

# GRAMMAR NOTE 6: APPOSITIVES ▪▪▪▪▪▪▪

In the simplest terms, an appositive renames something already mentioned in the sentence.

Henry, <u>the butcher</u>, has tired feet.

Here, "the butcher" is the appositive. It renames Henry. It is another way of identifying Henry.

More completely, an appositive is a noun, a noun phrase, or a noun clause that renames another noun or pronoun in the same sentence.

**Noun:** James Bacon, <u>an artist</u>, paints in the morning.

**Noun phrase:** The artist is James Bacon, <u>a talented man with gray hair and a shy smile</u>.

**Noun clause:** The belief <u>that help would arrive</u> kept them from giving up.

Usually, an appositive immediately follows the noun it renames, as in the examples just given. Occasionally, it appears in front. Less frequently, it follows the word it renames but is separated from it by other words.

**In front:** <u>A talented man with gray hair and a shy smile</u>, James Bacon was elected president of his group.

**Separated:** The models walked across the stage—<u>tall, elegant women with expressionless eyes</u>.

Appositives are usually set off by commas. Sometimes the dash or colon is used. Sometimes no punctuation is required.

## Dash

The dash is used either to prevent confusion or—as an element of style—to set off the appositive in a more forceful or dramatic way than commas do.

**To prevent confusion:** Three women—a lawyer, a doctor, and an engineer—were chosen.

With commas, the sentence might be thought to refer to six people, not three: Three women, a lawyer, a doctor, and an engineer, were chosen.

**For emphasis:** They sang an old song—a melody filled with the pain and suffering of the past.

## Colon

The colon is used, in formal writing, when the appositive comes at the end of the sentence.

Throughout his life, he practiced one simple idea: do no violence to anyone.

## No Punctuation

Some appositives do not require any punctuation. These are called restrictive appositives. A restrictive appositive is an appositive that is necessary to identify exactly the noun it renames. Here is an example:

Her sister Sandra is coming in June.

We do not know which sister is meant until we read the appositive, which is "Sandra." A more elaborate example is this:

Your comment that the soup was salty offended the cook.

In this case, we don't know what comment offended the cook until we read the appositive; thus no commas are used.

In sentence combining, you will see examples such as the following:

My boss praised my work.
My boss is a clever man. } My boss, a clever man, praised my work.

You could also write, "My boss, who is a clever man, praised my work." But in that case, the sentence contains an adjective clause, not an appositive.

He denied the fact.
The fact was that he had made a mistake. } He denied the fact that he had made a mistake.

She ordered these things.
The things were cheese, pretzels, wine, and a pound of caviar. } She ordered these things: cheese, pretzels, wine, and a pound of caviar.

He left his money to Gladys Sherman.
She is a woman of complete honesty. } He left his money to Gladys Sherman, a woman of complete honesty.

# GRAMMAR NOTE 7: COMPLEX SENTENCES AND DEPENDENT CLAUSES

A clause is a group of words that has a subject and a verb. There are two kinds of clauses, independent and dependent.

## Independent Clause

The independent clause is the same as a simple sentence. It can stand alone and communicate a complete idea. For example, the clause "The sun was shining" may be called either a simple sentence or an independent clause.

## Dependent Clause

The dependent clause has a subject and a verb—as all clauses do—but by itself it does not give a sense of completeness and cannot be punctuated as a complete sentence. For example, the clause "although the sun was shining" has a subject and a verb, but by itself it does not sound complete. What happened although the sun was shining? A dependent clause must be attached to an independent clause before a complete idea can be expressed: Although the sun was shining, her heart was sad.

## Complex Sentence

A sentence that includes at least one dependent clause is called a complex sentence. A dependent clause may act as an adjective, an adverb, or a noun in relation to the independent clause it is attached to. Grammar Notes 3, 5, and 11 consider each type of dependent clause separately.

# GRAMMAR NOTE 8: COMPOUND SENTENCES AND COMPOUND PARTS OF SENTENCES

The word *compound* means having two or more parts.

## Compound Parts of a Sentence

Various parts of a sentence may be compound. For example, a sentence may have a compound subject, verb, or direct object. Here are some examples:

| | | |
|---|---|---|
| George likes coffee. <br> Sylvia likes coffee. | } | <u>George and Sylvia</u> like coffee. (compound subject) |
| George washes the dishes. <br> George dries the dishes. | } | George <u>washes and dries</u> the dishes. (compound verb) |
| Sylvia reads magazines. <br> Sylvia reads books. <br> Sylvia reads papers. | } | Sylvia reads <u>magazines, books, and papers</u>. (compound direct object) |

**Punctuation Note:** When the compound part of a sentence has two parts, no comma is used. (George and Sylvia) But when there are three or more parts, a comma should follow each part except the last one. (magazines, books, and papers)

## Compound Sentences

A compound sentence is made up of two or more simple sentences (or independent clauses).

| | | |
|---|---|---|
| George washes the dishes. <br> Sylvia dries them. | } | George washes the dishes, and Sylvia dries them. (compound sentence) |

## Punctuating Compound Sentences

There are three ways to join the clauses of a compound sentence:

1.  a comma and a coordinating conjunction (and, but, or, for, so, yet)

    George is very neat<u>, but</u> he makes a lot of mistakes.

Notice that ''but'' is used when there is a contrast of some sort.

    Sylvia mowed the lawn<u>, for</u> she knew George wouldn't do it.

Notice that ''for'' is similar to ''because.''

George picked too many peaches, <u>so</u> Sylvia made peach jam.

Notice that "so" is similar to "therefore."

2.    a semicolon and a conjunctive adverb (also, besides, consequently, furthermore, however, indeed, likewise, moreover, nevertheless, otherwise, similarly, then, therefore, thus)

George is very neat; <u>however,</u> he makes a lot of mistakes.
George dislikes mowing the lawn; <u>therefore</u> Sylvia did it.
George picked too many peaches; <u>consequently</u> Sylvia made peach jam.

A comma after the conjunctive adverb is optional.

3.    a semicolon alone

George shouted in anger; Sylvia walked out of the room.

## Punctuation Summary

George shouted, so Sylvia left.
George shouted; therefore Sylvia left.
George shouted; Sylvia left.

Notice the different style or effect depending on the choice of punctuation. Notice also that a comma alone cannot be used.

**Incorrect:** George dislikes mowing the lawn, it bores him.

This error—known as the comma splice—occurs when two sentences (independent clauses) are improperly joined. A comma is not a "strong" enough mark of punctuation to do the job. The comma splice is a fairly common error and is also considered to be a serious error. See Grammar Note 14 for further explanation.

# GRAMMAR NOTE 9: GERUNDS

When a verb with an <u>ing</u> ending is used as a noun, it is called a gerund. In form, the gerund is the same as a present participle, but the function is different: the present participle is an adjective; the gerund is a noun.

In sentences, the gerund is most commonly used in these ways:

1. subject
2. direct object
3. object of a preposition

## Gerund as Subject

The gerund may be used as the subject of a sentence when an action <u>in general</u> is being discussed.

> <u>Driving</u> a car requires a license.
> <u>Drinking</u> good wine is a pleasure.

(An infinitive may be used instead of a gerund in both of the above examples. However, common usage would be to say "It requires a license to drive a car" or "It is a pleasure to drink good wine." It would generally sound too formal to say, "To drive a car requires a license.")

## Gerund as Direct Object

An example of a gerund as a direct object occurs in this sentence:

> I like <u>drinking</u> good wine.

It would be equally correct to use an infinitive instead of a gerund:

> I like to drink good wine.

**Usage Note:** However, there are certain verbs that must be followed by a gerund—not an infinitive—as the direct object. For example, one must say the following:

> He enjoyed talking with her.

"He enjoyed to talk with her" would be clear in meaning but not correct in form.

Here is a list of common verbs that require a gerund:

| | | |
|---|---|---|
| admit | enjoy | prevent |
| appreciate | finish | resent |
| avoid | forgive | resist |
| consider | imagine | risk |
| delay | miss | stop |
| deny | pardon | suggest |
| dislike | postpone | understand |

In addition, the gerund—since it is a noun—must be preceded by a possessive pronoun, not a pronoun in the objective case.

**Correct:** I can't imagine <u>his</u> being late.

**Incorrect:** I can't imagine <u>him</u> being late.

## Gerund as Object of a Preposition

After a preposition, a gerund—not an infinitive—must be used. This situation refers especially to verb-preposition combinations such as <u>insisted on,</u> <u>used to, thinking of, interested in,</u> but it also applies to prepositions in general. Some examples:

**Verb-Preposition Combinations**
>He insisted on driving.
>They were used to waking up early.
>We are thinking of buying a horse.
>She is interested in going to Bermuda.

**Gerund After Prepositions**
She is good at playing chess.
He suffered without crying.
Before diving, one should look for hidden rocks.
In spite of leaving early, he missed his plane.

In sentence combining, you will see this:

**Gerund as Subject**

[Something] is not easy.     ⎫    Being a good parent is not easy.
It is to be a good parent.   ⎭

It would be possible to use the infinitive instead of the gerund. "It is not easy to be a good parent" is correct, but here only gerunds are being considered.

**Gerund as Direct Object**

I would appreciate [something].   ⎫   I would appreciate your being on
You are on time.              ⎭   time.

She stopped [something].     ⎫   She stopped smoking cigarettes.
It was to smoke cigarettes.  ⎭

''Stop'' is one of those verbs that must be followed by a gerund. ''She stopped to smoke cigarettes'' would mean that she stopped in order to smoke, not that she stopped smoking.

**Gerund After a Preposition**

He is thinking of [something].        He is thinking of going home.

It is to go home.

# GRAMMAR NOTE 10: INFINITIVES

The infinitive is the form of a verb preceded by "to": for example, to wash, to sleep, or to study. The infinitive commonly functions in a sentence as an adverb, an adjective, or a noun.

## Infinitive as Adverb

When an infinitive functions as an adverb, it generally shows purpose.

> He left home to avoid an argument.

Here, the infinitive phrase "to avoid an argument" shows for what purpose he left home.

The infinitive also occurs after the word "only" in sentences such as this:

> He survived the operation only to die of pneumonia.

In this sentence, "only" does not suggest that the reason he survived was in order to die of pneumonia. One can use "only" followed by an infinitive to state a disappointing or negative event that comes after a more positive event. But "only" followed by an infinitive can also have its usual meaning of "no other." These two sentences show the different uses of "only":

> He returned from abroad only to find her. (He had no other reason.)
> He returned from abroad only to find her married to another man. (He was disappointed.)

Read the following sentence:

> He returned from abroad to find that his wife had given birth to a daughter.

The infinitive (without "only") connects two ideas (returning and giving birth) without the idea of disappointment.

## Infinitive as Adjective

An infinitive may follow a noun and show how that noun may be used or what is to be done with it.

> I have a sandwich to eat. (a sandwich that I can eat)
> I have a meal to prepare. (a meal that I must prepare)

## Infinitive as Noun

As a noun, the infinitive may be in a variety of positions in a sentence.

**1.** As the <u>subject</u> (or subjective complement) of a sentence, the infinitive is frequently encountered in old sayings or memorable quotations:

> To know him is to love him.
> To err is human, to forgive divine.
> To be or not to be—that is the question.

It is sometimes encountered in ordinary speech or writing as in the following:

> To make that mistake twice would be very unfortunate.

But the common use is shown in this version of the sentence:

> It would be very unfortunate to make that mistake twice.

Here, the infinitive is called the delayed subject, with "it" filling the usual subject position.

**2.** An infinitive may follow a linking verb as the complement of the subject (a <u>subjective complement</u>):

> His greatest wish is to live in harmony with the world.

**3.** The most common use of the infinitive is after the main verb of a sentence, as a <u>direct object</u>.

> He agreed to leave early.
> I decided to wait at home.
> We hope to finish before tomorrow.
> You should not refuse to listen.

Not all verbs can be followed by an infinitive-direct object. Here is a list of verbs that are commonly followed by infinitives:

| | | | |
|---|---|---|---|
| agree | consent | hesitate | promise |
| appear | decide | hope | refuse |
| arrange | demand | learn | seem |
| attempt | fail | plan | try |
| choose | forget | prepare | volunteer |

Sometimes the words <u>how, what, when, where, which,</u> or <u>whether</u> occur between the verb and the infinitive:

> We forgot how to use chopsticks.
> They learned when to ask for money.
> He found out where to buy cheap books.

When the verbs, <u>show</u>, <u>teach</u>, and <u>tell</u> are followed by <u>how</u> and an infinitive, some care is needed. First, <u>show</u> must have <u>how</u> between it and the infinitive:

He showed me how to change the tire.

But tell may or may not be followed by how, depending on the meaning:

He told me how to change the tire. (He taught me.)
He told me to change the tire. (He ordered me to do it.)

And sometimes a noun or pronoun comes between the verb and the infinitive:

I want him to leave now.
The man begged the judge to change his mind.
They like him to help them in the garden.

## The Incomplete Infinitive

Sometimes only one part of the infinitive is used. This is common after the verbs make and let, after which the to of the infinitive is omitted:

He let the children cross the street alone.
She made him drive for a long time.

But sometimes only the to of the infinitive is used:

Her boss asked her to work overtime, but she didn't want to.

In sentence combining, you will see situations such as these:

| | |
|---|---|
| I need a rag.<br>The rag is to wipe the table. | I need a rag to wipe the table. |
| He went to the bank.<br>[His going] was to cash a check. | He went to the bank to cash a check. |

(Remember, words in square brackets in this book are never used in the combined version of a sentence.)

| | |
|---|---|
| [Something] is difficult.<br>It is to learn Chinese. | It is difficult to learn Chinese. |
| He decided [something].<br>[The decision] was to cook breakfast. | He decided to cook breakfast. |
| They wanted [someone] to cut the grass.<br>He should cut the grass. | They wanted him to cut the grass. |
| The teacher told him to finish his work.<br>He didn't want to finish it. | The teacher told him to finish his work, but he didn't want to. |

**Usage Note:**  The split infinitive is something to avoid in careful writing. A split infinitive is one that has an adverb between the ''to'' and the verb, as in ''He tried <u>to carefully check</u> his homework. The sentence should be written in this way: ''He tried <u>to check</u> his homework carefully.''

# GRAMMAR NOTE 11: NOUN CLAUSES

One of the three types of dependent clauses is the noun clause. (The other two are adverb and adjective clauses. You may wish to read Grammar Note 7: Complex Sentences and Dependent Clauses before reading further.) The noun clause acts in all the ways a single-word noun can act. That is, in a sentence a noun clause may be in any of these positions:

subject
direct object
indirect object
subjective complement
object of a preposition
appositive

Here are some examples.

<u>Whoever buys this car</u> will be very lucky. (noun clause-subject)

"Whoever buys this car" is a noun clause. It has its own subject and verb ("whoever" and "buys") as all clauses do. And in this sentence, it acts as the subject of the verb "will be." Who will be very lucky? The answer (the subject) is "whoever buys this car." The word "whoever" is the subject of "buys," but the whole clause is the subject of the verb "will be."

The waitress dropped <u>what she was carrying</u>. (noun clause-direct object)

Here the noun clause functions as the direct object. What did the waitress drop? The answer is "what she was carrying."

Success comes to <u>whoever is ready for it.</u> (noun clause-object of preposition)

A preposition must have an object, and in this sentence the object is the clause "whoever is ready for it." The word "whoever" is the subject of "is," not a single-word object of the preposition.

His wild speech was <u>what frightened us away</u>. (noun clause-subjective complement)

The linking verb "was" requires a subjective complement to complete it. In this sentence, the subjective complement is the noun clause "what frightened us away."

The fact <u>that you were late again</u> made me angry. (noun clause-appositive)

In this sentence, "fact" is renamed by the clause "that you were late again." Such "renamers" of nouns are called appositives. (Grammar Note 6 discusses appositives in more detail.)

It is unfortunate <u>that you can't go with us.</u> (noun clause-delayed subject)

To understand this sentence, ask yourself what the subject is. "It" is where the subject usually is, but in this case, "it" is just filling the subject position. What is unfortunate? The answer is "that you can't go with us," the real (but delayed) subject. To say "That you can't come with us is unfortunate" is correct but extremely formal and rarely seen or heard.

**Usage Note:** The most common use of the noun clause is as a direct object. Often, the word "that" is left out of such sentences.

I forgot (that) you were coming.

For careful, formal writing, however, use "that."
Here is a list of words that commonly introduce noun clauses:

| | | |
|---|---|---|
| how | whether | who |
| if | when | whoever |
| that | where | whom |
| what | which | whose |
| whatever | whichever | why |

And here are some additional examples:

I don't know <u>why I like spinach.</u> (direct object)
<u>Whatever you decide</u> is OK with me. (subject)
They don't remember <u>when the exam is.</u> (direct object)
I wonder <u>if he's here yet.</u> (direct object)

In sentence combining, you will see examples such as these:

She remembered [something]. | She remembered that she had to
It was that she had to buy lettuce. } buy lettuce.

The square brackets ([ ]) indicate that you will not use the word "something" in your sentence. The "something" that she remembered is "that she had to buy lettuce." Thus it would be incorrect to say "She remembered something that she had to buy lettuce."

[Someone] came to him for help. | Whoever was in trouble came to
It was whoever was in trouble. } him for help.

[Something] saddened her. | It saddened her that she had never
She had never graduated from college. } graduated from college.
lege.

The fact left her helpless.
The fact was that the car was out of gas.
} The fact that the car was out of gas left her helpless.

Give the report to [someone].
It is whoever is in the office.
} Give the report to whoever is in the office.

# GRAMMAR NOTE 12: PARTICIPLES

Participles are verbs used as adjectives. There are two kinds: present participles and past participles.

The present participle has ''ing'' after the verb:
The <u>crying</u> baby spilled her milk.

The past participle has ''ed'' (sometimes ''n'' or ''t'').

The <u>baked</u> potato looked delicious.
The <u>broken</u> arm hurt.

Words such as ''crying'' and ''broken'' can also be used as verbs, of course, but here they are being considered only as adjectives.

In sentence combining, you might see this:

| | |
|---|---|
| The cat ate a mouse.<br>The cat is smiling. | The <u>smiling</u> cat ate a mouse. |

''Smiling'' is a present participle, an adjective describing ''cat.'' There are other ways to combine those sentences:

The cat that is smiling ate a mouse.
The cat that ate a mouse is smiling.

Both of those sentences are correct, but neither one has a present participle. ''Smiling'' is a verb in each sentence.

Participles can also be used in participial phrases:

<u>Hiding behind the tree,</u> George didn't see her coming.
The tree <u>broken by the storm</u> had no apples this year.

The participial phrase is correctly used in these ways:

1.  if it occurs at the beginning of the sentence, a participle must refer to the subject of the sentence:

    Lying on his back, Henry saw a falling star. (Henry was lying on his back.)

2.  if it is somewhere in the middle of the sentence, a participle must refer to the noun or pronoun in front of it:

    The baby, thinking her mother had left, began to cry. (The baby thought her mother had left.)

3.  if it is at the end of the sentence, a participle must refer to the subject of the sentence:

    The children sneaked into the house, worried about getting caught. (The children worried.)

See Grammar Note 15: Avoiding Dangling Modifiers for a common error in using participial phrases.

In sentence combining, you might see this:

Sylvia walked under the ladder.  }  Walking under the ladder, Sylvia
She heard her mother shout.           heard her mother shout.

Here is another group to combine, this time using a past participial phrase:

The apple had been baked in the sun.
The apple was delicious.

For this group, there are two choices:

Baked in the sun, the apple was delicious.
The apple baked in the sun was delicious.

But there is one version using the participial phrase that is not correct:

**Incorrect:** The baked in the sun apple was delicious.

That is, a participial phrase cannot come between an article (the, a, an) and the noun it modifies. A single-word participle can, however, as in ''the baked apple.'' (Occasionally you will see participial phrases such as this: What she enjoyed most was the baked-in-the-sun apple. It is correct but relatively uncommon.)

## Present or Past Participle?

The question of when to use a present participle and when to use a past participle is often troublesome to students learning English. A simple technique can help in the decision. Remember that participles are formed from verbs even though they are used as adjectives. Here are two rules:

1.   if the ''action'' of the participle/adjective happened <u>before</u> the action in the rest of the sentence, use the <u>past</u> participle.
2.   if the ''action'' of the participle/adjective is happening <u>at the same time as</u> the action in the rest of the sentence, use the <u>present</u> participle.

For example, look at these two sentences:

Henry is drinking <u>boiling</u> water.
Henry is drinking <u>boiled</u> water.

In the first sentence, Henry is in a lot of trouble because the water is boiling at the same time he is drinking it!

Another way of choosing between the past and present participles is to remember that the present participle is active—having an effect on something. The past participle is passive—something else has had the effect.

The news was surprising. (The news affected people; it surprised them.)
We were surprised. (We were affected by the news.)

# GRAMMAR NOTE 13: PUNCTUATION

Punctuation is not as complicated as some people believe. But punctuating correctly does require some familiarity with sentence structure. For example, it is useless to have memorized that a compound sentence requires a comma in front of the coordinating conjunction if you do not recognize a compound sentence when you have written one.

This grammar note reviews the most common uses of punctuation marks. For less frequent uses (such as single quotation marks within double quotation marks), see a complete handbook of English grammar.

● **The Period**

Everyone knows that a period comes at the end of a sentence. If recognizing when one sentence ends and another begins is a problem, you may find yourself writing run-on sentences—a common error.

**Incorrect:** The dog barked a cat was walking past.

For problems in recognizing the ends of sentences, see Grammar Note 14. Another trouble spot is the indirect question. A moment's study will demonstrate that the following sentence is a statement, not a question.

She asked him how to find the elevator.

**Incorrect:** She asked him how to find the elevator?

? **The Question Mark**

The question mark is used after a direct question:

How do I find the elevator?

It is not used after an indirect question:

**Incorrect:** She asked him how to find the elevator?

In conversations, notice where the question mark appears in relation to the quotation marks:

''Where is the elevator?'' she asked.
She asked, ''Where is the elevator?''

! **The Exclamation Point**

The exclamation point follows statements of surprise or strong feeling. Generally, it is not used (or only very rarely) in formal, academic writing.

**Rare:** Despite his small size, David defeated Goliath!

## The Semicolon

The semicolon separates the two clauses of a compound sentence when no coordinating conjunction (and, but, or, nor, for, so) is used.

He watched TV; she watched him.
They worked hard in the garden; nevertheless, nothing went right.
She finished her homework; then she began to write letters.

Words such as nevertheless (a conjunctive adverb) and then (an adverb) cannot be preceded by a comma in the middle of a compound sentence. An error called the comma splice is the result.

**Incorrect:** She finished her homework, then she began to write letters.

See Grammar Note 14 for a more detailed discussion of this error.

## The Colon

The colon, a rather formal mark of punctuation, introduces a list, an explanation, or an appositive. It should follow a complete sentence.

The reviewers disliked several aspects of the first play he produced: the acting, the scenery, the costumes, and the music.
He worked hard to explain his behavior to her: he had to show his family that he was worthy.
They needed only one thing: a new roof. (A dash or a comma would also be correct.)

**Incorrect:** The things we need are: nails, paint, and beer.

The colon in the preceding sentence does not follow a complete sentence. No punctuation is needed.

Correct: The things we need are nails, paint, and beer.

## The Dash

The dash should be used infrequently. It may be used instead of a colon to set off an appositive or an explanation. The dash may be used to make a sharp separation between the sentence and something that interrupts the flow of ideas.

Hot tea—the Chinese believe—cools the body on a hot day.
He spoke—hesitantly at first—of his childhood.

## The Apostrophe

The apostrophe is used to show possession:

a boy's bicycle
boys' bicycles
children's toys
the boss's daughter
the Smith's car

It is generally not used with nonliving things. "The bird sat on the branch of a tree" is more appropriate than "The bird sat on the tree's branch."

Several common errors occur in the use of the apostrophe.

**Incorrect:** That book is her's.

**Correct:** That book is hers.

Possessive pronouns (his, hers, its, ours, yours, theirs) show possession without an apostrophe.

**Incorrect:** The dog scratched it's back. Its flea season.

**Correct:** The dog scratched its back. It's flea season.

It's is a contraction for it is. Its is a possessive pronoun.

**Incorrect:** I don't know who's coat this is. Whose here?

**Correct:** I don't know whose coat this is. Who's here?

Who's is a contraction for who is. Whose is a possessive pronoun.

## The Comma

After the period, the comma is the most frequently used—and misused—mark of punctuation. Some people omit necessary commas. Other people use unnecessary commas. Most unnecessary commas come about from the belief that a comma should be used every time there is a slight pause in a sentence. It is true that a comma represents a pause. But using pauses as the sole guide for placement of commas brings about a great many errors, so that "rule" should be forgotten.

## The Comma with Coordinating Conjunctions

A comma must be used before a coordinating conjunction (and, but, or, nor, for, so) where the two clauses of a compound sentence are joined. (The second part of that sentence is underlined because it is often forgotten. More about that follows shortly.) Here are several examples:

He telephoned her, but she didn't answer.

You can call, or you can send me a postcard.

He repaired the car, and she painted the garage.

Forgetting the underlined portion of that earlier sentence leads to using a comma every time and or but is used. Most of the time, those commas are unnecessary and are considered errors.

**Incorrect:** She walked home in the rain, and got very wet. (This is not a compound sentence. It is a simple sentence with a compound verb and requires no comma.)

**Correct:** She walked home in the rain and got very wet.

**Incorrect:** Herb tried to study math, but was interrupted by his neighbors' loud party. (compound verb)

**Correct:** Herb tried to study math but was interrupted by his neighbors' loud party.

**Incorrect:** Three old friends from elementary school, and I are having lunch next Tuesday. (compound subject)

**Correct:** Three old friends from elementary school and I are having lunch next Tuesday.

If two parts of sentences (subjects, verbs, objects, etc.) are joined by a coordinating conjunction, no comma should be used. If you are confused, see the example above about walking in the rain.

## The Comma in Complex Sentences

A comma follows an adverb clause but does not precede one.

**Correct:** Because she was tired, she shouted at the children.

**Correct:** She shouted at the children because she was tired.

**Incorrect:** She shouted at the children, because she was tired.

A comma separates a nonrestrictive clause (one that adds information but is not needed to identify the noun it modifies) from the rest of the sentence.

My favorite pen, which I bought in Hong Kong, has been missing for a week.

Someone returned my favorite pen, which had been missing for a week.

**Incorrect:** All students, who withdraw from three courses, will be called in to see a dean.

Here, only certain students will have to see the dean, not all of them. The clause identifies the students being called in—those who drop three courses. No commas should be used:

**Correct:** All students who withdraw from three courses will be called in to see a dean.

A common error is to use a comma after a relative pronoun introducing a noun clause.

**Incorrect:** He believed that, the world is flat.

**Correct:** He believed that the world is flat.

## The Comma After Introductory Phrases

A comma follows a phrase at the beginning of a sentence.

After the long and heavy lunch, they tried unsuccessfully to get back to work.

Walking along the beach at sunset, Bob felt refreshed and at peace.

On the other hand, you may prefer a small hotel for its lower prices.

A short prepositional phrase (usually two words) is often not followed by a comma. This is one place where the ear may be used as a guide.

At breakfast he was silent.

He drinks coffee in the afternoon; at breakfast, he prefers tea.

## Commas in a Series

A series is a list of three or more words, phrases, or clauses. A comma should follow each item but the last.

Hamburgers, potato chips, and milkshakes were what he missed while he was sailing.

She lectured them about neatness, about promptness, about courtesy, and about good manners.

Her father was a lawyer, her mother was a doctor, and she was a perpetual student.

For commas between adjectives, see Grammar Note 2.

## Commas Around Phrases that Interrupt

Phrases that interrupt the usual pattern of a sentence should be set off by commas.

One of their children, to their great surprise, had no musical ability at all.

The beagle, for example, is a good pet and a good working dog.

**More Examples:** Here is a list of sentences illustrating correct uses of the comma and some common errors.

He waited patiently, and finally he saw her.
He waited patiently and finally saw her.

**Incorrect:** He waited patiently, and finally saw her.

**Incorrect:** He waited patiently, he finally saw her.

He asked her to be kind, gentle, and understanding. Because she had promised him to be faithful, she kept her word.

She kept her word because she had promised him to be faithful.

His favorite topic of conversation, which bored everyone, was golf.

The shirt that had the bloodstains fell out of the laundry basket.

**Incorrect:** The shirt, that had the bloodstains, fell out of the laundry basket.

She told him that she wanted to go home.

**Incorrect:** She told him that, she wanted to go home.

Waiting around the house, the children got bored.
To keep them occupied, he taught them to bake cookies.
In the hour after the storm, they saw a rainbow.
After that, lunch was not pleasant.

**Incorrect:** After that lunch was not pleasant.

For instance, noodles are popular in northern China.
Rice, on the other hand, is common in the south of China.
I like noodles and dumplings, not rice.

# GRAMMAR NOTE 14: AVOIDING RUN-ON SENTENCES, COMMA SPLICES, AND FRAGMENTS

The run-on sentence, the comma splice, and the fragment are all errors that result from uncertainty (or carelessness) about what a sentence is and where it ends. These are considered to be serious errors. If you habitually make them, it is worth your effort to solve the problem as soon as you can. Also, it would be useful at this point to review the grammar notes on compounds and dependent clauses if those terms are unclear.

## Sentence Fragments

A sentence must have two characteristics:

1.    it must have a subject and a verb;

2.    it must have independence or completeness.

If either of those characteristics is missing from a group of words written as a sentence (that is, beginning with a capital letter and ending with a period), the result is an error called the sentence fragment. A fragment is a piece of something, and a sentence fragment is a piece of a sentence.

Consider this short passage:

> Sylvia feels happy this morning. Because the sun is shining. She is leaving early to take a walk in the woods.

"Because the sun is shining" is really an adverb (dependent) clause, but it is written as if it were a sentence. It's easy to miss that it is a fragment because it makes sense that Sylvia feels happy because the sun is shining or that because the sun is shining she will leave early. The ideas flow in logical order. But this fragment violates the second characteristic of a sentence—completeness or independence. It is easier to see that a fragment is not independent or complete if it is separated from the sentences around it. There is a simple (though slightly silly) test for this. Imagine yourself walking down a sidewalk toward another person. As you pass, you say the group of words you are testing for completeness. For example, you might say, "Because the sun is shining." The other person is left waiting for the rest of the idea. What happened because the sun is shining? That is why fragments are considered errors. They are not complete ideas. Now imagine saying to that person on the sidewalk, "Sylvia feels happy this morning." The person might respond, "Good," or "Who cares?" or "Stop talking to me." But he or she would be responding to a complete idea.

In more formal terms, the sentence fragment usually comes about from punctuating one of these parts of a sentence as if it were a complete sentence:

adverb clause
adjective clause
participial phrase
infinitive phrase
a noun followed by a clause or phrase.

Here are some examples:

**Fragment:** I couldn't fall asleep. Although I was tired.
**Correct:** Although I was tired, I couldn't fall asleep.

**Fragment:** I bought a 16-pound turkey. Which wasn't enough food.
**Correct:** I bought a 16-pound turkey, which wasn't enough food.

**Fragment:** He couldn't see that movie. Being only 14.
**Correct:** Being only 14, he couldn't see that movie.

**Fragment:** I bought a 16-pound turkey. To feed 45 people.
**Correct:** I bought a 16-pound turkey to feed 45 people.

**Fragment:** I told my sister. A woman of great patience and charm.
**Correct:** I told my sister, a woman of great patience and charm.

## The Comma Splice and the Run-On Sentence

The comma splice results when two sentences (independent clauses) are joined only with a comma.

**Comma Splice:** John couldn't fall asleep, he was too worried.

Even though the ideas in these two sentences are closely related, punctuation rules in English say that a comma by itself cannot join them. (In some languages, the comma would be quite correct.) Here are the acceptable ways to write that sentence in English:

1.  John couldn't fall asleep, for he was too worried.
2.  John couldn't fall asleep. He was too worried.
3.  John couldn't fall asleep; he was too worried.
4.  Because he was too worried, John couldn't fall asleep.

The run-on sentence has no punctuation at all between the two clauses.

**Run-On:** John couldn't fall asleep he was too worried.

This may be corrected in the same ways as the comma splice is corrected, as shown in the four acceptable examples above.

Editing Exercise 6 in Chapter 6 gives further practice in correcting these errors.

# GRAMMAR NOTE 15: AVOIDING DANGLING MODIFIERS ■

A modifier (a word or phrase that describes some other word) must have something to modify. And it must modify the right word. If these things don't happen, the modifier is said to dangle—that is, to hang there loosely, ready (almost) to fall off the sentence.

The dangling modifier is an error worth avoiding. Errors of any kind, of course, bother the people who recognize them. But dangling modifiers are special. They are usually funny or ridiculous—by accident. It's one thing to make your reader laugh if that's what you planned. It's not so good to make your reader laugh when you were being serious.

Here is a dangling modifier. Try to see the error before you read the explanation.

**Incorrect:** Finishing the last of the wine, the room began to spin before John's eyes.

The sentence means (or tries to) that John finished the wine. But what it says is that the room finished the wine. The sentence, as it is written, is nonsense. A reader can figure out the intended meaning eventually, but no reader should have to work to do that.

The modifier that dangles is most often the participial phrase. Gerund phrases and infinitive phrases can also dangle. (Participles, gerunds, and infinitives are each discussed in a separate grammar note.)

## The Dangling Participial Phrase

This error occurs most frequently when a participial phrase comes at the beginning of the sentence. (Remember, however, that a participial phrase can be used correctly at the beginning of a sentence, as in "Lying on his back, Henry saw a beautiful falling star." This sentence is correct because the participial phrase describes Henry, the next word.) When a participial phrase dangles it usually modifies the wrong word.

**Incorrect:** Lying on his back, the falling star seemed beautiful to Henry.

After reading, "Lying on his back," people expect to find out immediately who was doing it. But what comes next in that incorrect sentence? "Falling star" does. The falling star was lying on his back? Impossible. "Lying on his back" is close to "falling star" and seems to modify it, but it really refers to "Henry," in this sentence, a word too far away from the participial phrase it is related to. That is the heart of the dangling modifier—in terms of grammar, it modifies a particular word, but in terms of logic, it cannot possibly modify that word. Another example:

**Incorrect:** Warmed by the morning sun, a drop of hope returned to my fearful heart.

A drop of hope was warmed by the sun? Not possible. The sentence means that the speaker was warmed by the sun. But notice that there is no "I" in that sentence. Thus the word that the participial phrase really modifies ("I") is not in the sentence at all. The word is in the mind of the writer, but not on the paper.

## Correcting Dangling Participial Phrases

There are two ways to correct dangling participial phrases:

1.  Provide the word that the phrase modifies and place that word close to the phrase.

2.  Rewrite the phrase as a dependent clause with its own subject and verb.

These corrections often require some changes in the rest of the sentence.

**Incorrect:** Sneaking into the house, my keys fell and woke the family. (The keys were sneaking?)

**Correct:** Sneaking into the house, I dropped my keys and woke the family. (I was sneaking.)

**Correct:** As I sneaked into the house, my keys fell and woke the family.

**Incorrect:** Covered with too much mustard, I could not eat the hot dog. (I was covered with mustard?)

**Correct:** Covered with too much mustard, the hot dog was inedible.

**Correct:** I could not eat the hot dog because it was covered with too much mustard.

## Dangling Gerund and Infinitive Phrases

Dangling gerund and infinitive phrases are quite similar to dangling participial phrases.

**Incorrect:** By working all night, my term paper was finished on time. (The term paper worked all night?)

**Correct:** By working all night, I finished my term paper on time. (I worked all night.)

**Incorrect:** To use the computer, instructions are needed. (The instructions will use the computer?)

**Correct:** To use the computer, you need instructions. (You will use the computer.)

Don't let the fear of writing dangling modifiers keep you from using introductory participial (or gerund or infinitive) phrases. Such introductions to sentences are important additions to effective writing. Just be aware that the introductory phrases have to modify the right word.

# INDEX